Rapid Response Reports

FA 1993
Butterworths Tax Planning

Rapid Response Reports

FA 1993
Butterworths Tax Planning

Butterworths
London, Dublin & Edinburgh
1993

United Kingdom	Butterworth & Co (Publishers) Ltd, 88 Kingsway, LONDON WC2B 6AB and 4 Hill Street, EDINBURGH EH2 3JZ
Australia	Butterworths, SYDNEY, MELBOURNE, BRISBANE, ADELAIDE, PERTH, CANBERRA and HOBART
Belgium	Butterworth & Co (Publishers) Ltd, Brussels
Canada	Butterworth & Co Canada Ltd, TORONTO and VANCOUVER
Ireland	Butterworth (Ireland) Ltd, DUBLIN
Malaysia	Malayan Law Journal Sdn Bhd, KUALA LUMPUR
New Zealand	Butterworths of New Zealand Ltd, WELLINGTON and AUCKLAND
Puerto Rico	Equity de Puerto Rico, Inc, HATO REY
Singapore	Butterworth & Co (Asia) Pte Ltd, SINGAPORE
USA	Butterworth Legal Publishers, AUSTIN, Texas; BOSTON, Massachusetts; CLEARWATER, Florida (D & S Publishers); ORFORD, New Hampshire (Equity Publishing); ST PAUL, Minnesota; and SEATTLE, Washington

A CIP Catalogue record for this book is available from the British Library.

ISBN 0 406 02648 3

Typeset by Doublestruck Limited, London
Printed and bound in Great Britain by Latimer Trend & Co Ltd, Plymouth

Preface

Practitioners will not need to be reminded that tax legislation, and the planning that goes with it, is ever-changing.

The Finance Bill/Act cycle, stretching over a five-month period, has always presented a problem for practitioners with the Finance Act 1993 being a particularly bad example of the genre. Its length and complexity have set an unenviable record and it will take tax practitioners many months (if ever) before they can feel confident about advising clients on the implications of the new legislation.

Butterworths Tax Planning recognises this by being in looseleaf format with regular updates. Yet even regular updating takes time. In order, therefore, to meet the needs of the tax practitioner for instant comment on the tax planning implications of the Finance Act proposals, Butterworths has commissioned this series of *Rapid Response Reports* on the most important aspects of the new legislation.

I hope that practitioners will welcome this new service.

Michael B Squires FCA FCCA FTII ATT
Tax Partner
KPMG Peat Marwick
Birmingham

Contributors

Chris Allen FCA is a chartered accountant specialising in VAT. He practises as an independent VAT consultant, providing a specialist advisory service to professional firms, and is a member of the ICAEW Tax Faculty's VAT Committee and of the VAT Practitioners' Group. A contributor to *De Voil: Value Added Tax*, and Tolley's *VAT Planning*, he is also the author of *VAT in Business* (CCH) and of numerous articles in the professional press. He produces a monthly magazine, *Allen's VAT News*, for users of his consultancy service.

Nina Buchan BA worked for a leading legal publishing house for a number of years. She then qualified as a solicitor in 1990 and joined the Corporate Tax Department of Wilde Sapte as an assistant solicitor after completion of her articles.

Carol Dempsey BComm AITI is a senior manager in the London office of Coopers & Lybrand where she specialises in personal tax. Her particular areas of interest include employee remuneration issues, taxation of company cars and offshore trusts. She is a frequent contributor to various Coopers & Lybrand publications.

Russell Jacobs LLB trained and worked for a number of years with another major city law firm before joining Wilde Sapte in 1992, when he became a partner in the firm's Corporate Tax Department. Concentrating on the banking and financial sector, he has been involved in the development of new debt, equity and hybrid products, both in the private placement and capital markets. He has written a number of articles and other publications on, among other things, the tax treatment of index-linked debt securities, foreign exchange gains and losses and equity notes.

Mihiri Jayaweera MA ACA is a supervisor in the London office of Coopers & Lybrand where she works in the personal tax department. Her particular areas of interest include taxation work for executives abroad.

Ian Nichol MA FCA ATII is a partner in the south coast practice of Coopers & Lybrand where he specialises in personal tax and growing businesses. He is a member of the firm's Compensation and Benefits skill group and writes and lectures frequently on Schedule E taxation.

Richard Pincher LLB is a barrister with McGrigor Donald, where he specialises in corporate taxation, with particular regard to VAT. He is a regular contributor to *Revenue* on EC tax matters and also contributes to the *Tax Journal, Estates Gazette, Law Society Gazette* and *Taxation.*

Anne Redston MA, ACA, ATII is the group tax manager at Allied Dunbar Assurance plc. She read history at Oxford, and then qualified in London as a chartered accountant and an Associate of the Institute of Taxation. After three years as a tax manager in Hong Kong she returned to the UK to take up her present position. She is a member of the Tax Panel of the Association of British Insurers.

Michael B Squires FCA FCCA FTII ATT is a tax partner with KPMG Peat Marwick in Birmingham and past president of the Institute of Taxation. He is author of *Tax Planning for Groups of Companies* (Butterworths), joint editor of *Butterworths Tax Planning Service* and a specialist contributor to *Simon's Taxes.*

Miles Walton MA (Oxon) ATII is the partner in charge of the Corporate Tax Department at Wilde Sapte. He has a particular interest in structured and asset finance work. Miles is co-author of *Taxation and Banking* (Sweet & Maxwell).

Neil Woodgate LLM is an assistant solicitor in the Corporate Tax Department at Wilde Sapte. He has a particular interest in structured finance and has considerable asset finance experience. Neil has co-written articles for the *British Tax Review* and *Butterworths Journal of International Banking and Financial Law.*

Contents

Chapter 4   Foreign exchange gains and losses
by Russell Jacobs and Nina Buchan

Chapter 5   Benefits in kind
by Ian Nichol, Carol Dempsey and Mihiri Jayaweera

Chapter 6   Relocation expenses
by Anne Redston

Chapter 7   VAT
by Chris Allen

CHAPTER 1

ACT

1 INTRODUCTION

1.1 Advance corporation tax (ACT) is charged on qualifying distributions made by companies. ACT used to be charged at a rate of tax equivalent to the basic rate of income tax so as to produce tax neutrality at that level of tax. The Finance Act (FA) changes introduce a mismatch for a year but tax neutrality will then be achieved at the lower rate of income tax.

1.2 The reason for reducing the rate of ACT was said to be to reduce the cash flow problems caused by ACT surplus. The changes also reflect Revenue protecting measures. In different circumstances, surplus ACT can be a short-term or a long-term, and possibly growing, problem. The recent changes can be regarded as mitigating this, cash flow, problem but will probably not remove it altogether. The proposals to introduce a special regime for foreign income dividends and international headquarters companies could provide a permanent solution.

1.3 The basic ACT regime has far-reaching consequences because it is built into other taxing provisions. These other provisions have also been amended.

1.4 In the text that follows all references are to the Income and Corporation Taxes Act 1988 unless otherwise specified.

The lower rate of tax

1.5 The lower rate of tax was introduced in the first Finance Act in 1992 (FA 1992 s 9). The lower rate of tax is 20% and, when introduced, was charged on the first £2,000 of taxable income but is now charged on the first £2,500 of taxable income (FA 1993 s 51(2)). The basic rate of income tax of 25% applies to the balance of taxable income up to £23,700 and the higher income tax rate of 40% applies to taxable income in excess of that figure.

2 ACT: INTRODUCTION

Companies paying dividends

1.6 ACT is a central element of the imputation system of tax introduced in the United Kingdom in 1972, the other element being the tax credits that are granted to recipients of dividends. UK-resident companies have to account for ACT at the relevant rate of tax on all qualifying distributions except to the extent that the company has franked investment income (FII) or where there is a relevant group income election in place. Qualifying distributions are widely defined (s 14(2)) and include deemed distributions (s 209). ACT is set against the company's mainstream corporation tax (MCT) liability when that becomes due for payment, usually nine months from the end of the company's accounting date. The ACT set-off was limited to an amount equal to the basic rate of income tax on the company's taxable profits. The maximum set-off is now limited to the intermediate rate of tax of 22.5% for the current year and the lower rate of tax liability on the profits thereafter. The ACT can be carried forward to set against future profits and carried back to be set against the previous six years' MCT. This can produce a short-term problem of ACT surplus when the company's dividend payments exceed taxable profits – the long-term ACT surplus arises because of a complicated set of circumstances explained further below.

Timing

1.7   ACT has to be paid 14 days after the end of the relevant return period. The relevant return periods end on the last day of March, June, September and December. Another return period ends with the company's tax accounting period if it is not one of these other dates.

1.8   Timing has always been elemental to ACT planning. The particular impact for charities under the new regime is discussed below. Because the rate of ACT has been reduced, the cash flow effects of ACT have likewise reduced. Delaying a dividend payment from the end of one return period until the beginning of the next, however, will still delay the payment of that ACT by almost three months with a consequential cash flow benefit. Special attention is required for the last return period in the company's accounting period when payment of the ACT will still be deferred by three months but credit for the ACT against MCT could be delayed by a year unless, for example, FII is expected in the first return period of the coming year that could frank the dividend.

Recipients of dividends

Individuals

1.9   Depending on the level of the recipient's taxable income and gains, dividends will now be taxed at either the lower rate of tax – so no further tax will be due because of the accompanying tax credit – or at the higher rate of tax with a credit for the lower rate of tax. Individuals are entitled to repayment of the tax credit, discussed further below (s 231).

Tax credits

1.10   UK-resident individuals and companies receiving dividends pay tax on the value of the dividend plus the amount of ACT but are entitled to a tax credit representing ACT. The effect was that basic rate taxpayers paid no further tax and higher rate taxpayers paid a further 15% of tax on the gross amount.

Franked investment income

1.11 UK-resident companies can also use dividend income (together with the tax credit called FII) to frank dividend payments (together with the accompanying ACT liability called franked payments) – that is to say the tax credit is set against the ACT liability. FII is discussed in more detail below.

3   CALCULATION OF TAX

What is the rate of ACT?

1.12 Since the financial year 1988, ACT has been paid at a rate related to the basic rate of income tax by the following formula

$$\frac{I}{(100 - I)}$$

when I was the basic rate of income tax charged for the year of assessment starting on 6 April in that financial year.

1.13 The rate of ACT has changed (FA 1993 s 78(1)). For the financial year 1993 the rate of ACT is limited to the intermediate rate of 22.5% of the gross dividend – $9/31$ of the net dividend. For the following financial years the rate of ACT is limited to the prevailing lower rate of income tax – currently 20% – when the fraction will be $1/4$.

1.14 The effect of the change on preference share payments should be checked. Usually the payment will be net of tax and the credit will automatically reflect the change in ACT rate. Gross payments will now cost the issuing company more in cash terms.

How are the changes of rate provided for?

1.15 Where the relevant rate of tax has not been set for any year, the rate set for the previous year applies until the later of:

1   the date the rate was set;
2   5 August.

1.16 In the past, the relevant rate for these purposes has been the basic rate of income tax; it is now the lower rate (FA 1993 s 78(2)).

4   LONG-TERM SURPLUS ACT

1.17   Long-term surplus ACT is a structural problem for some companies identifiable as those with a large proportion of foreign dividend earnings from jurisdictions with a tax rate not significantly lower than that of the UK. The UK company is credited with the foreign tax paid by its subsidiary – this reduces the MCT payable but strands the ACT paid when the profits are distributed – because there is no MCT to set ACT against. The solution is to reduce overseas profits – but thin capitalisation and transfer pricing rules will often constrain these arrangements. Thin capitalisation prevents overseas companies providing more than a commercial proportion of debt financing as compared to equity financing. Transfer pricing rules prevent overseas companies charging too high a price or paying too low a price for the product.

1.18   The long-term surplus ACT problem is sometimes emphasised if the UK company has foreign dividend income from both high tax and low tax jurisdictions. Because the maximum amount of ACT to be set against profits is calculated on a source-by-source basis, the maximum ACT set-off may not be achieved in relation to income taxed at higher rates overseas thus leaving ACT stranded. This problem is sometimes addressed by establishing a new offshore holding company – often referred to as a mixer company – in a jurisdiction that allows the foreign tax rates to be averaged and so reduces the overall tax take.

1.19   By reducing the rate of ACT the problems caused by long-term surplus ACT should be mitigated. But the problem is an incurable consequence of the imputation system as it currently operates and is unlikely to be resolved entirely simply by reducing the rate of ACT.

5   ACT AND LOSSES

1.20   The reliefs for ACT and losses, in particular the rules for carrying backwards and forward the reliefs, have developed piecemeal so that careful attention is now required to extract the full benefit of these tools. Setting losses against profit reduces the MCT payable and so in some cases the company's capacity to set-off ACT; the surplus ACT is then merely carried forward. Loss relief is limited by comparison to ACT relief because losses may be set only against profits of the same trade but ACT can be set against any MCT liability from whatever source including capital gains. It would therefore give companies greater flexibility in reducing future MCT if they converted losses into ACT. Losses can now be carried back three years and doing so might generate surplus ACT in those earlier years. That ACT may then be carried further back. A claim to carry back ACT has to be made within two years and so might be out of time in some cases. However, the losses carried back could generate ACT that could be carried forward to a year for which a claim could still be made to carry back ACT for up to six years going beyond the period in which the loss was made and into an earlier profitable period and so generate a tax repayment.

6 GROUPS

1.21 A parent company may surrender its ACT to its 51% subsidiary. A 51% subsidiary is defined in terms of control of the ordinary shares of a subsidiary and economic control – and includes a consortium company. Surrendered ACT may be used in priority to the subsidiary's own ACT to set against the subsidiary's MCT liability. This order of set-off can be used to achieve an effective carry back of the parent's ACT in the subsidiary. The subsidiary cannot carry back surrendered ACT but by receiving parent ACT its own ACT of the same amount may be released for carry back. (See Chapter 2 'Anti-avoidance' for new rules to prevent the acquisition of subsidiaries with ACT capacity with a view to using this technique.)

1.22 Groups may also elect to allow subsidiaries to pay dividends without accounting for ACT. This saves both the administration and the cash flow costs by having to account for ACT in these circumstances. Of course, the parent recipient benefits from no tax credit on the dividend either. The circumstances of the group should, therefore, be kept under review since the group income election is not always a benefit. For example, if the subsidiary receives FII in the same period as the parent pays a dividend then under the group income election the FII would be trapped and the parent would have to account for ACT whereas without the election the FII could frank the subsidiary's dividend and that would frank the parent's dividend. Another example of benefits of making a payment outside the election is where the subsidiary could use ACT to reduce previous years' MCT in which case the dividend outside the election would allow ACT to be carried back and produce a repayment.

7 THE NEW RULES FOR TAXING DIVIDENDS

1.23 In the future, individuals will not be taxed at the basic rate on dividend income. This also applies to personal representatives. In the case of individuals, this appears to extend the lower rate band up to the threshold for the higher rate of tax.

1.24 For the purpose of determining whether a person's dividend income is taxed at the higher rate of tax, dividend income is deemed to be the highest part of the individual's income. So, if an individual has £200 subject to tax at the higher rate and £300 of dividend income then that £200 will be treated as derived from dividends. The remainder of the dividend income will be taxed at the lower rate.

How to determine the highest part of a person's income

1.25 The new rules for taxing dividends are subject to existing rules to determine the highest part of a person's income. The income is calculated without accounting for (s 833):

1   payments on retirement or removal from office or employment (s 148);
2   gains arising from a beneficial interest in certain policies or contracts of an insurance or security nature (s 547(1)(a));
3   certain other chargeable sums connected with premiums for leases.

1.26   Those taxed on gains mentioned under point 2 above could claim top slicing relief when calculating the tax payable (s 550). The effect of the relief was to tax the receipt on the basis that it was spread over a certain number of years. That adjustment does not apply for the purpose of calculating the highest part of a person's income.

The effect of the new rules for taxing dividends

1.27   The tax consequences for UK-resident individuals will depend on their marginal rate of tax. Those taxed at the basic rate will be taxed on dividend income only at the lower rate and that liability will be matched by the accompanying tax credit. They will, therefore, pay less tax on dividend income than before. Because of the reduced tax credit that will accompany dividends in the future, those taxed at the higher rate will pay 5% more tax than previously.

1.28   The effect on higher rate taxpayers emphasises the benefits of asset sharing. A spouse paying tax at the higher rate on income including share income should consider transferring those shares to a basic rate taxpaying spouse.

1.29   The reduction in the liability for tax on dividends appears to make PEPs less attractive to shareholders paying tax at the basic rate but more attractive to those paying tax at the higher rate. PEPs, however, also appear to have possible income problems because of the changes relating to tax credit that are discussed further below.

1.30   Of course, companies also bear different rates of tax. Companies with profits below £250,000 pay tax at the rate of 25% – the small companies rate. Those with profits over £1,250,000 pay tax at 33%. Those with profits between those two thresholds benefit from a marginal relief at the rate of $^{1}/_{50}$th. The new treatment of dividends, however, does not affect the differing rates of tax applied to companies.

The big picture

1.31   To understand the consequences of the new ACT regime it may be helpful to analyse the effects of ACT. ACT is a mechanism to extract tax from profits when they are distributed by way of dividend – it does not necessarily realise the whole of the company's tax charge but passes on to the shareholder the amount charged as a tax credit.

So a company might have £100 of profits. Before the changes, it would pay a dividend of £67 carrying an ACT credit of £22.33. The shareholder would be deemed to have received income of £89.33 and any higher rate taxpayer would have a tax liability of £35.73 against which it could set a credit of £22.33. For sake of illustration, the company had a MCT liability of £33 against which it set £22.33 of ACT credit – leaving £10.67 of tax payable.

1.32 By reducing the ACT credit, the timing difference is reduced from the company's point of view because the company pays less of its MCT liability before it becomes due. The taxpayer, however, gets less of a tax credit – thus increasing the tax cost of operating business through a company when the dividend is taxed at the higher rate.

So, profits of £100 still produce a dividend of £67. With ACT at 25% the credit is worth £16.75. The higher rate taxpayer is deemed to have received a dividend of £83.75 giving rise to a tax liability of £33.50 against which can be set the tax credit leaving further tax payable of £16.75.

1.33 Whilst the rates of ACT and tax credit are different the tax take does not increase, but the mismatch emphasises the cash flow effects in the short-term. The company will prepay more MCT than the shareholder ever gets credit for – although the cash flow effect will end when the ACT is set against MCT.

Level of dividends

1.34 As a result of the change, companies may have to consider the level of their dividends in the future. Institutions, who gauge share values by earnings per share, may consider that the reduced tax credit has reduced that ratio. Previously, the company had produced a tax credit at a cash flow cost to itself. Supporting previous income levels to the institution in the future will be at a real cash cost to the company.

1.35 Companies with surplus ACT are in a different position. Because the rate of ACT is lower, the surplus will grow at a slower rate if the company maintains its dividend levels. If the company increases the dividend, maybe to make up for the lower tax credit, it will turn future ACT written off above the line into below-the-line dividends. Because of the reduced rate of ACT set-off, however, those companies with a short-term ACT surplus will now require more taxable profits to eliminate that surplus than would previously have been the case.

8   DIVIDENDS

What is a dividend?

1.36 Under the Companies Act 1985 a company may distribute its allowable profits and such a distribution can be of cash or otherwise but excludes bonus shares, share redemption, reduction of share capital or distribution on a winding up (Companies Act 1985 s 263). ACT is charged on distributions, except non-qualifying distributions, which means (s 209):

1   any dividend, including a capital dividend;
2   certain distributions out of assets;
3   certain redeemable share capital or securities not issued for new consideration;
4   certain interest or other distributions that represent more than a reasonable return;
5   certain interest or other distributions paid on:
    (a)   certain redeemable securities;
    (b)   certain convertible securities;
    (c)   securities where the return depends on the profits of the company;
    (d)   shares held by specified overseas associated companies;
    (e)   certain securities connected with shares in the company;
    (f)   equity notes held by associated companies;
6   certain transfers of assets or liabilities to members for no new consideration or less than the value of the asset or liability;
7   certain bonus issues following repayment of share capital.

Stock dividends

1.37   Stock dividends are treated as distributions received net of tax (s 249). Formerly the relevant tax rate was the basic rate of income tax, this is now to be the lower rate of tax (FA 1993 s 77(3)).

1.38   There are two categories of stock dividend (s 249):

1   share capital issued by a UK-resident company because a person exercises certain rights to receive a dividend in cash or shares;
2   bonus shares issued by a UK-resident company in respect of certain shares.

1.39   The recipient of a stock dividend, whether an individual or a trustee, is taxed as if he or they had received a cash dividend equal to the value of shares received net of tax. Formerly the recipient was not assessed to tax at the basic rate on the value of the stock dividend. That exemption now applies at the lower rate of tax. The recipient was also credited with having paid tax at the basic rate in calculating any higher rate tax liability. This credit is now also at the lower rate of tax. The tax deemed to have been paid is not repayable. Formerly, stock dividends were treated as income to which the lower rate did not apply but now they are treated as a dividend income subject to the same new rules for determining the tax rate applicable to dividends that are explained above.

1.40   Stock dividends are superficially attractive to companies because they plough profits back into the business. They do, however, present an additional administrative burden. Furthermore, institutional investors are often not disposed to take up the offer leaving many smaller shareholdings to be dealt with where the administrative burden is proportionately higher compared to the benefit to the company. Small shareholders appeared resilient to the imposition of a tax charge where no cash had been received but, in the case of higher rate taxpayers, this charge will increase with the reduction of the deemed tax credit accompanying the stock dividend. The result might be that stock dividends become less attractive to shareholders and to companies.

Loans to participators

1.41 If the appropriate assessment is issued, a close company that makes a loan to a participator has to account for tax on the value of that loan as if the value of that loan were a dividend so ACT has to be accounted for (s 419). This does not apply if the loan is made by the company in the ordinary course of its business. Where the loan is released, the recipient is treated as having received the amount of the loan net of tax – formerly at the basic rate (s 421) and now at the lower rate – and the recipient is taxed as if he had received dividends that will be taxed according to the new rules applicable to dividends described above (FA 1993 s 77(4)). This change applies for the year 1993 to 1994 and subsequent years (FA 1993 s 77(5)). The change in the rate of ACT will make loans to participators less expensive.

1.42 A close company is any company controlled by, either:

1   five or fewer participators; or
2   its directors,

or where such persons would extract most of the value of the company in a winding-up. The term does not include:

1   a non-UK-resident company;
2   certain registered industrial and provident societies;
3   certain companies controlled by or on behalf of the Crown that are not otherwise close companies;
4   certain quoted companies or companies controlled by quoted companies.

What is a participator?

1.43 A participator includes:

1   a person with a share or an interest in the capital of the company;
2   a person with, or entitled to acquire, voting control of the company;
3   a person with, or entitled to acquire, certain payments to loan creditors;
4   a person entitled to secure that income or assets be applied for his benefit.

Repurchase of shares

1.44 *Prima facie*, a repurchase of shares is treated as a distribution to the extent that the price paid exceeds the nominal value of the share (s 209(2)). This is not the case where, broadly, a trading company buys its own shares for the benefit of its business and from qualifying shareholders (s 219). Where the relief does not apply, following the changes to the taxation of dividends, companies may now be more inclined to repurchase shares because of the reduced ACT cost.

Foreign dividends

1.45   The new tax treatment of dividends also applies to foreign dividends in certain cases (FA 1993 s 77(2)). Foreign dividends are charged to tax under Case V of Schedule D being income from possessions outside the UK. The new treatment of dividends only extends to foreign dividends when the payment would be treated as a dividend if the company were resident in the UK.

1.46   The new treatment of dividends does not apply if the payment is subject to the remittances basis. The remittances basis is the regime applicable to certain individuals who are not UK domiciled or citizens of either the Commonwealth or the Republic of Ireland who are not ordinarily resident in the UK (s 66(5)(b)). Under the remittances basis the individual is only taxed on the dividend when it is remitted to the UK.

9   TAX CREDITS AND FII

1.47   A UK-resident individual or company that receives a qualifying distribution from a UK-resident company is entitled to a tax credit to set against its UK tax liability (s 231). Formerly the amount of that tax credit corresponded to the rate of ACT. For the year 1993 to 1994 that will not be the case – whilst ACT is charged at the intermediate rate corresponding to 22.5% the tax credit will only be allowed at the rate of 20% (FA 1993 s 78(3)).

Repayment of tax credits

1.48   In certain alternative circumstances companies resident in the United Kingdom are entitled to a repayment of the tax credit (s 231(2)). The company must be either wholly exempt from corporation tax or only subject to corporation tax on its trading income. Alternatively, the distribution may be specifically exempt. There is a general exemption from corporation tax on dividends (s 208) but that is not a relevant exemption for these purposes.

1.49   There is a specific restriction on the repayment of tax credits that relate to dividends from close investment companies in certain circumstances (s 231(2A)). For the restriction to apply, there must be, amongst other things, a purpose to obtain a repayment of tax. A close investment company is any close company that is not a trading company, a member of a trading group or a commercially-based property investment company (s 13A). Where the provision applies, the Inspector can limit the available credit to the extent that appears to him just and reasonable.

1.50   Those bodies that do recover tax credits – such as pension funds and PEPs – will suffer a 20% reduction in that source of income. Government estimates are that there will be a reduction in payments of tax credits to such as pension funds, charities and non-residents of:

Year	Amounts £m
1993–94	800
1994–95	1,000
1995–96	1,100

(Source: Budget Press Release 16 March 1993 'Taxation of Dividends')

1.51 As a result, PEPs may become less effective investment vehicles when compared to their previous performance. However, the change makes them relatively no worse than any other means of investment. Pension funds, however, may need to be topped up if they are to meet their investment objectives in the future.

1.52 Certain non-residents may recover the tax credit by virtue of a relevant double tax treaty. The UK has concluded double tax treaties with many countries. The treaty usually provides for repayment of some or all of the tax credit – the terms of any relevant treaty should always be confirmed. The credit afforded by double tax treaties will, however, be reduced in line with the tax credit available in the UK.

1.53 Investment trusts are likely to become less attractive. An investment trust is a quoted company, that is not a close company, and is approved by the Board of Inland Revenue (s 842(1)). An investment trust derives most of its income from shares or securities and invests no more than 15% of its fund in any one company. The investment trust must retain no more than 15% of the income it derives from shares and securities. Reducing the tax credit attached to dividends by comparison to the rate of MCT will make investment trusts less fiscally transparent and, therefore, probably less attractive.

1.54 Pushing down ACT rates relative to MCT rates may mean funders have more tax capacity. Tax capacity allows companies to get an immediate benefit from allowances or reliefs. Tax capacity has reduced because of the overall economic downturn so the relative change in ACT rates may not have any immediate practical consequence because of brought forward losses. Since this wider differential in rates appears to be a structural change in the tax system, however, it should mean that there is more scope for tax-driven finance deals in the future.

Accounting

1.55 The separation of the ACT rate and the tax credit rate disturbs established practice; mistakes can be particularly anticipated. A dividend paying company will pay, in advance, tax on its profits. The company will probably have to pay further corporation tax, because of the limited set-off mechanism that operates (see above). As a result of the changes in the taxation of dividends, companies taxed at the small companies' rate will now also have a liability to MCT even when they distribute all of their profits. Recipients never did get a full tax credit for the tax paid by companies taxed at more than the small companies rate – now companies taxed at the small companies rate will also be caught by that mismatch. The novel element is that for one year individuals will receive a credit not equal to the tax that the company has paid in advance.

Franked investment income

1.56   The changes made to the calculation of tax credits do not apply for the purposes of calculating FII (FA 1993 s 78(4)(a)). Calculation of the tax credit will, therefore, take account of the intermediate rate of tax whilst it applies and so will be calculated at the rate of 22.5%. The changes do apply in relation to the payment of any credit comprised in FII (FA 1993 s 78(4)(b)). FII is a device to allow ACT to flow through the hands of a company receiving and paying dividends. By not reducing the amount of FII in line with tax credits, this mechanism continues to operate. The limitation or repayments of credits comprised in FII is in line with the new treatment of tax credits.

What is franked investment income?

1.57   FII means dividend income of a UK-resident company where the recipient is entitled to a tax credit. The value of the income is the amount of the distribution plus the amount of the tax credit.

FII set-off and recovery

1.58   A company that has paid a dividend may set against that dividend the FII it has received in the same relevant period – called franking – and need only account for ACT on the difference.

1.59   Where FII exceeds franked payments in any return period (see above), the surplus may be carried forward to frank future payments. Where FII is received in a later return period but in the same accounting period as a franked payment, the FII may be set against the earlier dividend payment and the ACT can be reclaimed.

1.60   Certain companies, exempt from corporation tax, can recover surplus FII.

Franked investment income relief

1.61   This so-called relief (s 242) operates as a cash flow assistance. A claim may be made to treat FII as taxable profits so that the accompanying tax credit is paid to the company. This is potentially a benefit where the company has certain other deductions available to it. The deductions are then neutralised until the company generates ACT when the FII is used to frank that liability whereupon the other reliefs become available in the ordinary way. The relevant deductions are:

1   trading losses;
2   charges on income;
3   management expenses;
4   those capital allowances given by discharge and repayment;
5   setting losses on unquoted shares against income.

Special cases

1.62   Special rules apply in certain cases where the tax credit calculated on the new basis (as explained above) does not equal the tax credit comprised in the FII. In these special cases, the tax credit comprised in the FII is reduced to the amount which would result from the new basis of calculating tax credits, that is to say 20% rather than 22.5% (FA 1993 s 78(6)). Subject to what is explained further below in relation to the use of FII and claims, the special cases are where FII is referred to in the following.

1   *Calculating the small companies rate of tax.*   Companies with profits below a specified level, currently £250,000, are taxed at the rate equivalent to the basic rate of income tax. These profits include most FII received by the company, the excluded FII being that which is or could be covered by a group income election (s 13(7)).
2   *Exempt funds.*   Special rules apply where the recipient of a qualifying distribution:
     (a)   is entitled to 10% of the class of shares generating the payment; and
     (b)   is exempt from tax; and
     (c)   is entitled to recover the tax credit by virtue of that exemption (s 236).
     To determine whether the rules apply, it is important to determine the relevant profits and those include FII.
3   *Life assurance companies.*   A life assurance company may include FII as income taxable under Schedule D Case I and FII is included when calculating whether the company has made a loss on its life business (s 434). In general, FII may not be used to frank distributions to shareholders where FII has been included in policy holders' income (s 434(3)). This reference to policy holders' FII, however, is not within the rules relating to special cases; the FII will be calculated on the ordinary basis (FA 1993 s 78(11)).
4   *Pension business.*   The treatment of FII in the hands of a life assurance company's pensions fund is subject to special rules (s 438). The company's profits are taxable but the pension fund is exempt from tax except that its dealing profits are taxed under Schedule D Case VI. Without more, FII is treated as part of profits of the company which can then reclaim the tax credit. At the company's election, provided the company makes a profit, the shareholders' share of FII can be excluded from the calculation of the company's profits and used to frank the company's distributions. Where the company exercises this election, it follows that the relevant FII, together with the associated tax credit, is ignored for the purpose of calculating any provisional repayment of tax (Sch 19AB para 1(8)).
5   *Capital redemption business.*   Profits and losses derived from a capital redemption business include FII (s 458). Capital redemption business

consists of insurance (other than life or industrial insurance) by the provision of future payment or payments in return for premiums.

6   *Mutual business or no business.*   Distributions by companies carrying on a mutual business – certain insurance companies – or no business, are only taxed to the extent that they are made out of profits subject to tax or FII (s 490).

7   *UK insurance companies trading overseas.*   Insurance companies producing trading profits overseas are entitled to a limited credit for foreign tax suffered on dividends earned by that trade and received from overseas companies (s 802). That limit refers to the company's FII.

8   *Policy holders' share of profits.*   In allocating the profits of a life assurance company to the shareholders, a proportion of the company's FII may be deducted (FA 1989 s 89).

Use of franked investment income

1.63   The new legislation confirms that where the tax credit has been paid, or is payable, no further credit is available to frank dividends or to be treated as unrelieved FII even though the credit calculated under the new basis is not the same as the amount accounted for as ACT (FA 1993 s 78(7)). In other words, payment of the tax credit determines its value and prevents the recipient from claiming a higher value based on a different rate of tax. This new provision applies in the following circumstances.

1   *Calculating ACT where the company receives FII.*   In any accounting period, a company has only to account for ACT on the excess of its dividends over FII received (s 241(5)). In setting FII against franked payments a dividend-paying company will get the benefit of a tax credit at the rate of ACT. Where the rate of ACT is higher than the rate used in calculating tax credits on dividend income and the company has reclaimed the credit, it cannot then go on to claim further FII representing the difference between the two rates.

2   *Pensions business.*   Under the new regime (FA 1993 s 78(6)) in calculating the credit allowed to a life assurance company on its pensions business (s 438(5)).

3   *Overseas life assurance companies.*   Unless an overseas life assurance company is assessed to tax on its life business under Schedule D Case I, it is assessed under Schedule D Case VI. The overseas life assurance company is chargeable to tax on dividends it receives from UK companies and is entitled to a repayment of the tax credit only if an individual resident in the same country as the assurance company would be entitled to a tax credit (s 441A).

4   *Policy holders' share of profits.*   In calculating the unrelieved FII for the purpose of calculating the company's Case I profit (FA 1989 s 89).

Claims

1.64   Certain claims to set-off surplus FII are now limited to the amount of the surplus that would result from calculating the tax credit under the new method (FA 1993 s 78(8)).

1.65 The relevant claims are as follows.

1 *Set-off of losses against surplus FII.* Surplus FII may be treated as profits subject to corporation tax so that other reliefs may be used to reduce the MCT charge (s 242). This has been discussed above.
2 *Set-off of loss brought forward.* Certain financial operations may be taxed under special provisions on what would otherwise have been trading income. When that is the case, surplus FII can be set against losses brought forward in order to generate a repayment of the tax credit (s 243). The FII taken into account equates to the FII that would be allowed for the equivalent relief for companies assessed to corporation tax (see also s 393(8)) and the amount of that FII is now to be calculated using the new method of calculating tax credits (FA 1993 s 78(10)).

Carry forward surplus FII

1.66 Surplus FII accruing in any period may be carried forward (s 241(3)). From the financial year 1994 and for subsequent years, this is subject to change. Where a claim is made for the set-off of surplus FII against losses etc as described above, and surplus FII remains to be carried forward, then the amount to be carried forward will be reduced. The reduction will be the difference between the tax credits calculated on the new basis and the tax credits calculated without regard to the new basis (FA 1993 s 78(9)).

10 CONSEQUENTIAL CHANGES

1.67 The rate of ACT is relevant to many provisions of the taxing legislation. Those affected by the change to the tax treatment of dividends are noted here to provide a checklist to identify the extent of the new changes. Except where otherwise noted, the following changes have effect beginning in the year 1993 to 1994.

1 *Excess liability.* The reference to being charged to tax or chargeable to tax at the basic rate in calculating an excess liability in the following provisions is amended to include the new basis of calculating the tax on dividends.
   (a) The tax liability on beneficial loans (s 167(2A) and Sch 7 para 19(1)).
   (b) The relief for payments of interest, excluding MIRAS (s 353).
   (c) Mortgage interest payable under deduction of tax (s 369(3B)).
   (d) The liability of settlors to higher rate tax on certain settlements (s 683(2), s 684(2)).
   (e) The definition of excess liability for the purpose of charges referred to under (a) to (d) above are also relevant for calculating capital gains tax assessed at the higher rate (Taxation of Chargeable Gains Act 1992 (TCGA) s 6). The capital gains tax provisions are, therefore, amended to reflect the new definition of excess liability.
   (f) References, in certain instruments made on or after 3rd September 1939, to sums free of tax or net of tax (s 819(2)).

2   *Taxation of certain recipients and non-qualifying distributions (s 233).*
     Subject to any double tax treaty, a person (other than a company) not
     resident in the UK is liable to higher rate tax on the distribution paid
     without adding the tax credit but reduced by the amount of a basic rate
     liability on that value of the distribution – the excess liability. In certain
     other cases, a person receiving a non-qualifying distribution has an excess
     liability calculated on the same basis. The previous, deemed, basic rate
     tax credit is reduced to a deemed lower rate tax credit and the provision
     extended to discretionary trusts in calculating their liability to higher rate
     tax (s 686). The deemed credit is not repayable to the recipient of the
     distribution.

3   *Trusts.*
     (a)   The rate of tax applicable to trusts. A new definition of the rate of
           tax to be paid by trusts (s 686) – referred to as the rate of tax
           applicable to trusts – is the sum of the basic rate of tax plus the
           additional rate. This new term is also substituted for the former
           references to basic rate plus additional rate in the following
           cases.
           (i)   The calculation of profits by trustees in relation to the
                  chargeable event connected with an employee share owner-
                  ship trust (FA 1989 s 68(2)(c)) including charges connected to
                  borrowings by the trustees in such circumstances (FA 1989 s
                  71(4)(c)).
           (ii)   The rate of tax charged on trustees on deemed income derived
                  from convertible securities when transferred or redeemed in
                  certain circumstances (FA 1990 Sch 10 para 19(1)).
           (iii) Sums paid to settlors otherwise than as income. An anti-
                  avoidance provision applies to treat as income certain capital
                  sums paid or lent to the settlor (s 677). In calculating the
                  charge the amount of basic rate and the additional rate of tax
                  used to be taken into account.
           (iv)   Deep discount securities and trusts. Deemed trust income
                  arising from disposal of deep discount securities by trustees
                  was formerly charged at the basic rate plus the additional rate
                  (Sch 4 para 17) and now at the rate applicable to trusts.
     (b)   Whereas, previously, the additional rate paid by trustees in certain
           cases applied to increase the basic rate this has been amended to
           impose a liability to tax at the rate of the difference between the
           lower rate and the rate applied to trusts in the following
           circumstances:
           (i)   distributions of exempt funds (s 235);
           (ii)   disallowance of relief in respect of bonus issues (s 237).
     (c)   Payments under discretionary trusts. The recipient of a payment
           under a discretionary trust is deemed to receive a payment net of
           tax – formerly at the basic rate and additional rate – now at the rate
           applicable to trusts (s 687). An equivalent change has been made to
           the charge on trustees arising from distributions of accumulated
           income (s 694).

4   *Applicable rate.*   A definition of this term is inserted (s 701). It applies
     to determine the rate of tax applicable to certain interests in residue in
     connection with wills. The applicable rate is the rate that the income
     would have borne had it been taxed. The tax can be apportioned

between different persons with an interest in residue in a way that is just and reasonable, in relation to their different interests. Subject to that apportionment, the income derived from the residue is deemed to have been taxed at the basic rate before the lower rate. References to basic rate have been amended to refer to the applicable rate in the following cases:

(a)   limited interests in residue (s 695(4)(a));

(b)   absolute interest in residue (s 696(3)–(5));

(c)   certain other interests in residue (s 698).

5   *Cancellation of tax advantage from certain transactions in securities.*   In certain prescribed circumstances, connected with transactions in securities (s 704), a person obtaining a tax advantage is liable to be assessed to tax. The tax may be treated as ACT paid by the relevant company – where that appears just and reasonable. The deemed ACT is now calculated at the lower rate.

6   *Anti-avoidance: trustees.*   The charges on trustees:

(a)   connected with the transfer of securities that also apply to nominees (s 720); and

(b)   relating to offshore gains,

are amended to refer to tax at the rate applicable to trusts rather than the former basic rate plus additional rate.

7   *Manufactured dividends and interest.*   As an anti-avoidance measure, manufactured dividends and interest are taxed as dividends (s 736A, Sch 23A). Manufactured dividends and interest are also subject to the new regime for taxing dividends. The applicable tax rate (s 737) is amended to reflect the changes to the lower rate via the intermediate rate as appropriate. Certificates of deduction of tax may also be issued concerning manufactured dividends or interest and the new provision for calculating tax credits amends the older provision. These changes affect any payment of manufactured dividend or interest made after 6 April 1993.

8   *Total income.*   Total income is defined for the purposes of the Income Tax Acts partly by adding a tax credit to dividend income (s 835(6)(a)). This now reflects the new tax credit system.

9   *Assessment of public revenue dividends and foreign dividends etc.*   Tax is collected on these transactions at, formerly, the basic rate and, now, the applicable rate (Sch 3 para 6A). The applicable rate is, in these circumstances, not as defined above. It is the lower rate in the case of a foreign dividend that is neither interest nor any other annual payment other than a dividend and the basic rate in any other relevant case. This provision affects transactions after 6 April 1993.

11   AUTHORISED UNIT TRUSTS

Relevant rate of tax

1.68   The deemed rate of corporation tax applied to authorised unit trusts (s 468E) is reduced to 22.5% for the financial year 1993 and to the lower rate of income tax for the following years.

Distributions to persons chargeable to corporation tax

1.69   FA 1990 introduced special rules that applied in certain circumstances (s 468F) to calculate the corporation tax liability of a corporate holder of units in an authorised unit trust. The special rules apply when dividends are treated as paid to the unit holder in certain circumstances defined by s 468(2) in a distribution period ending after 31 December 1990.

1.70   Where the special rules apply, the payment is deemed to be an annual payment, but not a dividend or other distribution, for the purposes of calculating the corporation tax liability of the unit holder. Previously this deemed annual payment was treated as received net of tax at the basic rate. The deemed annual payment is now treated as received net of tax at the lower rate.

Unfranked portion

1.71   Whereas the rules explained in the previous paragraph used to apply to the whole of the payment, they now apply only to the unfranked portion of the payment, identified as U in the following formula

$$U = P \times \frac{I - D}{I}$$

where,

P   is the payment
I   is the amount of the trust's gross income in the relevant distribution period which amount was the basis of the distributions to the unit holders for that period
D   is the sum included in I that represents the FII of the trust.

The effect of this change is to remove a company's tax liability on authorised unit trust dividends that are themselves derived from UK dividends.

1.72   These changes apply to any payment made after 1 April 1993.

12   CAPITAL GAINS TAX

1.73   The rate of capital gains tax is equated to the rate of tax an individual suffers on his income (TCGA s 4). This has been amended to reflect the changes made to the taxation of dividends (FA 1993 Sch 6, para 22). The mechanism to determine the rate of tax applicable to chargeable gains is already contorted by virtue of previous amendments reflecting the introduction of the lower rate of tax. The changes resulting from the new treatment of dividends are, therefore, equally contorted.

1.74   In the first instance, capital gains tax is charged at the basic rate (TCGA s 4(1)). This rate is reduced to the lower rate to the extent that the individual's income does not exceed the lower rate band. The gains charged at the lower rate are referred to as the relevant amount (TCGA s 4(1A)). It is therefore necessary to determine:

1   whether the individual has any income; and
2   if so, how much.

In determining these two criteria for deciding a person's relevant income and so the rate of tax charged, it is now necessary to disregard:

1   income chargeable at the lower rate of tax by virtue of the new treatment of dividends; and
2   income that would be chargeable at the lower rate were it not chargeable at the higher rate (TCGA s 4(3A)).

That is to say, any dividend income within the new regime.

1.75   When, as a result of disregarding income because of TCGA s 4(3A), as described above, an individual is charged to tax on gains at the lower rate of tax (the amount of the gain being referred to as the amount of the lower rate gain), two consequences follow.

1   *Reduced basic rate limit.*   The basic rate limit is reduced by the amount of the lower rate gain. This applies for the purpose of calculating the liability to tax at the higher rate on both capital gains and income.

2   *Reduced higher rate tax charge.*   Where the taxpayer pays income tax at the higher rate, he has to pay capital gains tax also at the higher rate (TCGA s 4(2)). Now, however, the amount of the capital gain liable to higher rate tax is reduced by the amount of the lower rate gain. The effect of this is that the first slice of capital gains benefits from the lower rate band prior to any dividend income.

1.76   Trusts are also subject to a special regime applying to any capital gains that they realise and this has been amended to reflect the tax treatment of dividends. The trustees of accumulation and discretionary trusts were charged to tax at the rate equivalent to the basic and additional rates combined (TCGA s 5(1)). This is now amended to the rate applicable to trusts – as described above. The definition of excess liability in relation to certain tax charges is also re-defined (see excess liability above).

13   SMALL COMPANIES

Whether to incorporate

1.77   Sole traders have to face the question of whether to incorporate their business. Depending on the specific circumstances, financial requirements and intentions of the trader, there is a level of taxable profits beyond which it becomes tax effective to incorporate. Often incorporation is imposed on a trader by commercial concerns and those that do incorporate for short-term tax gains may later regret their decision on purely a financial basis. The ACT changes make incorporation less favourable from a tax point of view – all else being equal the profit threshold will have increased and, where most of the profits of the business are to be extracted, remaining unincorporated is likely to be the most favourable course in tax terms at any level of profits.

Salary versus dividend

1.78   Once incorporated, a private business can make considerable savings by paying the proprietors in dividends rather than salary. The changes have reduced that saving, as is shown below.

	Salary	*Dividend*	
		1992/93	1993/94
Company profits pre salary/dividend	1,000	1,000	1,000
Gross salary	906		
Net dividend of £150 grossed up $1/3$ or $1/4$		1,000	937.5
Tax			
Employer's NI	94		
ACT @ $1/3$ or $9/31$		250	217.7
CNT	Nil	Nil	32.3
PAYE @ higher value	362		
Higher rate tax on dividend		150	187.5
Net received by proprietor	544	600	562.5
Effective tax rate	45.6%	40%	43.75%
It is assumed that:	the small companies rate applies; there is no employees' NI; income tax is paid at 40%		

The example does not reveal the cash flow advantage of paying dividends rather than salary – the higher rate income tax is deferred. It also ignores the effect of reducing pensionable earnings.

Small companies rate

1.79   It will be a change of practice for companies taxed at the small companies rate to find that the tax credit for the shareholders is neither at the MCT rate nor at the rate of ACT. The ACT rate will be aligned after a year but mistakes can be anticipated. The MCT rate mismatch will emphasise the increased tax take from dividends – shareholders will have a stronger incentive to inject future funding by way of loans rather than equity.

14 CHARITIES

Introduction

1.80 Charities that do not pay tax may reclaim the tax credit attached to dividends. With the reduction in the rate of that credit they will suffer a reduced income for a given dividend – whether companies will increase their dividends is considered further above. To soften the impact of this anticipated drop in income, charities are provided with a transitional relief whereby they may claim from the Inland Revenue a fraction of any qualifying distribution they receive (FA 1993 s 80). The transitional relief applies to distributions after 5 April 1993 and before 6 April 1997.

1.81 The repayment is to be made out of funds specifically provided by the Government but is treated as a tax credit for the purposes of the provisions governing the use of tax credits.

Qualifying bodies

1.82 A body referred to as a section 505 body may qualify to make the claim. This term refers to the following bodies.

1   Charities; namely any body of persons or a trust established for charitable purposes only (s 506). The exclusivity of the purpose required should be given careful attention as this has caused problems in the past (*Guild v Inland Revenue Commissioners* [1991] STC 281).
2   Special heritage bodies; namely:
the Trustees of the National Heritage Memorial Fund;
the Historic Buildings and Monuments Commission for England;
the Trustees of the British Museum;
the Trustees of the British Museum (National History) (s 507).
3   Scientific research organisations; certain approved bodies that are appropriately constituted for qualifying purposes connected with scientific research (s 508).

1.83 In order to qualify for the relief the qualifying body must also qualify for repayment of tax credits. A charity is not eligible for a credit where its relevant income and gains exceed both £10,000 and its qualifying expenditure and it incurs or is deemed to incur other non-qualifying expenditure (s 5(3)).

Non-qualifying payments

1.84 In addition to the general limit on the payment of tax credits, the Board of Inland Revenue may determine that any particular distribution does not qualify for the relief. It may do so having regard to particular anti-avoidance provisions, namely the following:

1   *Distributions from exempt funds (s 235).* This provision prevents dividend-stripping operations by exempt funds. Where the recipient of the qualifying distribution would otherwise be entitled to the tax credit, but is exempt from tax and holds 10% or more of the shares on which the dividend is declared, then the exemption is lifted and the dividend brought into the charge for tax, possibly at the additional rate.

2   *Bonus issues etc (s 237).* The exemption from tax and relief for losses are restricted in relation to certain distributions which thereby become taxable, possibly at the additional rate. The relevant distributions are:
   (a)   certain distributions in excess of any new consideration received (s 209(3));
   (b)   bonus issues following the repayment of share capital (s 210);
   (c)   certain distributions not treated as repayments of share capital (s 211).

3   *Cancellation of tax advantage from certain transactions in shares (s 703).* This anti-avoidance provision has potentially wide-ranging application and is referred to above.

1.85   The Board may reach its decision to disallow the payment in whole or in part before or after the distribution is made. The Board's decision may be appealed to the Special Commissioners by written notice within 30 days of notification of the decision.

Qualifying fraction

1.86   The relief, geared to the amount of the distribution, tapers over four years. The fraction is as follows:

Year	Fraction
1993/94	$1/15$
1994/95	$1/20$
1995/96	$1/30$
1996/97	$1/60$

The period of a year referred to relates to payments after 5 April in the earlier year until the date before 6 April in the following year.

1.87   These dates and amounts appear arbitrary but may be significant – a day's delay will sometimes significantly affect the proportion of the distribution that may be claimed. The significant event is the making of the distribution – namely, when it became due and payable (s 834(3)). A final dividend is payable when it is declared, unless it is declared to be payable at a future date. An interim dividend, on the other hand, is not made until it is paid.

Recovery procedure

1.88   The relief is dependent upon a claim by the qualifying body. The claim must be made within two years of the end of the relevant body's relevant chargeable period. The chargeable period means, either, the accounting period or year of assessment.

1.89   The two-year time limit will probably be strictly enforced. In any case, for cash flow purposes, the qualifying bodies will not want to delay the reclaim – it would make sense to make the claim at the same time as claiming the tax credit associated with the distribution. But when making a claim for a period spanning one or more of the changes of rate that adjustment should not be overlooked.

15   DISCRETIONARY AND ACCUMULATION TRUSTS

Introduction

1.90   Trustees of certain trusts have a specific liability to tax on relevant income. The relevant trusts are those where payments are discretionary or where the trustees have the power to accumulate income and the income is neither the income of another person nor deemed to be that of the settlor or the income of a charity.

1.91   The trustees have formerly been liable to tax at the basic rate and the additional rate – there have been changes to the relevant provisions as are explained above. Income of a discretionary trust is now taxed at the rate applicable to trusts or, under the new regime applicable to distributions, at the lower rate (s 686(1)). These rates also apply to the trust's capital gains (TCGA s 5(1)). Where trustees receive qualifying distributions, the value of the distribution is deemed to be reduced by lower rate tax and the trustees are treated as having paid lower rate tax (s 233(1A)). The reference to qualifying distributions means as defined for the purposes of ACT as explained above. Trustees are not, however, entitled to repayment of the lower rate tax.

Order of expenses set-off

1.92   In calculating the tax charged on the income of the relevant trusts, certain expenses are allowed, namely those properly chargeable to income or that would be so chargeable but for an express provision of the trust (s 686(2)(d)). This permits only the deduction of what are regarded as income expenses under general law and not income defrayed in capital expenses (*Re Bennett, Jones v Bennett* [1896] 1 Ch 778; *Carver v Duncan, Bosanquet v Allen* [1985] STC 356). These expenses are now deemed to be set first against income chargeable under the new regime applicable to distributions before any other income.

Management expenses of non-resident trustees

1.93   Where trustees are not resident in the UK they are, in certain circumstances, not liable to UK income tax on certain income – non-taxed income. Provisions connected with double tax relief may deem trustees to be non-resident to the same effect.

1.94   Where a trust earns taxed and untaxed income, a proportion of its 'management expenses' will be disallowed. Management expenses is the term used to define expenses properly chargeable against income or that would be so chargeable but for some term of the trust. The proportion disallowed is the proportion the untaxed income bears to the income of the trustees; that proportion is calculated on a year-on-year basis.

Expenses planning

1.95   The rules for order of set-off and management expense relief appear to bear careful attention depending on the circumstances of the trust. For example, rippeling untaxed income and management expenses could achieve more effective relief for expenses. Untaxed income might be focused into one year out of three and the management expenses moved out of that year in order to maximise relief.

Non-qualifying distributions

1.96   Where a trust has received non-qualifying distributions, any liability of the trustees to tax on the distribution is reduced by the lower rate liability to tax on so much of the distribution that is taxed (s 233(1B)). A non-qualifying distribution means any distribution that is not wholly a qualifying distribution for the purposes of ACT (as defined above).

Payments under discretionary trusts

1.97   Special rules apply to tax income payments by trustees exercising a discretion. The relevant tax rate was formerly defined as the basic rate and the additional rate and is now referred to as the rate applicable to trusts. The recipient is treated as receiving income after deduction of tax at the relevant rate which tax the trustees are liable to pay. The charge applies when the recipient receives, maybe indirectly, what is income in his hands as a result of the action of the trustees – apportionments of capital may not trigger the charge (*Stevenson v Wishart* [1987] STC 226). The applicable rate, as defined relative to discretionary trusts, also applies to payments made by personal representatives to trustees of discretionary trusts.

Deductions

Tax paid by the trust

1.98   Certain amounts may be set-off against the liability of a person receiving a payment from a discretionary trust. As explained above, payments are treated as net of tax; formerly at the rate of the sum of basic rate tax and the additional rate tax and now at the rate applicable to trusts (s 687(2)). The tax deduction is treated as tax paid by the recipient of the payment – the applicable rate of tax has been amended appropriately (s 687(3)(a)). A new deduction allows a credit for tax charged on non-qualifying distributions (see below), the rate of credit being the difference between the lower rate of tax and the rate applicable to trusts (s 687(3)(aa)).

Stock dividends

1.99   The recent Finance Act has reinstated a former allowable deduction enacted by FA 1973 s 17(3) consolidated in s 687(3)(b) and repealed by FA 1989 Sch 17 Part V. The former provision read:

> 'The amount of tax at the additional rate on any sum treated, under section 426(2) as applied by Section 686(4) or under section 249(6) as income of the trustees'.

1.100   Section 426(2) applied the charge to income tax when there had been an apportionment of income to an individual under the close companies rules and applied to certain trusts by virtue of s 686(4). Apportionment has been repealed for accounting periods beginning after 31 March 1989, making these former references redundant when the provision is re-enacted.

The effect of s 249(6) is to extend the stock dividend rules to issues of such shares to trustees. Tax treated as paid in connection with stock dividends may also be deducted in calculating the tax charge on trustees.

Convertible securities

1.101   Another deduction is provided for tax treated as income of the trustees in connection with convertible securities (FA 1990 Sch 10 para 12). Such income is chargeable to tax at the sum of the basic rate and additional rate (FA 1990 Sch 10 para 19).

Rate of tax

1.102   The rate of tax referred to in s 687(3)(b) is also amended to the rate equal to the difference between the lower rate of tax and the rate applicable to trusts. This change is also made, where relevant, to the calculation of the other allowable deductions.

1.103   The rates of tax applicable to certain interests in residue have been amended to reflect the new regime – as explained above. There has also been a change to the tax charged on beneficiaries (s 698A). With a certain exception, where a beneficiary is treated as receiving income that has suffered tax at the lower rate that income shall fall within the new regime applicable to dividends for the purpose of determining the applicable rate of tax. The exception is when income is paid indirectly through a trustee in which case the trustee is treated as receiving Schedule F dividend income for the purpose of calculating tax under the new regime.

16   PROPOSALS RELATING TO FOREIGN DIVIDENDS

1.104   The Government announced, with the Budget, a consultative document ('Corporation Tax Surplus ACT Proposals for Reform'). This concerns the proposal of what is referred to as a foreign income dividend ('FID') to help overcome long-term ACT arising as a result of foreign taxed income. The consultation document also refers to international headquarter companies that the Government proposes to introduce regardless of the outcome of the consultation regarding foreign income dividends.

Foreign income dividends

The option

1.105   Companies would have the option whether or not to declare an FID. Since this right might unsettle the stock markets some companies might declare an FID policy but are unlikely to want to bind themselves more than is necessary. The company would be free to declare an FID and an ordinary dividend but it may not stream its dividends, that is to say paying ordinary dividends to those requiring a credit and FIDs to those not requiring a credit.

ACT

1.106   The company would pay ACT on its FIDs. The ACT could be set against MCT and might be surplus if there was sufficient ACT capacity. The surplus ACT attributable to foreign source profits would be repayable up to the amount of the surplus ACT for the period. ACT attributable to FIDs could be carried back for one year and so could generate a repayment of tax. ACT paid on an FID in the relevant accounting period would be repaid at the same time as the MCT became due.

1.107   The FID scheme will apply to foreign source profits. This means profits or gains charged to corporation tax and for which the company was allowed a foreign tax credit. The company will have to be able to demonstrate the allocation of FIDs to foreign source profits to recover ACT but will be able to choose between sources of foreign income. The company would probably choose to allocate FIDs to more highly-taxed profits first since that would generate the maximum ACT repayment.

1.108   FIDs would be taxed as income received after deduction of tax at the lower rate but would carry no repayable tax credit. This would also apply to trustees of discretionary trusts. The denial of a repayable tax credit would operate as a disincentive to those that reclaim the credit – this could also extend to foreign shareholders whose circumstances would have to be considered in relation to any particular applicable double tax treaty.

1.109   A company that receives an FID could use it to frank an FID it pays. But there will be no mixed franking either of normal dividends by FIDs or vice versa. Nor will the group income election apply to FIDs.

International headquarter companies

1.110 The FID scheme includes an inherent cash flow cost – the ACT has to be paid up front and though it may be repaid that may not happen for almost 21 months from payment. An international headquarter company would be allowed to pay FID without paying ACT. The international headquarter company will be defined by foreign ownership – it may have to be 80% foreign-owned – and number of shareholders – this may be no more than five.

CHAPTER 2

Anti-avoidance and the CGT reliefs

1 THE AVOIDANCE OR MINIMISATION OF ACT SURPLUSES

Background

2.1 The surplus advance corporation tax ('ACT') problem is well known and, in one form or another, has been with us since the introduction of the imputation system of corporation tax in the Finance Act 1972.

2.2 In recent years, there have been a number of important studies on the problem. See, for example, John Chown's 'Company Tax Harmonisation in the EEC' (The Institute of Directors, 1989), Barry Bracewell-Milnes' 'A Tax on Trade' (The Adam Smith Institute, 1989) and 'An ACT Against Trade' (The Adam Smith Institute, 1992), Malcolm Gammie's 'Imputation Systems and Foreign Income: The UK Surplus ACT Problem and its Relationship to European Corporate Tax Harmonisation' (Intertax, 1991/12) and Chris Higson's 'The Problem of Surplus ACT' (London Business School, 1992).

Other studies that are worth reading in this area include 'ACT: The Quoted Companies' by Robin D Joyce (Leigh Philip Publishing, 1992) and 'The Finance, Investment and Tax Decisions of Multinationals' by J Alworth (Blackwell, 1988).

2.3 While it is not possible in this section to discuss the surplus ACT problem in any detail, the following brief summary may be helpful in understanding the problem.

Basically, a UK-resident company accounts to the Inland Revenue for ACT at the prevailing rate whenever it makes a qualifying distribution (TA 1988 s 14). Provided the company pays sufficient corporation tax on its profits, the ACT represents no additional cost to the company (other than of a cash flow nature) since the ACT can be set against its corporation tax liability up to a specified maximum (TA 1988 s 239). In those cases where the company does not have a sufficient corporation tax liability, the ACT becomes surplus.

2.4 While it is wrong to generalise, surplus ACT usually arises as a result of one or both of the following two reasons.

(a) The level of dividends that a company pays is generally based on its accounting profits whereas a company's tax liability is based on its taxable profits. In those cases where a company's accounting profits are greater than its taxable profits, the company's corporation tax liability may not be sufficient (given the restrictions) to cover the ACT. This discrepancy between accounting and taxable profits was a particular problem when there was stock relief and widespread 100% first year allowances. Fortunately, such discrepancies between accounting and taxable profits normally right themselves over a period of time and the existing reliefs (see 2.6 below) are generally sufficient to ensure that surplus ACT is not a serious problem.

(b) The more serious problem relates to those companies that earn a substantial part of their profits abroad. These profits will often suffer overseas tax at a level that ensures, due to double tax relief, that little or no UK corporation tax is paid. Since ACT cannot be set off against foreign taxes, it represents an additional tax charge on the distribution of foreign profits. This type of surplus ACT is often of a more permanent nature than (a) above and rarely capable of much alleviation by the existing reliefs.

2.5 A surplus ACT problem may also arise where the dividends paid by a company are not justified by its profits (accounting or tax), perhaps being paid out of reserves. For example, during the recent recession many companies have continued to maintain their level of dividends even though their current profits have not justified it. Like (a) above, however, such surplus ACT is likely to be temporary with the existing reliefs generally being sufficient to avoid a long-term problem.

2.6 The legislation provides a number of ways for surplus ACT to be relieved, for example, by carry back to earlier accounting periods (TA 1988 s 239(3)), by carry forward to future accounting periods (TA 1988 s 239(4)) or by being surrendered to subsidiaries (TA 1988 s 240). Notwithstanding this legislation, however, for many companies the ACT remains surplus with little prospect of it ever being recovered. Conventional ACT planning is often of only limited benefit to such companies.

2.7 As a result of the above, many companies with an on-going surplus ACT problem have tried to eliminate or minimise it by embarking on arrangements that involve the acquisition from a third party of a company with ACT capacity. Usually, these arrangements have entailed:

(i) the surplus ACT company acquiring the ACT capacity company (perhaps after the company has been suitably 'packaged', for example, it will generally be dormant with net assets equal to its called up share capital);

(ii) interposing it between the surplus ACT company (generally the parent company of the group) and its operating subsidiaries;

(iii) the operating subsidiaries paying up an appropriate level of dividends to the ACT capacity company as group dividends (to give it sufficient reserves to fund its own dividends under (iv) below); and

(iv) the ACT capacity company paying a dividend up to the surplus ACT company outside of a group income election to provide itself with surplus ACT it can carry back to earlier years and the surplus ACT company with FII to offset against its surplus ACT.

2.8   Perhaps not surprisingly, the Inland Revenue have argued that these arrangements do not achieve their objectives and have tried to apply such provisions as the transaction in securities legislation to the arrangements (TA 1988 ss 703–709) or the *Furniss v Dawson* ([1984] STC 153) principle. They have now decided to tackle the problem by specific legislation.

The Finance Act 1993 changes

General

2.9   The Chancellor has attacked the surplus ACT problem in two ways:

(a)   by reducing the rate of ACT during 1993/94 and 1994/95; and
(b)   by proposing a foreign income dividend scheme.

Both of the above subjects are dealt with in the Report on Dividend Planning. Given that it is currently estimated that unrelieved ACT carried forward is some £5 billion (Hansard, 15 February 1993), the proposals have come not a moment too soon.

The Chancellor accompanied the above changes with an attack on the purchase and sale of the surplus ACT capacity company (FA 1993 s 81) and these changes are discussed below.

2.10   ACT can normally be carried forward to future years without restriction in that, unlike the case of trading losses, there is no requirement for the same trade to continue or, indeed, any trade. The only exception to this is to be found in TA 1988 ss 245 and 245A which broadly provide that where the beneficial ownership of a company changes hands and, roughly at the same time, there is major change in the nature, conduct or scale of its activities, the company's surplus ACT cannot be carried forward from the accounting period ending (either deemed or actual) with the change of ownership.

2.11   For the above purpose, the accounting period in which the change of ownership occurs is treated as two separate accounting periods, one ending and the other beginning on the date of change of ownership (TA 1988 s 245(2)). This deemed end and start to an accounting period also applies for the purposes of calculating relief against ACT payable by reference to franked investment income (TA 1988 s 241), setting ACT against a 'mainstream' liability (TA 1988 s 239) and determining return periods (TA 1988 Sch 13).

2.12   These provisions are very similar to those relating to the carry forward of trading losses in TA 1988 s 768 and, like those provisions, attempt to prevent the traffic in companies with surplus ACT. In certain respects, TA 1988 ss 245 and 245A are more necessary than TA 1988 s 768 in that, with trading losses, the Inland Revenue have always had the normal, albeit often ineffectual, argument that the same trade no longer exists to prevent the carry forward of trading losses (see, for example, such cases as *Gordon Blair Ltd v CIR* (1962) 40 TC 358 and *Robroyston Brickworks v IRC* [1976] STC 329).

2.13   Clearly, but for TA 1988 ss 245 and 245A, a company with surplus ACT could be acquired by another company or group with the aim of injecting a profitable trade or business into it to utilise the surplus ACT. While such surplus exists, the profitable trade or business would then only suffer corporation tax for the year ended 31 March 1993 at a 'net' rate of 8% (or 0% if a 'small company' within TA 1988 s 13).

2.14   The sections broadly apply if within any three year period there is:

(a)   a change in the beneficial ownership of the company, and, either earlier, at the same time, or later in the same period, or

(b)   there is a major change in the nature or conduct of its trade or business (TA 1988 s 245(1)(a)).

It also applies if after the scale of the activities in a trade or business carried on by the company has become small or negligible (and before any considerable revival in such trade or business) there is change in the beneficial ownership of the company (TA 1988 s 245(1)(b)).

2.15   A 'change of ownership' for the purposes of TA 1988 s 245 is defined by reference to TA 1988 s 769 (TA 1988 s 245(7)) and a 'major change in the nature or conduct of a trade or business' is defined in TA 1988 s 245 in a similar way to the definition of a trade in TA 1988 s 768 (although, of course, TA 1988 s 768 itself applies only to trading losses and not to surplus ACT).

2.16   The full definition of a 'major change in the nature or conduct of a trade or business' refers to:

'(a)   a major change in the type of property dealt in, or services or facilities provided, in the trade or business,

(b)   a major change in customers, outlets or markets of the trade or business,

(c)   a change whereby the company ceases to be a trading company and becomes an investment company and vice versa, and

(d)   where the company is an investment company, a major change in the nature of the investments held by the company.'

The change may be the result of a gradual process which began outside the 3 year period (TA 1988 s 245(4)).

Detailed legislation

2.17   What FA 1993 s 81 has done is to say that where, within the above provisions, the ownership of a company changes, not only can ACT not be carried forward from the acquired company but that company cannot carry back any ACT it pays in respect of distributions made in an accounting period ending after the change of ownership to set against corporation tax liabilities of an earlier period (TA 1988 new s 245(3A)).

2.18   For the above purpose, the change of ownership brings an accounting period to an end with time before and after being treated as two separate accounting periods.

2.19   The date of the change of ownership effectively brings down a wall which ACT on either side cannot cross.

2.20   The new legislation applies to changes of ownership on or after 16 March 1993 (TA 1988 new s 245(3B)).

Comment

2.21   What can a company still do to avoid a surplus ACT problem if the ACT proposals announced in the 1993 Spring Budget are of no, or little, assistance as will often be the case?

2.22   Clearly the company can reduce its dividends thereby reducing its ongoing ACT bill. Historically, UK companies distribute a larger percentage of their earnings to shareholders than their overseas competitors (see Alexander, I and Mayer, C 'Banks and Securities Markets: Corporation Financing in Germany and the United Kingdom', Journal of Japanese and International Economies 4, 1990). Reducing dividends is, however, rarely an attractive option for listed companies.

2.23   The company could pay distributions that do not give rise to an ACT liability (ie non-qualifying distributions) such as bonus issues and scrip/stock issues (eg gross stock dividends and dividend reinvestment schemes such as the currently popular BAT Industries arrangement, *Financial Times*, 23 March 1993).

2.24   Other options include debt push-down arrangements where UK debt is taken offshore to be borne by an overseas company with appropriate taxable capacity. This will increase UK profits and related corporation tax liability against which the surplus ACT can be set.

2.25   Restructuring the share capital can also achieve results. For example, by issuing shares to repay UK debt or by means of income access arrangements (examples include the SmithKline Beecham plc and Waterford Wedgwood arrangements of recent years). It is also worth considering equalisation arrangements (eg the Unilever arrangement) and the twin holding company structures (eg the Shell structure).

2.26   Where the surplus ACT problem is caused by the amount of foreign income, clearly the foreign income dividend scheme needs to be looked at closely. If, however, this is of only limited assistance other measures may need to be considered.

2.27   For example, can the company increase profits earned in the UK by a revision upwards of charges to overseas subsidiaries, eg management charges or goods sold? Note, however, the transfer pricing considerations in TA 1988 s 770. See also the OECD Reports in 1979 and 1984 'Transfer Pricing and Multinational Enterprises'. Failing this, can it reduce overseas group assets (by say a debt 'push-down' arrangement and/or cross-border arbitrage)? In certain cases it may be possible to minimise non-UK taxes (eg by the use of UK Case V companies, overseas mixers, local groupings, etc).

2.28 If desperate, a brave company may like to argue that the UK ACT system is in contravention of the EC parent/subsidiary directive (see 'The EC Parent-Subsidiary Directive and UK Advance Corporation Tax: Abuse by the Tax Authorities', European Taxation, October 1992).

2.29 Failing the above, it may still be necessary to consider more artificial possibilities. While many of these have been blocked by the Finance Act 1993 changes, there remain a number of other possibilities. For example, the acquisition of a surplus FII company (rather than an ACT capacity company) still seems possible.

2   CONTROLLED FOREIGN COMPANIES

Background

2.30 Since 6 April 1984, the Inland Revenue have in certain circumstances been able to issue a direction whereby the total income of a 'controlled foreign company' (a CFC) is apportioned to persons who had an interest in the company during the relevant accounting period (TA 1988 ss 747–756 and Schs 24–26). The main purpose of the legislation is to charge to UK tax those profits of non-UK companies that have been accumulated in low tax territories.

2.31 Broadly speaking, a controlled foreign company is a company that is:

(a)   resident outside the UK,
(b)   controlled by persons resident in the UK, and
(c)   subject to a lower level of taxation in the territory in which it is resident (TA 1988 s 747).

2.32 A company only came within (c) above, ie is subject to a lower level of taxation, if it is subject to local tax of less than 50% of the corresponding UK tax (ie the hypothetical corporation tax it would have suffered had it been a UK-resident company). The trouble with this definition is that in the financial year 1984 (the first year the provisions applied), the corporation tax rate in the UK was 45% whereas it is now 33%. Therefore, and accepting that respective tax rates are not what determines whether a company is a CFC (see 2.34 below), the overseas company originally needed to pay local tax of around 22.5% before it avoided being a CFC whereas it now only needs to pay local tax of approximately 16.5%.

2.33 The reduction over the years in the UK rate of corporation tax has taken many overseas companies out of the CFC net. In addition, many arrangements have been entered into by multinational groups to ensure (often by means of certain mixing devices) that the relevant overseas company keeps its local tax liability just above the 50% threshold.

2.34 It is important to appreciate that the 50% test is based not on respective tax rates but by a comparison of the tax that the company paid under the law of the territory in which it is resident and the 'corresponding United Kingdom tax' on those profits. While in doing this calculation there are a number of assumptions that have to be made, the corresponding UK tax is broadly the corporation tax (excluding tax on chargeable gains) which would have been payable for the accounting period if the company had been resident in the UK (TA 1988 s 750(2) and (3)). Therefore, even thought the local tax rate may exceed 50% of the UK rate, the availability of local reliefs and deductions may still bring the company into the CFC regime.

2.35   The Budget on 16 March 1993 contained an important change to the CFC legislation, making it vital for many groups to review their position both for the current accounting period and for their longer-term strategy.

The Finance Act 1993 changes

2.36   In relation to accounting periods beginning on or after 16 March 1993, a lower level of taxation will be defined as a tax charge which is less than 75% of the corresponding tax charge in the UK rather than 50% (FA 1993 s 118(1) and (2)).

2.37   This will bring some companies within the CFC rules for the first time, notably Channel Islands companies currently paying a 20% rate of tax and dual resident 'mixer' companies which are deliberately structured to pay tax at mixed rates in order to achieve an average rate which is slightly higher than the pre-Budget cut-off rate of 16.5%. Three quarters of the current UK rate is 24.75% although, as explained above, a comparison of respective tax rates is not how the calculation of a lower level of taxation is arrived at.

Comment

2.38   UK companies with subsidiaries which will fall within these rules for the first time will clearly need to consider their position. Some may be able to rely on:

(a)   the exemption within the CFC legislation relating to the activities of the foreign subsidiary ('the exempt activities test' – TA 1988 s 748(1)(b) and Sch 25 Pt II) so that in practice their position remains unchanged; or

(b)   the Excluded Country list (IR Press Release, 8 March 1991: List of excluded countries for the purposes of the controlled foreign companies legislation as amended by, for example, IR Press Release 26 April 1993).

2.39   In borderline cases, it will be important to examine forecasts of income and expenditure and to take action where appropriate to avoid the impact of the new limit by:

(a)   introducing additional transactions; or
(b)   abandoning or rescheduling proposed transactions.

It will rarely be sufficient to rely on an examination of the accounts of previous years, unless the pattern of the subsidiary's activities is exceptionally consistent from one year to the next. In particular, as it is not only the rate of UK and overseas tax which needs to be considered, differing rules as to the calculation of taxable profits may have a significant impact on the amount of the liability in each jurisdiction (such matters as capital allowances and interest payments may alter the liability substantially).

2.40 Care will need to be taken in respect of accounting periods which straddle 16 March 1993. For companies which only fall within the CFC legislation as a result of the Budget changes, this accounting period will be split into two:

(a) one ending on 15 March 1993, and
(b) the second beginning on 16 March 1993 (FA 1993 s 119(3)).

2.41 To avoid a direction for a CFC company, one of the defences is that the company has pursued an 'acceptable distribution policy' (TA 1988 s 748(1)(a) and Sch 25 Pt I). Although no dividend will need to be paid out of profits for the period to 15 March 1993 (as for that period the company will not be a CFC), one will need to be paid for the second period. As this period will be for less than one year, the Inland Revenue has an option to require the dividend to represent a proportion (90% or 50%) of profits computed under UK tax legislation rather than accounting profits (TA 1988 Sch 25 para 3(1) and (2)). This means that companies with high levels of non-tax deductible provisions and expenses may have to pay substantially higher levels of dividends.

2.42 It is assumed that the apportionment of total distributable and taxable profits between the period ended 15 March 1993 and the period beginning 16 March will be computed on a pro-rata basis according to the length of the periods. However, it may be worthwhile considering closing off the period at 15 March by drawing up audited accounts to that date to provide a more certain measure of the distributable and taxable profits for these periods, though a number of factors will need to be taken into account, including local company law restrictions and the possibility that closing off the period may advance the payment of overseas tax.

2.43 It should be noted that dual resident mixing companies cannot satisfy the acceptable distribution test and closing off accounting periods at 15 March may be the most effective way to preserve the old mixed rate for the first period, leaving the second period to be reviewed under the new rules.

3 CAPITAL GAINS OF GROUPS OF COMPANIES: CAPITAL LOSS BUYING

Background

2.44 The buying and selling of capital losses has been a favourite game for many years. Most of the large firms of accountants and lawyers (and others) have usually been able, on request, to match companies with large potential capital gains with companies that have capital losses they wish to sell.

2.45   The game stems from two basic principles of tax legislation in so far as they affect a group of companies.

(a)   First, the treatment of capital losses in a group is very restrictive. Broadly speaking, the capital losses of a company may only be set against its own chargeable gains arising either in the same or future accounting periods. It is not possible in a group of companies to surrender a capital loss to another company in the group, to carry the loss back to earlier years or to offset the loss against non-capital gains or income (see, however, TA 1988 s 573).

(b)   Second, transfers of assets within a group of companies are deemed to take place under TCGA 1992 s 171 not at market value or for the actual sales price but for a sales consideration which gives rise to neither capital gain nor loss to the transferor company.

2.46   In view of the above, it has become standard practice in a group of companies, immediately prior to the sale of an asset outside of a group of companies which will give rise to either a capital gain or loss, first to transfer the beneficial ownership of the asset to a specific company in the group (often referred to as the 'mother company'). That company then makes the sale outside the group. As a result of TCGA 1992 s 171, all gains and losses arising on assets transferred in this way end up being made by the 'mother company'. Often a company with significant capital losses is chosen retrospectively as the 'mother company'.

2.47   The trouble with this tax planning arrangement is that, while it ensures that group capital losses and gains can usually be set off against each other, a corporation tax liability will still arise on a capital gain if, when it arises, there are not sufficient capital losses available to offset against it.

Where such a potential liability may arise, a common practice arose of acquiring a company from outside the group which had a capital loss of an appropriate size prior to the sale of the asset that would give rise to the relevant corporation tax liability. Once the company had become a member of the group, the asset to be sold was transferred to it under TCGA 1992 s 171 prior to its sale outside the group.

2.48   An active market had built up over the years in the buying and selling of capital loss companies and it has, perhaps, been surprising that the practice was not stamped out earlier. Initially, this seemed to have been because the Inland Revenue believed that the *Ramsay* principle (*WT Ramsay Ltd v IRC* (1982) AC 300, [1981] STC 174 as amplified and extended by *Furniss v Dawson* (1984) AC 474, [1984] STC 153) put a stop to the practice. Indeed, the Revenue went so far as to say that provided the capital losses were not acquired from outside the group, the normal 'mother company' tax planning (as explained above) was not objectionable in their eyes and would not meet with a challenge under the *Ramsay* principle (CCAB TR 471).

2.49   Unfortunately for the Inland Revenue, the Ramsay principle was watered down by later cases (such as *Craven v White* (1989) AC 398, [1988] STC 476) before being exposed, at least in the capital loss company context, by the case *Shepherd v Lyntress Ltd* [1989] STC 617. The comments of Vinelott J in this case are prophetic:

'. . . It is surprising that losses can be bought and sold in this way, but if the law is to be changed it must be by the legislation and not by the courts' (1989 STC at p 650).

Now, some four years later, appropriate legislation has been introduced to curtail 'capital loss buying' (FA 1993 s 88 and Sch 8).

The Finance Act 1993 changes

General

2.50 In HM Treasury's background notes on the Finance Bill (issued as a Press Release on 14 April 1993), the purpose of FA 1993 s 88 and Sch 8 is said to be to:

> '. . . restrict the set-off of capital losses brought into a group of companies as a result of a company joining the group. The restriction will apply to losses set off against gains arising on or after 16 March 1993 where the losses came from a company which joined the group on or after 31 March 1987. The changes will end the practice of "capital loss buying" where by capital losses are brought in from other companies which have nothing to do with the purchasing group's own activities and where the purchasing group does not suffer the economic loss involved'.

To legislate for the above has taken 15 pages of complex legislation. It is far from clear why a simpler method could not have been devised based on overruling the decision in *Shepherd v Lyntress* [1989] STC 617.

2.51 Basically, the provisions insert a new Schedule, Sch 7A, into TCGA 1992 and restrict capital losses accruing to a company before it became a member of a group of companies as well as losses accruing on assets held by it at that time.

Detailed legislation

2.52 For the Schedule to come into operation, two conditions need to be satisfied:

(a) there must be a company which is or has been a member of a group, referred to as 'the relevant group', and
(b) that company has pre-entry losses (para 1(1)).

2.53 The term 'pre-entry loss' is defined as follows:

(i) any allowable loss that accrued to the company before it became a member of the relevant group, or
(ii) the pre-entry proportion of any allowable loss accruing to the company on the disposal of a pre-entry asset (para 1(2)).

While (i) above is fairly straightforward, and refers to the principal target of Sch 7A (ie bought-in realised capital losses), (ii) above is more difficult to understand as it refers to unrealised losses. It is (ii) above that has given rise to much of the complexity in the legislation.

2.54   An important point to bear in mind with these provisions is that the allowable loss on the pre-entry asset need not be realised by the company which held the asset when it came into the group. It is, therefore, no use transferring the asset post-acquisition to another group member before it is disposed of – the loss arising is still potentially restricted by the legislation. This is apparent from the definition of 'pre-entry asset' in para 1(3) – it is an asset which was held, at the time immediately before it became a member of the relevant group, by any company (whether or not the one which makes the disposal) which is or has at any time been a member of that group. This latter group member is the company by reference to which the asset is a pre-entry asset, and the time when it became a member of the relevant group is referred to as 'the relevant time' (para 1(5)).

2.55   Not all the loss realised on a pre-entry asset is a pre-entry loss. Only a proportion is a pre-entry loss and this is referred to as 'the pre-entry proportion' (para 2). The rules for determining the pre-entry proportion are complicated and are considered below.

For the purpose of these rules, two assets are treated as the same if one is derived from another (para 1(8)). Where a company has been a member of two or more groups, special rules determine which group or groups are the relevant group and how the pre-entry loss is calculated (para 9). The rules as to pre-entry losses do not apply to losses transferred from the public sector (para 11).

Where a pre-entry loss would accrue on an appropriation to trading stock, it is treated as accruing, regardless of whether the company concerned elects under TCGA 1992 s 161(3) for the appropriation to be at cost (para 10).

Restriction on set-off

2.56   Paragraph 7(1) lays down the rules restricting the set-off of pre-entry losses within point (i) at 2.53 above, ie losses which accrued before the company realising them joined the relevant group. The rules are that such pre-entry losses may only be set against the following gains:

(a)   gains which accrued to the company before it joined the relevant group,
(b)   gains which accrue to the company thereafter on assets which it had acquired before it joined the relevant group, or
(c)   gains accruing to the company on assets acquired thereafter provided the company acquired such assets from a non-group company and has used or held the assets throughout its ownership for the purposes of a trade which it has carried on since before it joined the group.

The broad effect of the above is to 'ring fence' pre-acquisition losses.

2.57   Paragraph 7(2) restricts the set-off of losses within point (ii) at 2.53 above, ie losses accruing on pre-entry assets brought into the group with latent losses in a similar way to para 7(1). Here a distinction is made between the company by reference to which the asset is a pre-entry asset and other group members. As noted above, the former is the company which brought the asset into the group and it is referred to as 'the initial company' (para 7(2)(a)).

2.58   The rules are that the pre-entry proportion of the losses can only be set-off against the following gains.

(i)   Gains realised by the initial company before it joined the relevant group. Since capital losses cannot be carried back (TCGA 1992 s 8) this only applies where both the gain and the loss are realised in the accounting period in which the initial company joins the group.

(ii)   Gains accruing on assets acquired by the initial company before it joined the group.

(iii)   Gains accruing on any asset which was acquired by the initial company from a non-group company and has throughout been used or held in a trade carried on by the initial company since before it joined the relevant group.

Again, the pre-entry proportion of the losses are 'ring fenced' by the legislation.

2.59   Special rules apply if the company was a member of another group when it joined the relevant group and one or more members of that other group joined the relevant group at the same time. These rules can be found in para 7(3). Broadly, a pre-entry loss within 2.56(b) above can be set against gains arising on assets held by those other companies when they joined the group. In addition, the pre-entry proportion of any loss within 2.58(b) may be set against a gain accruing on any asset acquired by any other member of the other group before the latter became a member of the relevant group. For the purposes of these provisions, the acquisition by any member of the other group counts as an acquisition by the initial company. These provisions provide a rare form of group relief for capital losses.

2.60   In relation to both paras 7(1) and 7(2), a major change in the nature or conduct of the trade carried on by a company in the same three-year period as it joins the relevant group has the result that the trade after the change is treated as a different trade (para 8(1)(a)). The same applies if the trade becomes small or negligible, and before it is revived the company joins the relevant group (para 8(1)(b)). Once the trade changes, or becomes small or negligible, the company loses the opportunity to use pre-acquisition losses against gains arising on assets acquired post-acquisition.

2.61   In summary, it may be said that bought-in realised or latent losses may only be set against gains accruing to the acquired company before it joined the group, gains accruing on assets it acquired before then and gains accruing on assets used in a trade started before then.

Mechanics of set-off

2.62   The mechanics of set-off are that where pre-entry losses of the current or a previous accounting period can be set against a gain, they are so offset in priority to other losses of the current or previous accounting periods (para 6(1)). Pre-entry losses of the current accounting period are deducted before those brought forward (para 6(1)(a)).

2.63   The company may elect the order in which current or (as the case may be) past pre-entry losses are deducted, and if no election is made, the losses are set against the gains in the order in which they accrue (para 6(2)(b), (4)). Any such election must be made within two years of the accounting period in which the gain to be offset accrues (para 6(3)(b)).

Pre-entry assets and the pre-entry proportion

2.64   As noted above, where a group acquires a company with unrealised losses, only the pre-entry proportion of the loss on any pre-entry asset is subject to the restrictions on set-off described above. There is a basic rule for determining the pre-entry proportion in para 2, which may be displaced by an alternative calculation under para 5 if the company so elects. Special rules, in paras 3 and 4, apply to pooled assets.

2.65   The basic rule is that the total indexed loss on a pre-entry asset is apportioned into segments, each segment corresponding to each item of indexed allowable expenditure. These segments are then each time apportioned on a straight-line basis between the periods before and after the company joined the relevant group. The aggregate of the segments apportioned to the period before the company joined the relevant group is then the pre-entry loss (para 2(1), (2) and (3)).

2.66   For these purposes, assets acquired on a no gain/no loss disposal are treated as acquired on the last disposal which was not such a disposal (para 2(5)–(7)). Losses treated as accruing on the disposal of qualifying corporate bonds, acquired on a reorganisation or similar transaction, are treated as accruing on the reorganisation (para 2(8)). There is an obscure provision relating to reorganisations etc which are subject to the identity of asset rule in TCGA 1992 s 127 (para 2(4)). This provision appears to deem consideration given on the reorganisation to have been given at the time of the acquisition of the original shares.

2.67   The alternative basis of calculating the pre-entry loss is simpler. On this basis, the pre-entry loss is the lesser of the actual indexed loss and the indexed loss which would have accrued on a market value disposal of the pre-entry asset when the initial company joined the relevant group (para 5(1), (2)). The alternative basis only applies if an election is made within two years of the accounting period in which the loss-making disposal occurs, or such longer period as the Revenue allows (para 5(8)).

2.68   Pooled assets are those assets which are subject to the CGT pooling rules. Pooling applies to shares and securities and other assets unable to be individually identified, all of which are generically referred to in TCGA 1992 as 'securities' (TCGA 1992 s 104). In relation to any class of securities, there are normally two pools: 1982 holdings, consisting of securities in the class acquired before 1 April 1982 and new holdings consisting of all such securities acquired thereafter (TCGA 1992 ss 104 and 109).

2.69   The problem posed by pooling in relation to pre-entry assets is that a company joining the relevant group may have one or more existing pools of securities, which are increased by the acquisition after the joining of other securities of the same class. So two securities held by the joining company may be transferred to a group member which already has a holding of the same class of securities. If in any such case some of the securities are disposed of at a loss, the problem is whether, and if so to what extent, the loss relates to the pre-entry securities.

2.70 One might have supposed that this problem would have been addressed by using concepts derived from the general CGT pooling rules. Thus, where on entry into a group a company owned a pooled asset, that asset could thereafter have been treated, for the purposes of determining the pre-entry proportion of any loss, as a notional separate pool. Rules of identification, such as last in, first out, could have been used where after entry into the group the actual pool was increased by further acquisitions.

2.71 For some reason, this relatively straightforward method has not been adopted. Instead, the key concept is whether all or any part of a pooled asset is 'referrable to pre-entry assets' (para 3(1)). A pooled asset is treated in incorporating a part referable to pre-entry assets if any of the securities in the pooled asset were owned by the initial company (ie the company joining the group) at the time it joined the group (para 3(2)).

2.72 The following rules apply (paras 3(3)–(5)).

(a) A part disposal out of a pooled asset is not treated as including pre-entry securities if the proportion disposed of is less than the proportion of the pool which is not referable to pre-entry securities.
(b) A part disposal is treated as including pre-entry securities if the proportion of the pool disposed of does exceed the proportion of the pool which is not referable to pre-entry securities. If on the disposal there is a loss, the pre-entry proportion of that loss is the amount which would have been the pre-entry loss if the excess was a separate asset.
(c) The same applies on a complete disposal of the pool if part only of the pool is referable to pre-entry securities. In this case the notional separate asset on which the pre-entry proportion of any loss is computed is the part of the actual pool referable to the pre-entry securities.
(d) Where the pool is wholly referable to pre-entry assets, the pre-entry proportion of any loss on either a part or a complete disposal is the amount which would have been the pre-entry proportion if the actual pool or part thereof disposed of had always been a separate asset.

In general, the pre-entry proportion of the loss on any of the notional separate assets arrived at under the above rules is computed under the basic rules in para 2, requiring time apportionment by each item of allowable expenditure (para 3(4)(b)).

2.73 It is assumed that the notional pool has always been a separate asset (para 3(6)), and acquisitions into the actual pool are in general identified with the notional pools on a first in, first out basis (para 3(7)). Where an actual acquisition as so identified was part of a larger acquisition, the acquisition costs are apportioned (para 3(9)). Assets treated as acquired as another asset was acquired (as on a reorganisation) are treated as acquired when the original asset was acquired (para 3(10)).

2.74   The alternative basis can, however, apply in determining the pre-entry proportion of the loss on a pooled asset (para 5(4)). In such an event, the notional assets referred to above still have to be identified. The loss on the deemed disposal treated as occurring on entry to the group is then the part apportioned to the notional separate asset of the loss that would have accrued had all the pool as it existed at entry then been disposed of (paras 5(5), (6)). As with the alternative basis generally, the pre-entry loss then becomes the lesser of the loss so computed and the actual loss accruing on the actual pool.

2.75   One characteristic of pooling is that in computing an actual gain or loss, average cost is used. Where a pool includes post-entry securities acquired for less than the pre-entry securities, this means the actual loss accruing on a part disposal of the pool is less than it would be if the part disposal were treated as including all the pre-entry securities. If in such a case the part disposal is of fewer than the post-entry securities (and so under rule (a) above would not result in a pre-entry loss), a pre-entry loss is treated as accruing equal to the difference between the actual indexed cost of the post entry securities and their average pool indexed cost (para 4(2), (9)–(13)). If the part disposal exceeds the post-entry securities, so that the excess is treated as a separate pre-entry asset under the rules described above, the pre-entry proportion is increased by the difference between pool average and the actual indexed cost of the pre- and post-entry elements (para 4(3), (5)).

2.76   The alternative method cannot as such displace these last mentioned rules (para 4(5)). Nevertheless, a company can elect that where those rules would otherwise apply, the pre-entry loss is computed on the basis that the disposal is wholly of pre-entry securities (save in so far as those securities are exhausted) and where it so elects, it can further elect that the alternative basis can be used in calculating such hypothetical loss (paras 4(6)–(8)). In the event of these elections being made, the pre-entry loss as so computed is deducted from the pre-entry loss computed under the alternative method on any subsequent disposal attributed to the same pre-entry securities (para 5(7)).

Commencement

2.77   Under FA 1993 s 88(3), the rules in the new Sch 7A apply to accounting periods ending on or after 16 March 1993. However, for an accounting period straddling 16 March 1993, they only apply in offsetting losses against gains in so far as the gains accrue on disposals on or after 16 March.

2.78   An important point to note is that Sch 7A applies even though the losses whose set-off is restricted accrued before 16 March 1993 and even if the company with the realised pre-entry losses or the pre-entry assets joined the group before then. Thus, the losses of a capital loss company purchased before 16 March 1993 cannot be used to offset gains accruing after 16 March. However, the realised pre-entry losses and the pre-entry assets of a company which joined the group before 1 April 1987 are ignored.

2.79   Paragraph 6(2)(a) of Sch 7A deals with the position where losses have been set against gains before 16 March 1993. Pre-entry losses are assumed to have been set against gains of the same accounting period before other losses, and pre-entry losses carried forward are assumed to have been offset before other losses. Otherwise the pre-entry losses brought forward to the accounting period ending on or after 16 March 1993 are identified with such losses as the company may elect.

Comment

2.80 Is the buying and selling of capital loss companies now finished? The answer to this question is probably yes and the value of any realised or unrealised capital losses in a target company or group is clearly significantly reduced. As regards the past, presumably those companies that bought capital losses on a contingency fee basis are safe from having to pay for the benefit of the restricted losses in the foreseeable future. Those that bought such companies on a fixed fee basis are not so lucky.

2.81 For the future, the new provisions do not mean that a company with a large potential capital gain can do nothing to avoid or minimise any potential corporation tax liability on the sale of an asset. The standard tax planning opportunities remain. Possibilities seem to fall into two categories:

(a)   tax planning that is unlikely to be objectionable to the Inland Revenue – 'acceptable' tax planning, and
(b)   tax planning that is more provocative and liable to challenge from the Inland Revenue.

2.82 Normal tax planning includes such areas as the following.

(i)   In relation to the sale of an asset within TCGA 1992 ss 152(1) and 155, seeing whether the roll-over provisions of TCGA 1992 ss 152–160 can be used to defer any liability. It is worth noting that roll-over relief may be available where the acquisition of the new assets is 'deemed' to be made at their capital gains cost to the vendor (for example, within TCGA 1992 s 171). To illustrate this, the relief may be claimed where one group company realises a gain on the sale of an asset used in its trade and acquires, for use in its trade, an asset from another group company, or where it acquires the trade and assets of another group company (see TCGA 1992 ss 152 and 175(1)). Clearly this possibility could be extremely useful where assets are unlikely to be acquired within the requisite time limit from outside the group.
(ii)   Making an enterprise zone investment in the relevant year of an amount that will cover the likely capital gain (CAA 1990 s 1).
(iii)   If shares or debentures are to be sold, seeing whether the paper-for-paper provisions are likely to be of assistance (TCGA 1992 s 135 etc).
(iv)   Since capital losses cannot be carried back to earlier years, crystallising any losses on other assets in the same or an earlier accounting period than the one in which the capital gain will arise. Where the assets are of negligible value, it may be possible to 'deem' a sale to take place without there being an actual sale (TCGA 1992 s 24). With indexation continuing to accrue, it is generally preferable to delay realising a capital loss until that loss is needed.

2.83   Failing the above, the following may be considered.

(a)   While capital loss companies cannot be acquired, the legislation does not seem to stop the acquisition of companies with surplus management expenses within ICTA 1988 s 75. Management expenses (including charges) can be set against total profits (including chargeable gains) for that period or succeeding periods.

(b)   There seems no reason why capital loss companies cannot acquire companies with assets pregnant with capital gains, ie the reverse of capital loss buying.

4   INTEREST PAYABLE WITHIN MULTINATIONAL GROUPS TO UK COMPANIES

Background

2.84   Interest (or other equivalent return such as discount) on a loan from a UK company to an associated non-resident company is generally taxed in the UK when it is received. Most of the UK's major trading partners, however, give relief to the borrower as interest accrues.

2.85   Not surprisingly, the above asymmetrical position has led to many UK members of multinational groups lending to overseas associates on terms such that the borrower would obtain relief on an accruals basis while the UK lender could defer liability until the interest was paid. In certain circumstances, such an arrangement of charging a market rate of interest (but not actually paying it) could also avoid problems under the transfer pricing provisions of TA 1988 s 770 (sales etc at an undervalue or overvalue) although the Inland Revenue are known to have resisted this line of argument.

2.86   Legislation is proposed to alter the basis of taxation to an accruals basis where the terms of the financial arrangements are such that in any 12-month period the amount of interest arising may be less than that accruing. The new rules apply also to the return on deep gain and deep discount securities.

The Finance Act 1993 changes

2.87   The legislation is to be found in FA 1993 ss 61–66 and applies to interest accruing from 1 April 1993 (FA 1993 s 63(12)).

2.88   Under FA 1993 s 63, qualifying debts are effectively brought within the accrued income legislation (albeit on an accelerated basis) such that interest is deemed to accrue on a day-to-day basis and taxed accordingly.

2.89   Broadly speaking, for a debt to be a 'qualifying debt':

(a)   a UK-resident company must be entitled to the debt (ie the lender);

(b)   the person liable for the debt (ie the debtor) must be either a 'qualifying company' or a 'qualifying third party';

(c)   the debt must not be an exempt debt (FA 1993 s 61(1)(a)–(c)).

2.90   A 'qualifying company' is any non-UK resident company which is associated with the company at (a) above (FA 1993 s 61(2)). For this purpose, a company is another's associated company if, at that time or within one year previously, one has control of the other or both are controlled by the same person or persons (FA 1993 s 61(7) adopting the definition in TA 1988 s 416).

2.91   There are provisions ensuring that a dual resident company which is treated as a non-UK resident company under the terms of a double tax treaty remains a non-UK resident company for the purpose of these provisions (FA 1993 s 61(3) and (7)).

2.92   A 'qualifying third party' is defined in FA 1993 s 61(4)–(6). It attempts to prevent back-to-back arrangements or a loan from going to an associated company via a non-connected third party, ie the rules apply equally where a third party is inserted between the UK company and the associated company.

2.93   Exemptions apply in the following circumstances.

(a)   A debt is an exempted debt at any time if each of the following conditions is fulfilled at that time, have been fulfilled throughout so much of the period of the debt as falls before that time and is likely to be fulfilled throughout so much of that period as falls after that time. The conditions are that any interest is at a fixed rate (or at a rate which bears a fixed relationship to a standard published rate or index of prices, say, LIBOR plus 1%), and is payable as it accrues at intervals of 12 months or less; and where either the debt must be redeemed within 12 months of its creation or the amount payable on redemption cannot exceed the original amount given for the debt, ie there is no premium (FA 1993 s 62(1)–(5)).

(b)   The inspector is satisfied that a 'motive test' is fulfilled and either he is also satisfied that an 'arms-length' test is met or a 'short-term adjustment' test is met. Basically, the motive test is that the possibility of the interest being taxable on a receipts basis rather than an accruals basis was not a main reason for the UK-resident company entering into the arrangements. The arms-length test requires the Inspector to be satisfied that the UK-resident company would still have created (or acquired or varied) the debt on the terms which exclude it from exemption under (a) above if the person liable for the debt were not a qualifying company, a qualifying third party or a person who would have been such a qualifying company or qualifying third party but for being resident in the UK. The short-term adjustment test is met where the terms of the debt are such that the debt must be redeemed before the end of the 'relevant period' (broadly 24 months beginning with the date the resident company created or acquired the debt on the qualifying terms) or provide for any interest accruing during that period to be payable no later than immediately after the end of that period, and for any interest subsequently accruing to be payable as it accrues at intervals of 12 months or less (FA 1993 s 62(6)–(11)).

(c)   The inspector is satisfied that the paying company is being, or is likely to be, wound up or has been or is likely to be dissolved under its domestic law on the grounds of its inability to pay its debts (FA 1993 s 62(10)–(12)). This is the hardship test. The exemption does not cover those cases where the lender is suffering temporary financial difficulties.

2.94   Although effectively taxing the owner of a security on the income accruing to him during his period of ownership, the tax charge under the accrued income scheme normally only arises on an actual transfer of securities, ie when the income is 'realised' (see TA 1988 ss 710–728). Under the new legislation, however, this charge is accelerated by deeming transfers and reacquisitions to take place at certain times.

2.95   Deemed disposals are treated as taking place on the last day of the resident company's accounting period and reacquisitions on the first day of the next accounting period.

2.96   In the case of a qualifying debt in existence prior to 1 April 1993, there is a deemed transfer at 31 March 1993 by the holder under the accrued income scheme which gives rise to a 'deemed sum' equal to the accrued interest for the interest period prior to that date. On 1 April 1993, there is a deemed transfer to the holder under the accrued income scheme which gives rise to relief equal to the deemed sum at 31 March 1993. At the end of the accounting period there is a further deemed transfer by the holder for the purposes of the accrued income scheme, again giving rise to a deemed sum equal to the accrued interest for the interest period to that date. On the first day of the new accounting period there is a deemed transfer to the holder; relief equal to the deemed sum at the end of the accounting period thus falls into the next period.

2.97   The deemed sum under the accrued income scheme at 31 March 1993 only gives rise to a tax charge at the time the security is eventually redeemed etc by virtue of s 63(5), ie it effectively remains within the current tax regime. Therefore, with regard to a security on which there are many years' outstanding interest, the proposals do not affect any income accrued prior to 31 March 1993.

2.98   Where, after 1 April 1993, the terms of a debt alter and cause it to become a qualifying debt or cease to be a qualifying debt, a deemed disposal and reacquisition occur. This causes the interest accruing during the proportion of the accounting period that it is a qualifying debt to come within charge under the accrued income scheme.

2.99   Under s 63(4)(c), any security which is in existence prior to 31 March 1993 is deemed to be a variable interest rate security for the purposes of TA 1988 ss 717 and 718. Under s 717, the Revenue has the power to determine the accrued interest by means of a 'just and reasonable apportionment'. This would seem to allow the Revenue to treat all securities, whether variable or not, on the same basis.

2.100   Similar rules apply to the return on deep discount and deep gain securities (FA 1993 ss 64–65).

Comment

2.101 Clearly, UK companies with loans to overseas associates who do not pay interest at least every 12 months will be taxed on income not received. In some cases, a mismatch will arise if an overseas associate only obtains an interest deduction on a paid basis (as is generally the case in the USA). Where such a mismatch arises it may be possible to argue that there is a good commercial reason why interest has been rolled-up and, therefore, the loan is on arm's-length terms and constitutes an exempt debt.

2.102 Companies which are insolvent but not yet being dissolved will not be exempt from these provisions.

2.103 It may, of course, be possible to revise the terms of existing loans in order to bring them within the exemptions. If overseas associates do not have sufficient cash to pay interest, consideration may need to be given to capitalising existing loans and waiving accrued interest (capitalisation of accrued interest will give rise to a UK tax charge, TA 1988 s 582).

2.104 Consideration should also be given to making future loans interest free although the transfer pricing provisions of TA 1988 s 770 will need to be considered, ie the Inland Revenue may try and impute interest.

5 CAPITAL GAINS TAX AND THE ENTREPRENEUR

A Roll-over relief for shares

Background

2.105 Many people have argued that an effective capital gains tax rate for individuals of up to 40% discourages entrepreneurs from starting up new businesses or investing in existing businesses.

Whether or not this is true, there can be no doubt that the entrepreneur who is currently sitting on shares in a company that are pregnant with capital gain has a strong incentive to retain those shares. He is effectively locked in since, should he sell those shares, he will be faced with a capital gains tax liability of up to 40% and can only reinvest elsewhere the net of tax proceeds of approximately 60%. It does not take much financial acumen to realise that the return from retaining the existing 100% investment will generally outweigh the possible return from investing 60% elsewhere. The absence of capital gains tax on death (TCGA 1992 s 62) further encourages such inertia.

2.106 In many areas, this reinvestment problem has been recognised by Government. For example, a business (whether in the corporate or unincorporated sector) can generally sell trading assets and reinvest the proceeds in new trading assets without crystallising a tax charge. These are the well-known roll-over relief rules to be found in TCGA 1992 ss 152–160.

Equally, in certain circumstances, paper-for-paper exchanges can take place without giving rise to a capital gains tax liability (TCGA 1992 ss 135–138).

2.107   The lack of some kind of roll-over relief for the entrepreneur who sells shares in one company and reinvests in another has always been seen as something of an anomaly. Strong representations in this area were made by the British Venture Capital Association in their 1992/93 Tax Submission supported by a number of other professional organisations. In this regard, the paper 'The Plight of the Golden Goose – or Why Capital Gains Tax on Entrepreneurs at 40% is a Mistake' by Andrew Joy, Chairman of the Taxation Committee of the British Venture Capital Association, should also be noted.

The Finance Act 1993 changes

General

2.108   For disposals of shares after 15 March 1993, relief will be available which allows individuals to defer the payment of capital gains tax on the sale of shares in their own companies where the proceeds are reinvested in other qualifying trading companies (FA 1993 s 87 and Sch 7 Pt II).

2.109   Conditions regarding the companies, the individual and the period and size of ownership of the shares will all have to be satisfied. The conditions seem to represent a combination of conditions already seen in the retirement relief, roll-over relief and business expansion legislation. This has led to the new legislation being referred to as a legislative hybrid.

While the legislation will undoubted be welcomed by those taxpayers affected, it is a matter of regret that it needed over 20 pages of legislation to introduce it.

The relief

2.110   The relief applies where an individual (companies cannot claim the relief), who is referred to as 'the re-investor', makes a material disposal of shares or securities and acquires what is called a 'qualifying investment' within a period referred to as 'the qualifying period' (s 164A(1)). The relief can also apply on a re-investment by trustees (s 164B).

2.111   The qualifying period is the same as under roll-over relief for the replacement of business assets, ie it begins 12 months before the material disposal and ends three years thereafter. As with that legislation, the Revenue has discretion to extent the period (s 164A(9)).

2.112   The meaning of 'material disposal' and 'qualifying investment' are exhaustively defined and are considered below. In broad terms, however, a material disposal is a disposal of shares or securities which would attract retirement relief if the re-investor were 55 or over and retirement relief were unlimited in amount. A qualifying investment is, again in very broad terms, a holding of at least 5% in an unquoted trading company as defined for the purposes of the Business Expansion Scheme. It is far from clear why the legislation should look to the retirement relief provisions on the disposal of shares or securities whereas the acquisition looks to the Business Expansion Scheme provisions. Indeed, much of the complexity in the legislation is caused by this strange transplanting of legislation from other, unconnected, reliefs.

2.113   In essence the new relief applies to individuals who have built up and sold one trading company and reinvest all or part of the proceeds in another such company.

2.114   Where the relief applies, the mechanics are the same as for all roll-over reliefs. A reduction is made both in the proceeds of the material disposal and in the acquisition cost of the qualifying investment (s 164A(2)). The reduction is broadly the lesser of the chargeable gain otherwise accruing on the material disposal and the acquisition cost or market value of the qualifying investment (s 164A(2)(a)).

2.115   Individuals who are eligible for the new relief and for retirement relief can claim either relief or a combination of the two. As with all roll-over reliefs, the present relief has to be claimed and, in an important new departure, the claim may specify that the relief applies only to an amount less than the gain on the material disposal or the cost or value of the qualifying investment (s 164A(2)(a)(iv)).

The material disposal

2.116   A disposal of shares or securities is a material disposal if certain conditions are satisfied throughout a period of one year ending with the date of the disposal (s 164A(3)(a)). These conditions are as follows (s 164A(4)):

(a)   the company must be a trading company or the holding company of a trading group;
(b)   the company must be unquoted;
(c)   it must be the re-investor's personal company; and
(d)   the re-investor must be a full-time working officer or employee of the company or of the group or commercial association of companies to which the company belongs.

A disposal of shares in a quoted company can be a material deposit if, when it ceases to be an unquoted company, all the above conditions were satisfied in the previous twelve months and the shares were acquired when it was unquoted. The company is broadly treated as if it remains an unquoted company (s 164A(6)–(7)).

2.117   Apart from the requirement that the company be unquoted, these requirements are the same as for retirement relief (see TCGA 1992 s 163(5)), and the same definitions apply (s 164M(3)), including the new definitions of 'personal company' and 'full-time working officer or employee'. As with retirement relief, where the company ceases to be a trading company within the permitted period before the disposal, the disposal is material if the conditions are satisfied in the year prior to the cessation (s 164A(3)(b)). The permitted period is the same as in retirement relief, ie one year or such longer period as the Revenue may allow (TCGA 1992 Sch 6 para 1(2)). Also, as with retirement relief, easing off is allowed – relief applies if the re-investor has at one time been a full-time working officer or employee and has since been an officer or employee devoting at least ten hours per week to the company (s 164A(5)).

2.118   One of the more tiresome aspects of retirement relief is the chargeable business asset test, and this too is incorporated in the present relief (s 164C). Both retirement relief and the present relief are restricted to what is called 'the appropriate proportion' of the gains on the material disposal (s 164C(1)). The appropriate proportion is the proportion which the company's or, as the case may be, the group's chargeable business assets bears to its total chargeable assets (s 164C(2) and (3)). If the company or group has no chargeable assets, the appropriate proportion is 100% (s 164C(4)). If the group has 51% subsidiaries which are not wholly owned, only a fraction of the chargeable assets and chargeable business assets of such subsidiaries are brought into account (s 164C(7)).

2.119   As with retirement relief, a chargeable asset is an asset on which any gain would be chargeable (s 164C(5)). A chargeable business asset is any asset used for business purposes by the re-investor, any personal company of his, or by any trading subsidiary in a group of which the parent is his personal company (s 164C(9)). In a group structure, shares held in subsidiaries do not count as either chargeable assets or chargeable business assets (s 164C(6)(b)).

The qualifying investment

2.120   The new investment is a qualifying investment if it satisfies the following conditions (s 164A(8)).

(a)   The investment must be eligible shares, ie ordinary shares in a company with no present or future preferential rights (s 164N(1)). Shares are not eligible shares if their acquisition is relieved under the Business Expansion Scheme (s 164M).
(b)   The eligible shares must be shares in a qualifying company. A qualifying company is an unquoted company which exists wholly for the purpose of carrying on of one or more qualifying trades (apart from certain insignificant activities) and/or is the holding company of one or more qualifying subsidiaries, ie subsidiaries which themselves carry on qualifying trades (s 164G(2), (4)).
(c)   The re-investor must hold at least 5% of the eligible shares in the qualifying company either at any time after making the acquisition or within three years of the material disposal or such longer period as the Board of Inland Revenue allows.
(d)   The qualifying company must not be the same company as, or in the same group as, the company whose shares were subject to the material disposal.

2.121   As mentioned above, these requirements are based on the Business Expansion Scheme rather than on retirement relief, and thus are different from the requirements relating to the material disposal. In particular, the re-investor can, but does not have to, be an officer or employee in the qualifying company and the required level of his participation is effectively determined by whether he has 5% or more of the ordinary shares rather than by whether the company is his personal company. Equally, the qualifying trade requirement does, as will be seen below, exclude some companies whose shares could be comprised in a material disposal.

2.122 The following points may be noted about the definition of 'qualifying company'.

(i)   There is no requirement that the company be incorporated in the UK.

(ii)   A company cannot be a qualifying company if it is controlled by another company or by another company and a person connected with that company. Equally, it cannot be a qualifying company if it is a 51% subsidiary of another company without being controlled by it (s 164G(3)(b)).

(iii)   A company cannot be a qualifying company if it has any subsidiary which is not a qualifying subsidiary (s 164G(3)(a)), and a subsidiary is not a qualifying subsidiary unless it and the parent are members of a group of which all members (or all members apart from the parent) exist wholly for the purpose of carrying on a qualifying trade (s 164G(4)). This means the only permitted group structure is that of the qualifying company plus directly owned trading subsidiaries. 'Group' has its normal CGT meaning (s 164N(2)).

(iv)   As with the Business Expansion Scheme, property companies cannot be qualifying companies (s 164H). A company is not a qualifying company if it (or the group as a whole) holds interests in land worth over half the company's (or the group's) total chargeable assets. In determining the value of the interests in land, there may be deducted debts secured on the land, unsecured debts not due for repayment for more than 12 months and amounts paid up on shares carrying preferential rights in a winding-up (s 164H(2)). In contrast to the Business Expansion Scheme, the comparison is between the net value of the interests in land and the total chargeable assets – it is not a comparison with all assets. This could cause difficulty if, for example, a trading company with only modest holdings of land has invested surplus cash in gilts.

2.123 The term 'qualifying trade' is defined in substantially the same terms as for the Business Expansion Scheme (s 164I). There are two basic requirements.

(a)   The trade must be carried on on a commercial basis with a view to the realisation of profits (s 164I(9)). Activities of research from which it is intended that a trade will be derived are included (s 164I(1)(b)).

(b)   The trade (or a substantial part of it) must not consist of one or more of a list of forbidden activities (s 164I(2)).

2.124 The list of forbidden activities at (b) above is as follows.

(i)   Dealing in land, in commodities or futures, or in shares securities or other financial instruments.

(ii)   Dealing in goods otherwise in the course of an ordinary trade or wholesale or retail distribution. Tests as to whether goods are so dealt in are laid down in s 164I(3) and (4), in the same terms as apply to the Business Expansion Scheme under TA 1988 s 297(3).

(iii)   Banking, insurance, money-lending, debt factoring, hire-purchase, financing, or other financial activity.

(iv)   Leasing (including letting ships on charter or other assets on hire) or receiving royalties or licence fees. Film production companies and research and development companies are exempted from this head (s 164I(5) and (6)), as are certain companies chartering ships registered in the UK (s 164I(7) and (8)).

(iv)   Providing legal or accounting services.

(v)   Providing services for any trade with (i)–(iv) above if the same person has a controlling interest both in that trade and in the trade of providing the services. The meaning of 'controlling interest' in this context is given in s 164J.

(vi)   Property development.

(vii)   Farming.

This list of forbidden activities is the same as applies for the Business Expansion Scheme under TA 1988 s 297, save that (i) above includes dealing in financial instruments, and oil extraction activities are omitted.

Anti-avoidance

2.125   There are three important restrictions of the relief conferred by ss 164A to 164N.

(a)   *Non-residence.*   The relief does not apply if the re-investor is non-resident when he acquires the eligible shares, or non-resident under a Double Tax Treaty (s 164K).

(b)   *Arrangements*   Shares are not treated as eligible, and relief is thus denied, if the arrangements for or surrounding their acquisition include certain forbidden matters (s 164L(1)). These matters are arrangements 'with a view to the subsequent acquisition, exchange or other disposal of the shares'; arrangements for the cessation of the qualifying company's trade or the disposal of its chargeable business assets; and arrangements for the return of the value of the re-investor's investment to him.

(c)   *Claw-back.*   The relief is clawed back if
(i)   the eligible shares cease to be eligible;
(ii)   the qualifying company ceases to be qualifying;
(iii)   the re-investor becomes non-resident; or
(iv)   the eligible shares are exchanged for qualifying corporate bonds in such circumstances that the reorganisation relief in TCGA 1992 s 116 applies (s 164F(2)).
The shares are treated as ceasing to be eligible if all or part of the re-investor's investment is returned to him (s 164L(2)). The claw-back only applies if the event triggering it occurs in what is called the relevant period, which ends three years after the acquisition of the eligible shares (s 164F(12)). The claw-back does not apply if the eligible shares have already been disposed of, unless the disposal is to the re-investor's spouse, in which case she stands in his shoes (s 164F(3)–(5)). Non-residence does

not trigger the claw-back if it is for full-time employment and lasts less than three years (s 164F(9)).

2.126 The return of all or part of the re-investor's investment to him is at the heart of these anti-avoidance provisions, for arrangements for such a return prevent the relief applying at all and the happening of such a return triggers the claw-back. The following events are treated as a return of the investment (s 164L(3)).

(a) The repayment, redemption or repurchase by the qualifying company of any of its shares or securities which belong to the investor.
(b) The repayment by the qualifying company of any debt owed to the re-investor and incurred before the re-investor acquired the eligible shares.
(c) Any payment by the qualifying company to the re-investor for giving up his right to any debt on its extinguishment.
(d) The release or waiver by the qualifying company of any liability of the re-investor, or the discharge by the qualifying company of any liability of the re-investor. A liability is treated as waived if not discharged for over 12 months (s 164L(5)).
(e) The provision by the qualifying company of any benefit for the re-investor.
(f) Disposals by the qualifying company to the re-investor at below market value.
(g) Acquisitions from the re-investor at above market value.
(h) Any payment by the qualifying company to the re-investor.
(i) Any loan made by any person to the re-investor which would not have been made had he not acquired or been proposing to acquire the eligible shares (s 164L(4)).

2.127 A payment by the qualifying company to the qualifying investor is not a return of the investment if it is a qualifying payment (s 164L(3)(h)). A debt or liability is also ignored if its discharge by the company would be qualifying payment, as is a benefit if it would be a qualifying payment if conferred in money (s 164L(7)). The term 'qualifying payment' is defined in s 164L(8) and, in broad terms, includes reasonable remuneration, dividends or interest which represents a reasonable return on the investment and reasonable commercial payment for goods or services provided.

2.128 Although the 'qualifying payment' concept narrows the scope of a return of investment, it is broadened by s 164L(9). This deems any payment or disposal to the order of or for the benefit of the re-investor to be to him. More significantly, references to the re-investor are deemed to include his associates. 'Associate' has its close company meaning (s 164N(1)), except that brothers and sisters are excluded. However, it still includes spouses, parents, children and settlements of which the re-investor is settlor.

Extensions of the relief

2.129 The new roll-over relief is extended by s 164D to situations where the re-investor disposes of his eligible shares and acquires eligible shares in another qualifying company. The former are referred to as 'the acquired holding' and the latter as 'the replacement shares', and somewhat confusingly the gain originally rolled into the acquired holding is called 'the held-over gain'. In such a case, the disposal of the acquired shares may well not itself be a material disposal and so relieved under s 164A, as, for example, where the re-investor is not a full-time officer or employee of the original qualifying company. Where this is the position, the held-over gain may be rolled into the replacement shares, provided the latter are acquired within the relevant period, which in this case starts 12 months before and ends three years after the disposal of the acquired holding (s 164D)(10)).

2.130   Where a disposal takes place within the well-known share-for-share provisions of TCGA 1992 s 135 such that TCGA 1992 s 127 applies (ie no disposal is treated as taking place), it is now possible to make an election to disapply these provisions and come within the new roll-over relief rules instead. As a result, the new relief can be claimed on the gains arising on shares up to the day that they are involved in an exchange so long, of course, as the other conditions for relief apply (s 164E).

2.131   Section 164B extends the relief to settled property. The relief may be claimed by trustees if they both make the material disposal and acquire the eligible shares in the qualifying company. However, a disposal by trustees is only material if the company is the personal company of a relevant beneficiary and he is a full-time working officer or employee (s 164B(2)). A relevant beneficiary is a beneficiary who has an interest in possession in the shares or securities which are comprised in the trustees' disposal, and, for relief to apply, he must also have such an interest in the eligible shares (s 164B(3), (7)). As will be apparent, these restrictions mean that the relief is of restricted application to trusts, in that it only applies if:

(a)   the trust is a fixed interest trust; and
(b)   the life tenant owns 5% of the original company personally, and works full-time for it.

Comment

2.132   While clearly the legislation is to be welcomed, its complexity is not. It is not difficult to imagine many circumstances where relief will not be available simply because of some detailed restriction in the legislation. It is particularly regrettable that the restrictive Business Expansion Scheme conditions have been imported into the new legislation.

2.133   Nevertheless, in certain areas, the relief is generous. For example, to obtain a full deferral of the chargeable gain, the relevant individual need only reinvest an amount equivalent to the chargeable gain. He is not required to reinvest the entire disposal proceeds as is necessary with the existing roll-over relief for business assets. The ability to restrict the amount to be deferred is also useful as it may preserve the availability of other CGT reliefs (eg the annual exemption) in certain circumstances.

2.134 Interestingly, the legislation only talks of a 'qualifying investment' being acquired. It would seem to be possible, therefore, for shares to be acquired by way of gift and still obtain a deferral of tax. If this is so, the re-investor can retain the cash received on the material disposal and still obtain relief under the legislation.

2.135 Arguably, the share roll-over relief acts, in part, as a replacement for the business expansion scheme which comes to an end on 31 December 1993. Nevertheless, the relief is merely a deferral of capital gains tax rather than a relief from charge.

2.136 It is interesting to note that the press release describing the proposals issued at the time of the Budget suggested that the cost to the Treasury would only be £50million in a full year. Clearly the Government do not believe they are being particularly generous with this relief.

B Retirement relief

Background

2.137 The retirement relief rules are well known and the relevant legislation can be found in TCGA 1992 ss 163–164 and Sch 6.

Broadly speaking, where a taxpayer aged 55 or above realises a capital gain on the disposal of:

(a) the whole or part of a business, or
(b) shares or securities in a family company, or
(c) assets owned by him and used in that business or company, or
(d) assets used by him in his employment,

a relief, generally called 'retirement relief', is in certain circumstances given to reduce or eliminate the amount of gain chargeable to capital gains tax. It is not necessary in most circumstances for the taxpayer to retire to be eligible for the relief, although the disposal will often take place on retirement.

Relief is also available in certain cases to taxpayers under 55 years old who retire because of ill health.

2.138 The relief was probably instituted in recognition of the fact that many small businessmen depend on the proceeds of sale of their business or family company for a sum which can be invested to provide income for their retirement, since the requirements of the business may have precluded adequate pension provision. The availability of the relief is not, however, affected by any other pension arrangements the taxpayer has made.

2.139 The relief operates by exempting from tax a proportion or the whole of the capital gain arising on the disposal. The relief affects the disposer only, and has no effect on the cost to the person who acquires the transferred assets.

Nevertheless, where the disposal is by way of gift (see TCGA 1992 s 165) and the donor elects to hold over his chargeable gain, the base cost of the donee is effectively increased by the donor's retirement relief.

2.140   Retirement relief is a valuable relief from capital gains tax in that it extinguishes the liability on a gain permanently (rather than merely deferring it). The maximum relief is £150,000 plus one-half of the excess over £150,000 and below £600,000 with a maximum possible cash saving therefore of £150,000 (ie (£150,000 + (½ × (£600,000 – £150,000))) × 40%).

2.141   There are a number of conditions that have to be complied with before relief can be obtained (see, in particular TCGA 1992 Sch 6). The two conditions that have been affected by the Finance Act 1993 are as follows.

Condition One

To be the taxpayer's family company it was formerly required that the taxpayer must be able to exercise:

(a)   at least 25% of the voting rights of the company; or
(b)   at least 5% of the voting rights of the company, provided that over 50% of the voting rights are exercisable by the taxpayer together with members of his 'family' (as defined) (TCGA 1992 Sch 6(1)(2)).

Condition Two

In addition, the taxpayer had to be a 'full-time working director' of the family company (TCGA 1992 s 163(3) and Sch 6(1)(2)). This is a director who is required to devote substantially the whole of his time to the service of the company in a managerial or technical capacity.

The Finance Act 1993 changes

2.142   There are three changes proposed by FA 1993 s 87 and Sch 7 (Part I).

(a)   The family company test has been abolished. The reference in the legislation to the taxpayer's 'family company' has been replaced with a reference to his 'personal company' (para 1(1)).
(b)   A company is an individual's personal company if he can show that not less than 5% of the voting rights in that company are exercisable by him at the relevant time (para 1(2)). The alternate 25% and 5%/50% tests are, therefore, now combined into a single 5% test.
(c)   The need to be a 'full-time working director' during the relevant qualifying period is replaced with a requirement to be a 'full-time working officer or employee' (para 2).

2.143   The change at (a) above is simply cosmetic and recognises that, given the reduction at (b) above to 5% in the required shareholding necessary to qualify for retirement relief, the company will not always be a 'family' company in the way normally understood. This change is rather similar to the change made by FA 1989 s 53(2)(a) to the heading of TA 1988 Part II from 'higher paid employees' to 'employees earning £8,500 or more' in recognition of the fact that an employee on £8,500 can no longer be thought of as being a higher paid employee.

2.144 It should be noted that the replacement of the 'family company' test with the 'personal company' test also applies for the purposes of TCGA 1992 s 157 (trade carried on by a family company: business assets dealt with by an individual), part of the roll-over legislation, and TCGA 1992 s 165 (relief for gifts of business assets), the gift hold-over legislation.

2.145 A 'full-time working officer or employee' in relation to one or more companies means any officer or employee who is required to devote substantially the whole of his time to the service of that company, or those companies taken together, in a managerial or technical capacity (para 2(4)).

The new provisions apply for disposals on or after 16 March 1993 (FA 1993 s 87(2)).

Comment

2.146 Clearly, more taxpayers will now be potentially eligible for retirement relief than hitherto, particularly 'outsiders' (such as managers and others who work in the business and may, for example, have received shares via a share option scheme). To this extent, the changes are welcome. The changes also remove the somewhat artificial distinction of who is or is not a member of the 'family'.

2.147 Subject to the above, the available tax planning possibilities remain very much the same post-16 March 1993 as they were previously.

2.148 It is obviously even more important than previously to consider retirement relief in a wide range of circumstances. However, the availability of the relief will not always be clear. As a general rule, in the personal company context, the potential availability of the relief should be considered wherever a taxpayer who has 5% or more of the shares or securities in a company is about to sell those shares.

6 TAX RELIEF FOR EMPLOYERS' CONTRIBUTIONS TO PENSION SCHEMES

Background

2.149 Conventional wisdom as set out in most of the standard tax textbooks has always been that the deduction of a pension expense for corporation tax purposes is solely on a paid basis. This view stems from TA 1988 s 592 (exempt approved schemes) and, in particular, s 592(4) which states that:

> 'Any sum paid by an employer by way of contribution . . . shall, for the purposes of Case I or II of Schedule D and of sections 75 and 76, be

allowed to be deducted as an expense, or expense of management, incurred in the chargeable period in which the sum is paid'.

In the Inland Revenue's view s 592(4) provides the only basis for claiming a deduction for pension contributions to an approved pension scheme.

2.150 However, since the adoption of SSAP 24 (accounting for pension costs) under which companies are required to recognise a portion of their unfunded pension liabilities on an accruals basis, this treatment has been called into question. Following the introduction of SSAP 24, it has been possible to argue that a tax deduction is permissible on an accruals basis although the Inland Revenue have consistently refused to accept that this is so.

2.151 Broadly speaking, SSAP 24 requires companies to recognise in their accounts:

'. . . the expected cost of providing pensions on a systematic and rational basis over the period during which they derive benefit from the employees' services' (para 77).

The ways in which this expected cost is to be recognised are set out in paras 78–92 and, in particular, para 86 provides:

'. . . if the cumulative pension cost recognised in the profit and loss account has not been completely discharged by payment of contributions or directly paid pensions, the excess should be shown as a net pension provision'.

SSAP 24 is effective for accounting periods beginning on or after 1 July 1988.

2.152 Under general principles, two conditions usually need to be complied with before an amount that is accrued in the accounts of a company can be deductible:

(a)   the amount must be revenue and not capital expenditure; and
(b)   its deduction must not be specifically prohibited by legislation (normally by TA 1988 s 74 which contains 16 specific provisions disallowing various types of expenditure but there are also a number of other sections that prohibit a deduction in appropriate circumstances). Specifically, in the case of a trading company, the expense must have been incurred wholly and exclusively for the purposes of the trade.

2.153 It has generally been accepted that (a) above rarely gives rise to any difficulty in relation to an accrual in the accounts for an unfunded pension liability. The main areas of doubt have always been:

(i)   with the accounting treatment (for example, has the amount been specifically quantified to provide a reliable figure complying with the correct principles of commercial accounting) – SSAP 24 seemed to have removed most of the potential worries in this area; and
(ii)   whether TA 1988 s 592(4) still prevents a deduction from being made.

It has been possible to argue that TA 1988 s 592(4) does not displace the normal right to claim a deduction for an accrued expense and this right continues except in so far as a deduction has already been taken under s 592(4), ie the intention of s 592(4) is to permit a deduction in circumstances where a deduction is not otherwise allowable.

2.154 Support for this view goes back to the fact that the original enactment of s 592(4) was in FA 1921 s 32 (with little changes to the wording in the intervening years). Pre-1921, a right clearly existed to deduct pension expenses on an accruals basis and it is argued that nothing in the then legislation, or subsequent enactments, altered this fact (see, for example, *Atherton v British Insulated and Helsby Cables* (1926) 10 TC 155). All the 1921 legislation did was to implement a statutory framework for superannuation funds which was put in place around that time. The argument runs that, in its original form, s 32 was intended to be a relief and nothing has happened since to turn the section into a restriction. While the right to a deduction on an accruals basis has clearly fallen into disuse over subsequent years, mere disuse does not act as a bar to using or reviving that right.

The Finance Act 1993 changes

2.155 Whatever the likelihood of their views being successful, the Inland Revenue have clearly decided to take no chances. Accordingly, they have introduced FA 1993 s 112 to make it clear that with effect for accounting periods ending after 5 April 1993 (and for any year of assessment the basis period, as defined, for which ends after that date), tax relief under TA 1988 s 592(4) will be due only for sums paid into exempt approved pension schemes and not for provisions or accruals in respect of such payments.

2.156 The way the Revenue have enacted the changes is by adding at the end of TA 1988 s 592(4) the words:

> 'but no other sum shall for those purposes be allowed to be deducted as an expense, or expense of management, in respect of the making, or any provision for the making, of any contribution under the scheme' (FA 1993 s 112(1)).

The changes apply:

(a) in the case of companies, for any accounting period of the employer ending after 5 April 1993, and
(b) in the case of other employers, for any year of assessment the employer's basis period for which ends after 5 April 1993 (FA 1993 s 112(2)).

'Basis period' for the purpose of (b) above is defined in FA 1993 s 112(6)) and basically means the accounting period that gives rise to the profits or gains taxable in the relevant year of assessment. Where, therefore, a sole trader has a 30 June year end, the first year of assessment to be affected will be 1994/95 as the first basis period ending after 5 April 1993 will be 30 June 1993.

2.157 In addition, no deduction can be allowed for sums actually paid into an exempt approved scheme after 5 April 1993 to the extent that provisions in excess of contributions actually paid have already been allowed for tax purposes (FA 1993 s 112(3)–(5)). This is clearly to avoid the possibility of an employer obtaining double relief:

(a)   once on the amount accrued in the accounts (assuming the Revenue lose their argument), and
(b)   again under the above provisions when the premium is actually paid.

EXAMPLE

Accounting period to 31 March 1993

Annual pension contribution actually paid	£58,000
Provision for pension fund deficit	£16,000
Profit and loss account charge	£74,000

Tax relief was claimed and allowed on the full £74,000.

Accounting period to 31 March 1994

Annual pension contribution actually paid	£62,000
Actual payment to reduce pension fund deficit	£30,000
Profit and loss account charge	£92,000

Tax relief would be given in the year ended 31 March 1994 as follows:

Actual payments made		£92,000
Total previous allowed	£74,000	
Less relevant maximum	£58,000	
		£16,000
Relief available on		£76,000

This is the same result as the 31 March 1994 payments (£92,000) less the provision allowed previously (£16,000).

An exempt approved scheme is defined in FA 1993 s 112(6) by reference to the definition in TA 1988 s 592(1).

Comment

2.158   The introduction of the new provisions suggests that the Inland Revenue are not as confident of success as they say. Nevertheless, whatever the chances since 1988 of successfully arguing that a pension accrual is tax deductible, it has always been prudent to avoid the issue wherever possible by paying the appropriate pension contribution before the end of the company's accounting period. This has then put the tax deductibility beyond doubt.

2.159   In those cases, however, where for whatever reason this has not been done, it clearly remains open to a company (where the tax liability for the relevant year is not yet final and conclusive and it is beneficial to do so) to argue for a tax deduction on an accruals basis. It is likely to be of most relevance to accounting periods beginning on or after 1 July 1988 and ending before 5 April 1993.

Companies should be aware, however, that the Inland Revenue will:

'continue to resist claims for relief on any basis, other than for payments into schemes' (IR Press Release 30 March 1993).

In the Inland Revenue's view, the changes do no more than 'put the matter beyond doubt' and it is understood that they will be taking a case on this principle in the near future.

2.160 It should, however, be borne in mind that an accruals basis will not always be to a company's advantage.

EXAMPLE

A company has a £90,000 deficiency in its exempt scheme. It wishes to fund this deficiency by three annual payments of £30,000. The average service life over which the deficiency must be spread is ten years and regular pension costs are £11,000. Accordingly, under SSAP 24 the profit and loss charge must be £11,000 plus £90,000 divided by ten.

This produces the following results:

Year	Profit and loss charge	Cash paid
1	20	41
2	20	41
3	20	41
4	20	10

In this situation, the accruals basis would clearly not be beneficial.

CHAPTER 3

Capital allowances

1 SECTION 113

Summary

3.1 Initial allowances for the construction costs of industrial buildings were withdrawn in the 1980s (other than for buildings in Enterprise Zones). Section 113, in an attempt to encourage investment in capital business assets, has introduced, for a limited period, an initial allowance of 20%; this allowance applies to industrial buildings and to qualifying hotels but not to commercial buildings or structures.

Existing law

3.2 Writing-down allowances at 4% per annum on a straight line basis are available in respect of capital expenditure incurred in constructing an industrial building or qualifying hotel. At the end of the chargeable period, the taxpayer must be entitled to the 'relevant interest' in the building and the building must, at that time, in 'in use' for one of the purposes (manufacturing etc) set out in the Capital Allowances Act 1990 (CAA 1990) s 18.

3.3 Allowances are generally available only for the person who incurred the costs of construction of the building. However, by CAA 1990 s 10, a person who incurs expenditure on buying the relevant interest before the building has been brought into use is entitled to the allowances, based, in most cases, on the price paid for the acquisition of that interest.

The Finance Act 1993 provisions

3.4 Section 113 inserts s 2A into CAA 1990. This provides that:

(a) an initial allowance is available for industrial buildings and qualifying hotels;
(b) the allowance is at the rate of 20% of expenditure;
(c) the capital expenditure must be incurred under a contract which is entered into between 1 November 1992 and 31 October 1993 or which is entered into later but so as to ensure that obligations under a contract entered into during that period are complied with;
(d) the building must be brought into use by 31 December 1994; if it is not, any allowance given will be withdrawn.

62

3.5   A new section, s 10C, in CAA 1990 makes provision for the purchase of unused buildings.

(a)   The section applies where expenditure is incurred under such a contract as is described at 3.4(c) above and, before the building is used, the relevant interest in it is sold.

(b)   If the contract for sale is entered into between 1 November 1992 and 31 October 1993, the seller is a land dealer and that dealer was entitled to the relevant interest before 1 November 1992, the expenditure incurred by the seller must have been incurred under a contract entered into at any time before November 1993.

(c)   Where the section applies, the actual expenditure incurred is left out of account and the purchaser is deemed to have incurred, on the date when the purchase price becomes payable, the lower of the actual expenditure incurred by the seller and the net price paid by the purchaser (the 'deemed expenditure'). Where the sale is by a dealer in land, the deemed expenditure is the net price paid.

(d)   The deemed expenditure is apportioned between that which qualifies for s 2A allowances and that which does not.

(e)   The new provisions apply in relation to chargeable periods ending after October 1992.

Planning

3.6   The intention of the Government in introducing the initial allowance was to give a boost to industry. However, extra allowances are useful only where there is tax capacity. As a result of the recession, fewer companies than before have the capacity to absorb large allowances. Moreover, finance lessors are in a similar position and whereas in more prosperous times they may have been interested in a 20% allowance, this has not been the case in relation to the initial allowance.

3.7   Nevertheless, an allowance will be of use at some time, if not initially. If the company which is entitled to the allowance cannot see a use for it but can see a group member with a need for it in the future, it may be worth disclaiming the allowance so as to increase writing-down allowances in the future which can then be group-relieved. The mere carry forward of the initial allowance would restrict its use to within the claimant company.

3.8   Clear planning points involve the dates. Either the contract under which the capital expenditure is incurred must be entered into between the two dates or the contract must be to secure the performance of a contract entered into before those dates. The time of the incurring is not irrelevant in that regard.

3.9   The new provisions do not specify the type of contract to be entered into and a contingent contract would appear technically to suffice. The Inland Revenue have stated, however, that options will not be sufficient; any expenditure incurred on exercise of an option will, they say, be under a separate contract.

3.10   In any event, the building or structure must, to enable the expenditure to qualify for the initial allowance, be brought into use by the end of December 1994.

3.11   An initial allowance is available in a chargeable period whether or not it is 'in use' (subject to the December 1994 point made above). In this it differs from the writing-down allowances. If, however, the building or structure is also in use at the end of the chargeable period in which the initial allowance is available, the person incurring the appropriate expenditure is entitled to both the initial and the writing-down allowance, a total of 24%.

2   SECTION 115

3.12   This section enacts the measures announced by the Chancellor of the Exchequer in his Autumn Statement (made on 12 November 1992) in relation to enhanced capital allowances for machinery and plant. This measure was, and is, intended to stimulate capital investment and expedite economic recovery (in the traditional Keynsian manner).

3.13   This measure has been widely commented on in the press and was discussed in tax publications prior to the Budget.

Section 115(1)

3.14   This section inserts into CAA 1990 s 22 the new limit of 40% to a first-year allowance arising by virtue of the newly-inserted CAA 1990 s 22(3B) (which is introduced by s 115(2) and considered below); this effectively prevents a 100% first-year allowance which would otherwise apply.

Section 115(2)

3.15   This section inserts new sub-section 22(3B) into CAA 1990 s 22 and provides a wholly new basis for a first-year allowance (of 40%) within the existing capital allowance code set out in CAA 1990. Although the new allowance is set at 40%, it is a 'first-year allowance' for all other purposes of the CAA 1990 (subject to the amendments set out in FA 1993 Sch 13 introduced by s 115(4) and considered below).

There are two new bases for a 40% first-year allowance.

Timing of expenditure

3.16   First, expenditure incurred in the period beginning with 1 November 1992 and ending with 31 October 1993 and second, any additional 'VAT liability' which arises by virtue of expenditure incurred in that period may qualify.

The normal rules as to when expenditure is incurred apply for this purpose, except that express provision is made for CAA 1990 s 83(2) to be disregarded.

(This provision stipulates that, for the purposes of CAA 1990 Pt II, expenditure is deemed to be incurred on the first day a trade is carried on where it is incurred prior to the commencement of that trade.)

Planning – commencement of trade

3.17 A preliminary point to note is that where a trade commences during the calendar year commencing on 1 November, expenditure incurred prior to that period will not qualify for the new 40% first-year allowance.

3.18 Therefore, to the extent possible, a would-be trader who intends to commence trading during this period should try actually to incur capital expenditure (in accordance with CAA 1990 s 153) after the trade has commenced (and before 1 November 1993); this deferral should enable that expenditure to qualify for the 40% first-year allowance, rather than a 25% writing-down allowance.

Planning – incurral of expenditure

3.19 The date on which expenditure is incurred for this purpose is set out in CAA 1990 ss 159(2)–(6). Broadly speaking, these provisions stipulate that expenditure is incurred on the date upon which the obligation to pay it becomes unconditional (provided this is not more than four months prior to when it must actually be paid).

3.20 It would therefore be advisable to ensure that material payment obligations become unconditional within the new first-year allowance period.

3.21 This strategy is, of course, subject to the anti-avoidance provisions set out in CAA 1990 s 159(6), where payment obligations are tailored solely or mainly to obtain a tax advantage.

3.22 It can also be noted here that the provisions of CAA 1990 s 60(1)(b) deem expenditure to be incurred under certain contracts (such as hire-purchase contracts) as incurred when the machinery or plant is brought into use.

3.23 Expenditure to be incurred between 1 November 1992 and 31 October 1993 under these types of contracts will qualify for the 40% first-year allowance, provided the machinery or plant is brought into use within this period.

3.24 Subject to the 'sale and leaseback' provisions in CAA 1990 ss 75 and 76, which deny a first-year allowance (including the new 40% first-year allowance), there is no requirement that the machinery or plant be new or unused to qualify for the 40% first-year allowance.

Section 115(3)

3.25 This section introduces a further exception to CAA 1990 s 22(4)(c) which would otherwise deny a first-year allowance in respect of expenditure (incurred between 1 November 1992 and 31 October 1993), unless the machinery or plant in question were used for a 'qualifying purpose' throughout the 'requisite period'.

3.26   However, this section does provide for two alternative restrictions of the availability of the new 40% first-year allowance in relation to leased machinery or plant.

3.27   First, where CAA 1990 s 42 ('foreign leasing') would apply, no 40% first-year allowance will be available.

3.28   Second, the other restriction consists of three conditions:

(a)   the expenditure is incurred on or after 14 April 1993;
(b)   it does not appear that the machinery or plant would be used for a 'qualifying purpose' throughout the 'requisite period' (subject to minor qualifications); and
(c)   the lessee or an associate used the machinery or plant prior to its provision for leasing.

3.29   This restriction is therefore not quite the same as CAA 1990 ss 75 and 76 in that those sections are more widely drawn, but are subject to the exceptions set out in CAA 1990 ss 76(3) and (5).

3.30   For example, this restriction on the new 40% first-year allowance would apply where a local authority or a charity entered into a sale and leaseback transaction with a finance lessor after 14 April 1993: the equipment would not be used for a 'qualifying purpose' (if the lessee did not carry on a trade) but would continue to be used by the local authority or charity (as lessee rather than owner).

3.31   The new 40% first-year allowance would not be denied to this type of arrangement by reason of CAA 1990 ss 75 and 76.

Section 115(4)

3.32   This section introduces the consequential amendments set out in FA 1993 Sch 13.

3   SCHEDULE 13

Paragraph 1

3.33   This paragraph introduces the following amendments to CAA 1990.

Paragraph 2

3.34   This paragraph provides for the exclusion of the new 40% first-year allowance from the Inland Revenue notification provisions in CAA 1990 s 23:

these provisions require the notification of the Inland Revenue where machinery or plant qualifying for first-year allowances ceases to be used for a 'qualifying purpose' during the 'requisite period'. Such notification would be otiose, as the availability of the new 40% first-year allowance is not dependent on such a use.

Paragraph 3

3.35 This paragraph cross-references the new restriction on CAA 1990 s 30(2)(c) (special provision for ships) set out in CAA 1990 s 46(8)(e) (introduced by paragraph 9 – see further below).

Paragraph 4

3.36 This paragraph ensures that assets qualifying for the new 40% first-year allowance are not excluded by CAA 1990 s 38(m) from 'short-life asset' treatment. This is necessary because the new first-year allowance is not a 100% allowance.

Paragraph 5

Paragraph 5(1)

3.37 This paragraph extends the 'qualifying purpose' set out in CAA 1990 s 39(2)(a) so as to include the availability of the new 40% first-year allowance and so ensures parity of treatment for this purpose.

Paragraph 5(2)

3.38 This paragraph inserts a reference to the new 40% first-year allowance into the anti-avoidance provision set out in CAA 1990 s 39(8) (meaning of 'qualifying purpose'): if one of the main objects of a 'wet leasing' arrangement (within CAA 1990 s 39(6)) was to obtain the new 40% first-year allowance, such an arrangement will not constitute a 'qualifying purpose'. (This in turn may mean that CAA 1990 s 42 may apply.) This places the new 40% first-year allowance on the same footing as a 25% writing-down allowance in this context.

Paragraph 6

3.39 This paragraph inserts a new sub-section, sub-s (9), into CAA 1990 s 42 (foreign leasing).

3.40 This new provision ensures that, where CAA 1990 s 42 applies to a leasing arrangement which had qualified for a new 40% first-year allowance, that allowance will be withdrawn on the same basis as a writing-down allowance would be withdrawn under CAA 1990 s 42(4) (broadly, a balancing charge in an amount equal to the excess allowance in the period in which the allowance is to be withdrawn). This ensures that the mechanics of these 'foreign lease' claw-back provisions can apply to the new 40% first-year allowance.

Paragraph 7

Paragraph 7(1)

3.41   This paragraph excludes the new CAA 1990 s 43(4) (introduced by paragraph 7(2)) from the conditions for application set out in CAA 1990 s 43(1) (joint lessees: new expenditure), as its operation is not intended to be dependent on these conditions.

Paragraph 7(2)

3.42   This paragraph introduces the new sub-s (4) into CAA 1990 s 43 (joint lessees: new expenditure).

This provision prevents CAA 1990 s 22(6A)(a) (introduced by s 115(3)) from excluding expenditure on machinery or plant from the new 40% first-year allowance where the conditions set out in CAA 1990 s 43(1) and (2) (joint lessees: new expenditure) are satisfied and provides for the determination and apportionment (if any) of the new 40% first-year allowance on the same pro-rating between 'foreign' and 'non-foreign' use basis as is provided for in relation to writing-down allowances under this section.

Paragraph 8

3.43   This paragraph inserts the new sub-s (5) into CAA 1990 s 44 (further provisions in relation to joint lessees in cases involving new expenditure).

3.44   This section provides for the application of CAA 1990 s 44 to expenditure qualifying for the new 40% first-year allowance on a similar basis to that which applies for expenditure qualifying for writing-down allowances and ensures parity of treatment. In outline, this section provides for the basis of supplementary adjustments to capital allowances made or to be made in relation to changes of use by joint lessees during the 'requisite period'.

Paragraph 9

3.45   This paragraph introduces the new sub-s (8) into CAA 1990 s 46 (recovery of allowances made in respect of plant and machinery subsequently let to a foreign resident).

3.46   This section provides for the application of CAA 1990 s 46 to expenditure qualifying for the new 40% first-year allowance on a similar basis as it applies to expenditure qualifying for writing-down allowances. In outline, this section also provides for an adjustment to capital allowances made where the 'foreign leasing' occurs during the 'requisite period' by way of a balancing charge at that time.

Paragraph 10

3.47   This paragraph introduces the new sub-s (7) into CAA 1990 s 48 (information provisions in relation to joint lessees in cases involving new expenditure) and ensures that these provisions also apply to expenditure qualifying for the new 40% first-year allowance.

Paragraph 11

Paragraph 11(1)

3.48   This provision amends the definition of 'old expenditure' to ensure that expenditure qualifying for the new 40% first-year allowance does not constitute 'old expenditure' by reason of it falling within CAA 1990 s 22 (as amended by s 115) and so will constitute 'new expenditure' for the purposes of CAA 1990 Ch V.

Paragraph 11(2)

3.49   This paragraph introduces the new sub-s (4A) into CAA 1990 s 50 (interpretation of CAA 1990 Chapter V) and which ensures that references to expenditure qualifying for the new 40% first-year allowance in CAA 1990 Ch V are deemed to include expenditure partly so qualifying.

Paragraph 12

Paragraph 12(1)

3.50   This paragraph introduces the new sub-s (1A) into CAA 1990 s 81 (assets used for purposes not attracting capital allowances and assets received by way of gift) which ensures that the provisions in that section also apply to expenditure on assets qualifying for the new 40% first-year allowance. Broadly, this section enables capital allowances to be claimed where assets are newly brought into use for the purposes of a trade (calculated by reference to their open market value at that time). The new 40% first-year allowance will be available (subject to the restriction in pargraph 12(2)), where assets are so brought into during the period from 1 November 1992 to 31 October 1992.

It would therefore be beneficial, where machinery or plant is to be appropriated to a trade, for this to occur in this period.

Paragraph 12(2)

3.51   This paragraph introduces a restriction on the availability of the new 40% first-year allowance under CAA 1990 s 81 in relation to machinery or plant brought into use on or after 14 March 1993. The appropriation to a trading use is deemed to be an acquisition from a connected person for the purposes of CAA 1990 s 75(1) – this section will deny a first-year allowance unless one of the exceptions to it set out in CAA 1990 s 76(3) or (5) applies.

Paragraph 12(3)

3.52   This paragraph limits the effect of paragraph 12(2) to cases where machinery or plant is brought into use on or after 14 April 1993.

Paragraph 13

Paragraph 13(1)

3.53   This paragraph ensures that where an allowance is made in respect of any expenditure CAA 1990 Part I, III, V, VI or VII no new 40% first-year allowance may also be made under CAA 1990 s 22.

This preserves the entitlement to choose under which provision a claim is made, where it could qualify under more than one provision.

Paragraph 13(2)

3.54   This provision ensures that where a new 40% first-year allowance is made, no allowance may be made under any other part of CAA 1990. This also preserves the entitlement to choose (under which provision a claim is made).

4   SECTION 116

Section 116(1)

3.55   Section 116(1) inserts the following italicised words into the second sentence of CAA 1990 s 40(4) (part of the definition of 'requisite period').

3.56   The definition of 'requisite period' now reads as follows:

'40(4) For the purposes of this Chapter the requisite period is -
(a)   in the case of expenditure not falling within paragraph (b) below, the period of four years beginning with the date on which the machinery or plant is first brought into use by the person who incurred the expenditure; or
(b)   in the case of:
   (i)   new expenditure; or
   (ii)   old expenditure as respects which section 70(3) of the Finance Act 1982 had effect, the period of ten years beginning with the date on which the machinery or plant is first brought into use by the person who incurred the expenditure;
except that where the machinery or plant is used for a qualifying purpose, this subsection shall have effect with the substitution for each reference to ten years of a reference to four years.
   If the circumstances are such that machinery or plant is used for a qualifying purpose, then this subsection shall have effect *for the purposes of sections 31(2) and 37(6)* with the substitution for each reference to ten years of a reference to four years.'

Context – the purpose of the term 'requisite period'

3.57 The definition of 'requisite period' interrelates with that for 'qualifying purpose', which continues to be defined in CAA 1990 s 39.

In outline, machinery or plant is used for a 'qualifying purpose' at any time when:

(a) it is leased to a lessee who uses for the purposes of a non-leasing trade and either:
   (i) the expenditure was 'old expenditure' (as defined in CAA 1990) s 50(3) and again generally speaking, the lessee could have claimed a first-year allowance in respect of it had it incurred the expenditure; or
   (ii) the expenditure was 'new expenditure' (as defined in CAA 1990 s 50(3)) and the lessee could have claimed a writing-down allowance in respect of it, had it incurred that expenditure;
(b) the owner uses the machinery or plant for 'short-term leasing' (as defined in CAA 1990 s 40(1));
(c) the machinery or plant is leased to a person who uses it for 'short-term leasing' and that person is either resident in the United Kingdom or carries on a trade here (note that this test no longer corresponds with the test now set out in CAA 1990 s 42(1)(b), as substituted by s 116(2);
(d) the owner uses the machinery or plant for the purposes of a trade otherwise than for leasing;
(e) subject to certain restrictions (including obtaining a 25% writing-down allowance as a main object), the machinery or plant is a ship or aircraft leased to an operator on what are commonly referred to as 'wet leasing' terms;
(f) it is a transport container let on certain prescribed terms.

3.58 It is generally regarded that trading lessees who are liable to pay tax in the United Kingdom can satisfy the test outlined at 3.57(a)(ii) above and, correspondingly, that foreign lessees can not.

3.59 It should also be remembered that, it is generally accepted by practitioners and the Inland Revenue that, in the context of CAA 1990 s 42, the 'lessee' is the end-user, in the case where there is a 'chain' of leases on similar terms (for example, where there is an owner/lessor, intermediate lessor/lessee and sub-lessee/end-user), it is the last person to whom one must have regard; the intermediate lessor is disregarded and so, even though it is 'a lessee', it may be foreign.

3.60 These two definitions interrelate for the purpose of various restrictions in relation to capital allowances in CAA 1990 and the definition of 'requisite period' prescribes a period of either four or ten years for which an asset must be used for a 'qualifying purpose' to avoid these restrictions.

3.61 These restrictions include restrictions on the availability of the following.

(a) First-year allowances (other than the 40% first-year allowance introduced by s 115) as a first-year allowance, (CAA 1990 s 22(4)).

(b)   Allowances carried forward, as first-year allowances, under the 'free depreciation' regime for ships (CAA 1990 s 30(2)(c)).

(c)   'Single ship trade' treatment for domestically leased ships (CAA 1990 s 31(1)(b)).

(d)   'Short-life asset' treatment (CAA 1990 ss 37 and 38).

(e)   writing-down allowances for assets subject to 'foreign leases' (CAA 1990 s 42 et al).

3.62   Practitioners have tended to regard the second sentence of this definition as ambiguous and raised doubts as to how long an asset had to be used for a 'qualifying purpose' 'to avoid these restrictions – four or ten years: some advised that after four years' use for a 'qualifying purpose' an asset was free of its 'requisite period' and could therefore be used for any purpose without these restrictions applying. Other practitioners took the contrary view that a ten year requisite period could revive, if an asset ceased to be used for a 'qualifying purpose' after four years.

3.63   This issue can be illustrated by an example. If the four year 'requisite period' interpretation were correct, an aircraft lessor could lease an aircraft to a domestic airline for four years (as noted above, this could be a 'qualifying purpose' under CAA 1990 s 39(2)(b))) and then lease the same aircraft to a foreign lessee without infringing the restrictions in CAA 1990 s 42 or 46; had the 'requisite period' not ended, these provisions would have applied. The Inland Revenue are of the view that, in this example, the aircraft should be leased to a domestic airline for ten years before the potential application of CAA 1990 ss 42 and 46 would be exhausted and so this amendment has been introduced to put this point beyond further doubt.

(This is the example given in the Inland Revenue's Budget Press Release dated 16 March and headed 'Capital Allowances: Assets Leased Overseas' and the principal intended effect of the amendment.)

The effect of the amendment

3.64   The new amendment removes from the four or ten year 'requisite period' debate all provisions apart from newly-excepted ss 31(2) and 37(6) of CAA 1990.

Several consequences would appear to follow.

Impact on foreign leasing – CAA 1990 s 42

3.65   In order to avoid what practitioners commonly refer to as the 'foreign leasing' provisions, an asset must not be subject to a 'foreign lease' (infringing CAA 1990 s 42(1)) for ten years from the date of first use by the lessor; a lessor can no longer rely upon the argument that four-year's use of the asset for a 'qualifying purpose' will end the (four-year) 'requisite period' for that asset and then enter into a 'foreign lease' of that asset (with, for example, a foreign lessee).

3.66   As noted above, this is the expressly intended effect of the amendment in relation to 'foreign leasing' entered into prior to the effective date of this legislation (16 March 1993); it would perhaps be unwise to expect that the Inland Revenue will simply accept that the 'four-year' interpretation applies, as the ambiguity only of this provision was noted.

3.67 'Foreign leasing' is considered further below, in relation to the amendment made to CAA 1990 s 42(1)(b). However, in this context it should be noted that as CAA 1990 s 42 applies in relation to machinery or plant only for the 'requisite period' and so planning for the 'requisite period' of an asset to end (after four, rather than ten, years) was one of the ways of limiting the application of this section (to a four rather than ten-year period), where the other exceptions could not be relied upon (these other exceptions are satisfying CAA 1990 s 42(1)(a) or (b) and 'short-term leasing' or the 'wet leasing' exceptions each set out at the end of CAA 1990 s 41(1).

3.68 This planning technique has now been effectively blocked and given that CAA 1990 s 42 can impose a severe limitation on what would otherwise be a very lucrative financing market, especially in relation to large value, core assets, such as aircraft, ships and satellites, it is to be expected that other methods of avoiding the restrictions imposed by this section will receive a heightened degree of attention and focus. Some of these other exceptions and planning techniques to avoid them are considered further below, in relation to the amendments made to this section by s 116(2).

CAA 1990 ss 31(2) and 37(6)

3.69 An implied consequence is, perhaps, that the original ambiguity in the second sentence of the definition of 'requisite period' has now been resolved for practical purposes, in the situations where it still applies (CAA 1990 ss 31(2) and 37(6)). Although the ambiguous text has not been redrafted (and so in one sense is no less ambiguous), it is arguable that the amendment would not have been necessary had the 'four-year' interpretation been incorrect. The Inland Revenue may now accept that, for the purposes of CAA 1990 ss 31(2) and 37(6) only, four years' use for a 'qualifying purpose' will end the 'requisite period' for that asset.

However, even if a four-year 'requisite period' were applicable, planning opportunities would be rare.

3.70 In the case where the operation of a ship ceased to be used for a 'qualifying purpose' within the 'requisite period' (and so cased to constitute a 'single ship trade') a balancing allowance may not be claimed, as the residual expenditure is deemed to be added to the owner's pool of qualifying expenditure and the consequences of CAA 1990 ss 42 and 46 still have to be avoided for another six years.

3.71 Similar consequences apply in relation to CAA 1990 ss 37 and 38 in relation to 'Short-Life Assets'.

Impact on the other restrictions

3.72 It may also be noted that the amendment also removes the possibility of a four-year 'requisite period', in most cases, in relation to CAA 1990 ss 22(4) and 30(2)(c), even though this is not an objective expressly stated in the Inland Revenue's Budget Press Release.

3.73   In relation to CAA 1990 s 22(4), this consequence will have little practical effect as this section is now of limited effect – see CAA 1990 s 22(2) and (3) which provide transitional relief for certain regional projects; it should be noted here that CAA 1990 s 22(4)(c) (which denies a first-year allowance unless it appears that an asset will be used for a 'qualifying purpose' for the 'relevant period') does not apply in relation to the new 40% first-year allowance introduced by s 115. The restrictions on this allowance are considered further in the commentary on the section.

3.74   In relation to CAA 1990 s 30(2), it should be noted that a ship must be used for a 'qualifying purpose' for ten years to claim the benefit of this section.

Neither of these consequences is of great significance.

Two 'requisite periods'?

3.75   One further complication would appear to be that 'requisite period' could in certain circumstances have two meanings, both four and ten years (ie four years for the purposes of CAA 1990 s 31(2) or 37(6) and ten years for other purposes).

3.76   For example, if a shipowner leased a ship it would have to be used for a 'qualifying purpose' for four years to avoid the consequences of CAA 1990 s 31(2) (deemed disposal event and re-pooling), but ten years to avoid the 'foreign leasing' provisions.

Section 116(2)

Substitution of new CAA 1990 s 42(1)(b)

3.77   Section 116(2) substitutes a new s 42(1)(b) into CAA 1990 (with effect from 16 March 1993).

3.78   CAA 1990 ss 42–46 provide for restrictions on the availability of 25% writing-down allowances to lessors in relation to (what practitioners commonly refer to as) 'foreign leasing'. If these provisions are infringed within the period of ten years after the machinery or plant is brought into use, then these allowances are restricted to 10% or denied altogether. If 25% writing-down allowances have been made, then they are clawed back (through the mechanism of an adjusted balancing charge in respect of the period in which the infringement occurs (see CAA 1990 ss 42(4) and 46 in relation to 'new expenditure').

Context – CAA 1990 s 42 generally

3.79   CAA 1990 s 42 will apply where machinery or plant is used for the purposes of being leased to a person who is either not:

(a)   resident in the United Kingdom – see CAA 1990 s 42(1)(a) (broadly, a company is resident in the United Kingdom if it is incorporated in the United Kingdom after 15 March 1988 or its 'central management and control' is located in the United Kingdom); or

(b)   he can not satisfy the test set out in CAA 1990 s 42(1)(b) (this is considered in detail below);

unless the leasing is either 'short-term' leasing or the leasing of a ship, aircraft or transport container which is used for a 'qualifying purpose' within CAA 1990 s 39(6)–(9) (broadly, these provisions cover 'wet leasing' and not finance leasing).

3.80   Therefore, unless any one of the United Kingdom tax residence test, the CAA 1990 s 42(1)(b) test, the 'short-term leasing' test or the 'wet leasing' test is satisfied for the whole of the 'requisite period', CAA 1990 s 42 (or s 46) may apply.

3.81   Where CAA 1990 s 42 does apply, then, unless the restrictions set out in CAA 1990 s 42(3) can be avoided, no writing-down allowances are available.

3.82   This rather awkward structure is a function of the history of this provision: it was originally enacted as s 70 of the Finance Act 1982. The Inland Revenue had originally intended to limit writing-down allowances to 10% on all 'foreign leasing'; however, it became apparent, during the late stages of the 1982 Finance Bill, that finance leases to 'foreign lessees' could still be structured without being unduly prejudiced by this 10% limitation proposal and so what is now CAA 1990 s 42(3) was rather hurriedly added.

3.83   Practitioners have since struggled with its unfortunate lack of clarity and very few 10% 'foreign leases' have been successfully written. It can be noted here that the precise nature of the terms of these leases (and related documents) are jealously guarded as industrial secrets of the most proprietary nature.

The new s 42(1)(b) of CAA 1990

3.84   Prior to this change, CAA 1990 s 42(1)(b) read as follows:

'[used for the purpose of being leased to a person who . . .]

(b)   does not use the machinery or plant for the purposes of a trade carried on there [ie in the United Kingdom] or for earning profits or gains chargeable to tax by virtue of section 830(4) of the principal Act.'

(Broadly s 830(4) extends the scope of the United Kingdom tax charge to certain oil or gas exploration activities on the continental shelf.)

3.85   The new s 42(1)(b) reads as follows:

'[used for the purpose of being leased to a person who . . .]

(b)   does not use the machinery or plant exclusively for earning such profits or gains as are chargeable to tax (whether as profits or gains arising from a trade carried on in the United Kingdom or by virtue of Section 830(4) of the principal Act.'

3.86   Section 116(3) sets out a partial definition of the phrase 'profits or gains chargeable to tax' – see further below – it can be noted here that a person who is entitled to claim tax relief in respect of profits by reason of a double taxation agreement does not have profits or gains so chargeable.

Purpose of the amendment

3.87   This amendment corrects one of the defects in this section well known to many practitioners. The original intention of s 42 was to restrict the allowances available to lessors who leased assets to lessees who did not pay tax in the United Kingdom (this was seen as a politically unacceptable subsidy of foreign business by the United Kingdom taxpayer).

3.88   Certain lessees, notably international airlines and ship operators, could satisfy s 42(1)(b) (prior to its amendment) as they maintained a branch in the United Kingdom (and so were, prima facie, liable to tax on the profits arising therefrom). However, those enterprises did not actually pay tax on those profits by reason of a double taxation agreement provision (for example, an article in the form of Article 8 the OECD Model Convention which exempts branch profits of international airlines and ship operators in such circumstances).

3.89   The new s 42(1)(b) will prevent the exploitation of this defect.

The effect of the amendment on 'foreign leasing' generally

3.90   Several points of note arise.

None of CAA 1990 s 42(1)(a) and the 'short-term leasing' or 'wet leasing' exceptions set out at the end of s 42(1) has been amended. These are still alternative exceptions.

3.91   CAA 1990 s 42(1)(b), as substituted, now requires the relevant machinery or plant to be used exclusively for earning profits or gains chargeable to tax in the United Kingdom. Therefore, an asset used partly for earning profits elsewhere will not satisfy this test (for example, an asset which is used partly in connection with a foreign 'permanent establishment' cannot satisfy this CAA 1990 s 42(1)(b) test).

3.92   Lessees with overseas branches who now enter into tax-based leases should carefully consider whether or not they can satisfy this test, if they are unable to satisfy any of the others. It may be advisable to ensure that the contractual lessee is resident in the United Kingdom (by virtue of being incorporated here).

3.93   Where the contractual lessee is not the operator, the 'end-user' test (referred to above) and the 'joint lessee' provisions (in CAA 1990 ss 43 and 44) will have to be considered.

3.94   Assets employed in businesses which are not taxable otherwise than by reason of a double taxation agreement may now also fail this test (for example, a charity).

3.95   It should also be noted that, although the substituted s 42(1)(b) refers to 'use . . . for earning . . . profits or gains', which might, at first, appear to be wider than the original requirement of 'use . . . for the purposes of a trade' and include non-trading use (for example by an investment company), this expression is still qualified by the following phrase (in parenthesis): the 'profits or gains' in question must still arise from a trade carried on in the United Kingdom (or from a deemed branch or agency under s 830(4) of the Income and Corporation Taxes Act 1988 ('TA 1988').

3.96   The Inland Revenue Press Release states that 'foreign leases' are limited by CAA 1990 s 42 to 10% writing-down allowances and then goes on to add that 'in certain circumstances' s 42 also provides that 'no writing-down allowances are available'. As noted above, the restrictions on 10% writing-down allowances set out in s 42(3) are extremely onerous: for example, it is quite difficult to write an economically viable finance lease within these constraints and so qualify for 10% writing-down allowances.

3.97   It should also be noted that foreign enterprises which can not satisfy CAA 1990 s 42(1)(b) as substituted will not be able to enter into finance leases on the same terms as their United Kingdom counterparts; although the effect is discriminatory, the 'Non-Discrimination' article in any double tax agreement may not help. See, for example, Article 24 of the OECD Model Convention.

Planning

3.98   This area of the law presents lucrative planning opportunities: where a financial structure can secure 25% or even 10% writing-down allowances for a 'foreign lease', that structure is liable to be regarded as highly confidential and proprietary by its originator. Practitioners in this area will be aware that the two amendments (in s 116(1) and (2)) have effectively stopped two viable routes to structure 25% allowance-based tax leases for 'foreign lessees'.

3.99   On the basis that practitioners will continue to view this area with interest, it can be anticipated that attention will now be focused on the remaining exceptions to CAA 1990 s 42 and the other material sections.

3.100   As noted above, CAA 1990 s 42(1)(a) has not been amended and neither have the 'short-term leasing' nor the 'wet leasing' exceptions (the latter two exceptions probably present too great a commercial problem in the context of large value core asset finance).

3.101   Also, given that two 25% writing-down allowance routes for foreign leasing have been closed, further focus will be applied to situations where, although s 42 does apply, the constraints of s 42(3) (which denies the lessor writing-down allowances altogether) can be avoided and 10% writing-down allowances secured.

3.102   To avoid CAA 1990 s 42(3):

(a)   rent payments must be annual (or more frequent);

(b)   only periodical payments may become due and payable under the lease (or agreements collateral to it);

(c)   payments (due from the lessee) under the lease must be equal in amount except to the extent that they are varied by reference to change in:

    (i)   the rate of tax;

    (ii)   the rate of writing-down allowances;

    (iii)   the rate of interest on inter-bank loans; or

    (iv)   insurance premiums;

(d)   the lease must not exceed 13 years or be capable of exceeding 13 years at the inception of the lease;

(e)   asset value support (other than insurance proceeds) may not be provided to the lessor (this would normally be necessary for a 13-year 10% writing-down allowance based tax lease.

3.103   It should be noted again that these restrictions, as indeed with this section in its entirety, apply only during the 'requisite period' (which lasts for ten years from the first use of the machinery or plant or until its disposal by the lessor).

3.104   Whilst it is generally thought not to be possible for a finance lease with a 'foreign lessee' on standard United Kingdom market terms to avoid these restrictions (for example because irregular indemnity payments may be required by the lessor, the permitted variation provisions are insufficiently sophisticated, a lease of longer than 13 years may be required by the lessee of its core assets and the (irregular, 'unequal') termination payment will normally be required in the event of any early termination of the lease), it should still be possible to structure a leasing transaction to avoid them, particularly where there are additional parties to the transaction and, having regard to the potential benefits, the lessor and lessee are prepared to be more flexible than they otherwise might be.

3.105   In summary, although the opportunities for planning around and through CAA 1990 s 42 have been further limited by the provisions of s 116, they have not been altogether extinguished.

Section 116(3)

New definition of 'profits or gains chargeable to tax'

3.106   This section introduces into CAA 1990 s 50, as CAA 1990 s 50(3A), a new partial definition of the expression 'profits or gains chargeable to tax' for the purposes of Ch V of CAA 1990. This expression is used only in the substituted s 42(1)(b), and although similar expressions are used elsewhere in Chapter V, they would not appear to be effected.

3.107   It should be noted that the term 'profits or gains chargeable to tax' expressly excludes profits or gains arising to a person who claims or can claim relief under a double taxation agreement. Therefore, whether or not such a person does claim relief is immaterial.

3.108 The definition is not exhaustive; profits or gains not chargeable to tax otherwise than by reason of a double taxation agreement will also be outside the definition (for example, the profits of a charity carrying on a trade which is exempt under TA 1988 s 505(1)(e) or the profits of an international body carrying on a trade which is exempt under an order made under TA 1988 s 324).

Section 116(4)

Commencement of s 116

3.109 This section provides that the provisions apply to machinery or plant for leasing under leases entered into on or after 16 March 1993.

3.110 Leases entered into prior to this date are not therefore affected. Arrangements then existing should not be affected, unless altered (a new lease can be regarded as arising as a result of these alterations under normal contractual principles).

3.111 In relation to the amendment made by s 116(1), however, it should be noted that the Inland Revenue regard this as the removal of a 'possible ambiguity'; this might be thought to leave open the possibility of arguing that the amendment did not actually change the law at all, but only clarified it.

5 SECTION 117

Summary

3.112 The capital allowances legislation affords certain reliefs to taxpayers who wish to transfer assets to persons who are connected with them. Broadly, the reliefs enable the transfer to take place without resulting in balancing adjustments for the transferor. The first part of s 117 extends those reliefs to assets not previously covered.

3.113 There are certain restrictions placed on the use of these reliefs. The second part of s 117 extends those restrictions to cover perceived abuses. It is accepted, however, in the Budget Press Release announcing the changes that they will have negligible revenue effect.

Existing law

3.114 The general rule for capital allowances is that where an asset on which allowances have been claimed is disposed of, the sale or insurance proceeds or other capital sums received by the transferor are brought into account in computing whether the transferor will suffer a balancing charge or be given a balancing allowance. The major exceptions to that rule concern sales between controlled or connected persons and sales, the sole or main benefit of which is to obtain an allowance or a deduction or a greater allowance or deduction or the avoidance or reduction of a charge. These rules are contained in CAA 1990 s 157; they do not apply to plant and machinery allowances given pursuant to CAA 1990 Pt II, which contains its own rules.

3.115   Sections 157 and 158 work together. Where there is a sale of any property and the buyer is a body of persons over whom the seller has control, or the seller is a body of persons over whom the buyer has control, or both the buyer and the seller are bodies of persons and some other person has control over both of them or the buyer and the seller are connected with each other (within the terms of TA 1988 s 839) and the property is sold at a price other than open market value, the capital allowance consequences for both parties are based on the open market value.

3.116   Initial points to note in relation to s 157 are as follows.

(a)   'Control' is defined in s 161 in terms, broadly, of power to ensure that the affairs of the target are conducted in accordance with the wishes of the controller.
(b)   A 'body of persons' includes a partnership.
(c)   The provisions apply in relation to a sale even if they are not fully applicable for whatever reason, including the non-residence of any party to the sale.
(d)   As noted above, s 157 has no application to plant and machinery allowances available under Part II. It has limited application to patents and no application to know-how.
(e)   Although the reference in the sections is to a sale, various provisions extend the effect of this section to 'transfers': see, for example, CAA 1990 s 21(7) in relation to industrial buildings. In any event, 'sale' includes 'exchange' by virtue of CAA 1990 s 150(4).
(f)   In relation to certain allowances, there are slight modifications of the basic position in s 157: see, for example, s 129 (agricultural buildings).

3.117   The legislation provides, however, that the potentially onerous provisions of s 157 can be mitigated where the parties agree.

Section 158 provides that where the circumstances are as described in 3.115 above (ie sale etc between controlled or connected persons), the sale is not one where the sole or main benefit is to avoid tax (as described in 3.114 above) and the parties elect not later than two years after the sale, then:

(a)   the price at which the property is deemed to be sold (for the purposes of s 157) is the lower of the open market price and a sum referred to in s 158(2); and
(b)   on a subsequent event, any balancing charge which would have been made on the seller, had the seller continued to own the asset, will be made on the buyer.

3.118   Under current law, the sum referred to in s 158(2) is:

(a)   in relation to an industrial building or structure, the residue of expenditure;
(b)   in relation to a qualifying dwelling-house, the residue of expenditure; and
(c)   in relation to mineral extraction allowances, the excess of expenditure over (broadly) allowances made and disposal receipts.

No specific reference is made to any other type of capital allowance.

3.119 The section provides that elections may not be made in certain circumstances: first, where any party is not resident in the United Kingdom and no allowance or charge under the industrial buildings, dwelling-houses, mineral extractions, dredging or scientific research provisions can or could be made on the seller; second, where the buyer is a dual resident investing company; and third, in the case of dwelling-houses, unless both buyer and seller are and were approved bodies within the Housing Act.

FA 1993 changes

3.120 The main purpose of s 158 is to prevent a charge arising in circumstances where transfers are effected for good commercial reasons and where the possibility of a tax charge is not removed on the transfer. Accordingly, the Government has, where the existing law is inadequate, provided for an extension of the relief in some circumstances.

3.121 The first change is to include, where reference is made to industrial buildings and structures, a reference to qualifying hotels and commercial buildings or structures. 'Qualifying hotel' is defined in s 19, 'commercial building or structure' in s 21(5). This change is necessary because the definition of 'industrial building or structure' in s 18 does not include hotels or commercial buildings. Accordingly, under the current legislation, any elections would have no practical effect, there being no sum in s 158(2) to apply in making the necessary comparison with the open market price.

3.122 Second, scientific research allowances are brought in. CAA 1990 Pt V provides for a trading deduction to be available for both non-capital expenditure and capital expenditure on scientific research. Accordingly, the whole of the expenditure is written off for tax purposes in (broadly) the chargeable period in which it is incurred (CAA 1990 s 137).

If connected parties seek to transfer a relevant asset without producing a balancing adjustment, the transfer which would be needed pursuant to s 158 must take place at nil; any greater sum will be taken into account as a trading receipt in accordance with s 138. Accordingly, the new provision, the insertion of a new paragraph (d) in sub-s 158(2), provides for the sum to be taken into account under s 158 to be nil in respect of an asset representing allowable scientific research expenditure of a capital nature which has qualified for an allowance under s 137.

The provision also suggests that capital expenditure on an asset may give rise to an allowance for scientific research expenditure under a section other than s 137 and that, where that is the case, the relevant sum for s 158 is the amount of that expenditure. It is uncertain what the intention of the Inland Revenue is in this regard.

3.123 Section 158 contains restrictions on the use of the election procedure: see 3.119 above. In place of the first restriction, namely, that s 158 cannot apply where one party to the transaction is not resident in the UK at the time of the sale and the circumstances are not at that time such that an allowance could be made on that party in consequence of the sale, a more restrictive provision is being introduced.

The existing provision clearly cannot apply unless one party is not resident in the UK. This left open certain arrangements involving dual residents not caught as dual resident investing companies and companies which were connected but where one of them was not liable to pay corporation tax. It is unlikely that much loss of tax was seen in this area but the new provision would appear to have been introduced to prevent any such avoidance.

3.124   The new provisions apply to sales and other transfers made on or after 16 March 1993 other than any made in pursuance of contracts entered into before that date or contracts entered into for the purpose of securing that obligation under contracts entered into before that date are complied with.

Planning

3.125   This is not a particularly fruitful area for planning; the changes have effect for only small numbers of taxpayers. Moreover, the helpful provisions of s 158 apply only where the sole or main benefit of the disposal is not to obtain, avoid, etc an allowance (s 158(1) and s 157(1)(b)).

3.126   The greatest use of ss 157 and 158 is in commercially-driven intra-group reorganisations. The vendor company may receive no monetary consideration for the transfer and would thus have to look to its reserves to pay any tax; moreover, where the group is effecting a reorganisation for commercial reasons, there is no logical reason why a tax charge should be made. The introduction of provisions to deal with qualifying hotels, commercial buildings and structures and scientific research assets will clearly assist any company with those assets wishing to effect a reorganisation.

In this regard, it should be remembered that ss 157 and 158 apply to most assets on which capital allowances have been claimed but not all such assets. For example, plant and machinery and know-how each has its own code. It will be important to ensure that the appropriate rules for each code are adhered to, for example, anti-avoidance, time limits for claims, status of transferee, etc.

3.127   Even in a reorganisation, the election will not always be beneficial. Where the market value of the asset is higher than the tax written-down value of the asset, an election is likely to be worthwhile to prevent the mismatch of balancing charge (fully taxable on the transferor) and allowances (available at a rate less than 100% for the transferee). Where, however, market value is lower than tax written down value, it may be beneficial to allow the provisions of s 158 to take effect, for the vendor to claim a balancing allowance (if appropriate) and the purchaser to claim allowances on market value.

3.128   Where either s 157 or s 158 applies, the price actually paid is, in most cases, irrelevant (at least for allowance purposes). Accordingly, if there is a reason not to move funds between the companies, or to pay something other than market value or the s 158 (2) sum, this can be done without allowance consequences. Sometimes, there is a need or desire to transfer value between companies for good commercial reasons.

3.129 Where a transfer of assets is needed and s 158 is not available, because, for example, of a restriction, it may be worth considering whether the sale or transfer can be routed via an entity which is not controlled or connected (in each case as defined). Provided that the sole or main benefit is not to avoid etc tax, the market value provisions will not apply and the actual proceeds will be taken into account for allowance purposes.

3.130 In terms of timing, the new anti-avoidance provisions, which will become s 158(3)(a), apply to transfers on or after 16 March 1993 except provisions to certain earlier contracts. If a transfer could be effected pursuant to such a contract and it would be beneficial for other (non-tax) purposes, but would be caught under the new provisions, the election should still be possible.

CHAPTER 4

Foreign exchange gains and losses

1 INTRODUCTION

4.1 Sections 60, 92–95 and the whole of Chapter II of Part II of the Finance Act 1993 introduce an entirely new tax regime relating to the tax treatment of exchange gains and losses. Although a vast amount of detail remains to be published by the Inland Revenue, largely through delegated legislation, it is already clear that the new rules introduce one of the most fundamental and sweeping changes made in recent years to the United Kingdom tax system. The rules represent a significant departure in this system, blurring the traditional distinctions between income and capital and receipts or payments and accruals; furthermore, they suggest a move towards an accruals basis for measuring a company's taxable profit or loss.

4.2 The tax system of the United Kingdom, in common with that of other countries, was not put in place at a time of floating exchange rates, and so was not designed to cope with them. As a result, when floating exchange rates came into being after the abandonment of the *Bretton Woods* agreement in the early 1970s, the tax and economic treatment of exchange differences started to diverge. This divergence was particularly marked in tax systems, such as that of the United Kingdom, which were largely predicated on real movements of value and distinguished between transactions on capital and on revenue account. Other countries, such as the United States of America, where the tax treatment also draws this distinction, have over time introduced amendments to their tax system to accommodate, inter alia, floating exchange rates; but, until now, the United Kingdom has perhaps remained the one major trading nation whose tax system does not reflect the commercial realities of foreign exchange risk.

4.3 The asymmetries, and consequential fiscal iniquities, which have arisen in the United Kingdom from the tax treatment of exchange gains and losses have, therefore, caused considerable concern for some time. This concern has particularly increased in the last decade or so, as many companies in the United Kingdom have expanded their overseas activities, and as treasury management techniques have become more sophisticated in order to help United Kingdom companies compete more effectively in international markets. The anomalous tax treatment of foreign currency transactions has sometimes proved to be expensive for commerce and industry, especially at times of exchange rate volatility (such as that which has recently been experienced by a number of EC currencies, both within and outside the Exchange Rate Mechanism).

4.4 In addition, the lack of a coherent basis for the tax treatment of foreign exchange gains and losses is one of the factors which has discouraged many large multinational companies from setting up treasury functions in the United Kingdom. For example, the finance vehicles of a number of major United Kingdom groups, because they have been unable to claim foreign exchange losses as expenses of management, have been forced to raise funds offshore in suitably tax-neutral jurisdictions (such as the Netherlands) in order to avoid the asymmetries inherent in the present regime when foreign currency funds are required in the United Kingdom or overseas. Other companies have moved or concentrated their treasury functions in places such as Belgium (through coordination centres) or Ireland (through Irish financial service companies in the Dublin Docks).

4.5 The progressive step represented by the new rules, set against the background of several years of consultation between the Inland Revenue and numerous, and diverse, representative bodies, still comprises only part of the legislation required to keep the United Kingdom tax system in step with the development of the modern financial markets and the vast range of financial instruments commonly used by companies in this country to hedge, keep pace with or even beat the vicissitudes of the foreign currency and derivative markets. Equally important is the anticipated legislation relating to financial instruments. However, it is uncertain when this related legislation will be introduced. As the Inland Revenue appraises itself (both directly and through the consultation process) of the range of financial instruments and other hedging and investment techniques used by companies in the financial markets, and gradually comes to understand the underlying economic and fiscal rationale for such techniques, it has become apparent to the Inland Revenue that a wide-ranging review of financial instruments is required. That this review is continuing suggests that much broader legislation than was originally envisaged in the Inland Revenue's Consultative Document dated 29 August 1991 in respect of financial instruments may be introduced.

4.6 There appears, however, to be no genuine unanimity amongst corporate taxpayers – or at least amongst their various representative bodies – supporting even the new rules on exchange gains and losses. It is believed that, up to the end of May 1993, a number of substantive objections were raised by the so-called Group of Nine representative body. It appears that the Group was concerned, among other things, about the absence of the all-important regulations to be promulgated under the new statutory rules. It is understood that these objections jeopardised the introduction of the new rules which may instead have been replaced by less flexible provisions.

4.7 As it is, we appear to have ended up with a skeleton regime, on to which a significant amount of flesh remains to be added, probably over a number of years. Whether or not the new rules are introduced before the end of 1994/95, when it is believed the Inland Revenue intend the regime to be fully operational, depends largely upon the reaction of industry, commerce and professionals and the willingness of interested parties to work alongside, rather than against, the Inland Revenue in order to build up a fair but practical set of rules which can operate on a stand-alone basis but which will also dovetail with the forthcoming legislation on financial instruments.

2   THE BACKGROUND TO THE NEW LEGISLATION

4.8   It is not possible even to start to try to understand the new rules without first taking a brief look at the existing tax treatment of currency gains and losses. To do so requires a systematic look at the fundamental difficulties which have arisen under the present regime. Some of these were identified by Mr Anthony Nelson, the Economic Secretary to the Treasury, during the House of Commons Standing Committee consideration of the new provisions on 18 May 1993:

> 'The main problems with the present system are, first, that for trading companies, exchange differences on capital liabilities – that is, mainly long-term borrowings – and on capital monetary assets, such as loans to subsidiary companies, are not generally taken into account for tax purposes. The lack of tax relief for exchange losses on capital borrowings is seen as onerous, given that they are genuine business financial costs that must be borne.
>
> Secondly, for non-trading companies, exchange differences on any borrowings are disregarded for tax purposes, but exchange differences on investments which are chargeable assets for capital gains tax are recognised in calculating capital gains or losses – this can create a mismatch. That underlines . . . the difference between trading and non-trading companies and the problems that can arise in that area for non-trading companies.
>
> Thirdly, for both kinds of companies, the hedging of currency risks may be made ineffective because the exchange difference on the hedging instrument may be treated differently from the difference on the underlying transaction. For example, a gain on a currency instrument used for hedging a loan may be taxed but a loss on the loan itself not allowed.
>
> Fourthly, for companies operating in the United Kingdom which prepare accounts in foreign currency, there is a good deal of uncertainty over how to compute the sterling measure of their trading profits for tax purposes.'

4.9   In summary, the existing tax treatment of exchange gains and losses requires a strict analysis of each relevant transaction. While no substantial difficulties arise in respect of transactions on revenue account, problems are acute in respect of foreign currency transactions on capital account, because of (inter alia):

(i)   the technical distinction drawn between the two different classes of monetary assets; sterling is not treated as a chargeable asset and so falls outside the scope of capital gains tax, while all foreign currency is treated as a chargeable asset and so potentially within the capital gains tax regime;

(ii)   the difference between the tax treatment of exchange gains and losses on chargeable assets (which are generally taxable or relievable, as appropriate) and exchange gains and losses on liabilities (which are ignored for capital gains tax purposes and so are treated as 'tax nothings'); and

(iii)   the different bases on which gains and losses on capital assets and income profits and gains are recognised; the former are generally recognised on a realisation basis, while the latter are usually recognised on an accruals basis.

The reasons for the existing anomalies are considered further below.

The distinction between transactions on capital account and transactions on revenue account

4.10 In answering the question of whether a borrowing transaction is entered into on revenue or capital account, it is, in essence, necessary to decide whether the funds raised augment the borrowing company's circulating or fixed capital. The vast majority of borrowings – possibly other than overdraft or short-term debt or, in the case of financial institutions, some medium- and long-term debt – will be on capital account. The distinction ultimately turns on questions of fact and, to some extent, the borrower's underlying commercial motive. For example, where a United Kingdom company raises long-term foreign currency funds to fund its general business activities (in order, say, to purchase a business asset or to add the funds raised to its overall working capital) the transaction will normally be on the company's capital account. However, the line can often be much more difficult to draw, particularly in complex transactions. It is sometimes extremely difficult to predict with confidence the tax treatment of transactions which fall within the 'grey area' between what is on revenue and what is on capital account.

4.11 These difficulties have made the capital/income distinction – which is largely based on old case law offering inadequate parallels with modern commercial and financial practice – unacceptable as the principal benchmark of one of the most important, and certainly one of the most complex, areas of the United Kingdom tax system.

The distinction between the tax treatment of gains and losses on assets and gains and losses on liabilities

4.12 The capital/income distinction, as it applies to the treatment of foreign exchange gains and losses, causes what is commonly known as 'tax fragmentation'; for example, as a result of the different tax treatment between, on the one hand, gains and losses on assets and, on the other, gains and losses on liabilities. Broadly, capital gains on most assets (other than, for example, sterling cash) are potentially chargeable; conversely, capital losses on those assets are generally allowable. However, capital gains and losses on liabilities – arising, for instance, where a US dollar loan is repaid at a time when the dollar has either depreciated or appreciated against sterling since the loan was taken out – are not recognised by the United Kingdom tax system and so fall outside the tax net. This is so even when the borrower is economically matched; that is, where it is in no better or worse an overall economic position before or after the relevant transaction because it has hedged against its liabilities either by entering into a currency swap or similar financial derivative or by acquiring a matching currency asset which it intends to hold to the maturity date of the funding liability.

4.13 Thus, with foreign currency being treated as a potentially taxable asset but sterling and foreign currency debt liabilities falling outside the tax net, the obvious divergence between the economic and fiscal effects of capital borrowing and investment has tended to highlight the potentially inequitable tax treatment of transactions which have largely the same commercial end result but, owing to the legal structure of the transaction, may produce significantly different tax results. This divergence has only been partially mitigated by the impact of the *Marine Midland* case and the introduction by the Inland Revenue of Statement of Practice 1/87, which are discussed in more detail below.

The recognition problem

4.14   The anomalies in the tax treatment of currency gains and losses are further exacerbated by the fact that the rules relating to the taxation of chargeable gains are triggered by the actual or deemed acquisition and disposal of assets (although not liabilities or obligations), the values of which have to be fixed and recognised in the borrower's accounts and translated into quantifiable tax profit (or loss). By depending on actual or deemed events to crystallise such profit or loss, rather than measuring the taxpayer's overall commercial position, asymmetries emerge both in terms of the timing and of the actual quantum of tax payable. These mismatches are sometimes increased by the application of accounting and tax rules which translate the assets (but not always liabilities or obligations) so acquired and/or disposed of into sterling equivalent benchmark values for the purpose of determining a company's accounting and tax profit.

The translation problem

4.15   The rules relating to tax on chargeable gains, which are predicated on the disposal of assets, do not sit neatly with two further rules: firstly, that sterling is (in most cases) the only acceptable currency in which a United Kingdom company can draw up its accounts upon which its taxable profit is then calculated; and secondly, that, although profit and loss cannot be anticipated, tax profit is normally derived from accounting profit. The Inland Revenue tends to insist that a company's taxable profit derives almost exclusively from its statutory accounts, give or take one or two statutory adjustments for such things as depreciation and certain disallowed expenditure. As a result of the application of Statement of Standard Accounting Practice 20, *Foreign Currency Transactions* ('SSAP 20'), which translates *unrealised* differences – including those on foreign currency assets, such as a non-sterling loan to a subsidiary – into sterling-equivalent profit or loss on the balance sheet date, has been relied upon by the Inland Revenue to legitimise its attempt to seek to tax unrealised exchange gain differences in circumstances where a genuine commercial profit has not been recognised – even when it is unlikely to be realised because of the existence of collateral financial hedges.

The hedging problem

4.16   Many of the difficulties discussed above are illustrated by the tax fragmentation resulting from the difference between the treatment of a financial hedging transaction (such as a standard currency swap or forward currency contract) and that of the underlying borrowing, the currency exposure on which that hedge is intended economically to eliminate.

Chargeable assets and unrelievable liabilities do not necessarily 'net out' in tax terms, even though this may be their *economic* objective and result.

Marine Midland: the matching principle

4.17   A number of these difficulties were considered by the House of Lords in the case of *Pattison v Marine Midland Ltd* [1984] STC 10, in which the depreciation of sterling against the United States dollar gave rise to a loss on a capital borrowing which was used to fund short-term loans in the course of the taxpayer's specialist banking trade. The Inland Revenue ended up losing its claim that it was entitled to tax (under Case I of Schedule D) the appreciation in value of the company's dollar assets without offering tax relief for the equivalent loss on the company's matching capital liability. The taxpayer successfully argued that it had made neither a profit nor a loss because, by holding the same amount of dollars during the transaction, it was commercially, and so fiscally, matched throughout.

The 'matching' concept which emerged from this case was given only limited recognition by the Inland Revenue's subsequent Statement of Practice, SP1/87, but has now been adopted as an important element of the new proposals.

Statement of Practice 1/87

4.18   Following the House of Lords' decision, the Inland Revenue issued SP1/87 which offered its interpretation of the *Marine Midland* decision. Until now, SP1/87 has provided the only official guidance on certain aspects of the tax treatment of foreign exchange gains and losses.

4.19   The Statement of Practice permits a limited degree of matching of foreign currency assets and liabilities. Where matched, regardless of whether the items are on capital or revenue account, no tax adjustment will have to be made for any exchange differences.

4.20   However, SP1/87 applies only to the computation of *trading* profits. It does not apply to non-trading companies, such as investment companies. Nor does it apply to exchange gains and losses on capital liabilities, which are currently still outside the scope of United Kingdom tax. Moreover, chargeable assets for the purposes of tax on chargeable gains remain chargeable to tax on a realisation basis.

4.21   Thus, SP1/87 has been criticised, in the authors' view quite rightly, for its failure adequately to resolve many of the particular difficulties described above.

Two examples of how problems arise on hedged borrowings

Currency swap

4.22   UK plc wants to borrow to fund its business in the United Kingdom, but wants to tap cheaper sources of funds, which are available in the US public medium-term note market because US LIBOR is 3% against UK LIBOR of 6%. UK plc enters into the following transactions:

4.23

Day 1	borrows $200m for 7 years
	swaps $200m for £100m when exchange rate is US$2:£1
Year 7	swaps back sterling for dollars at the day 1 spot rate by selling sterling and receiving dollars. However, in the meantime sterling has weakened against the dollar and the actual exchange rate is US$1.5:£1
	repays $200m on borrowing

UK tax computation in respect of currency swap

			£m
Day 1	Disposal:	UK plc sells US$200m for sterling (at US$2:£1) and receives	100
	Cost:	UK plc acquires US$200 from bond issue at imputed cost (at US$2:£1)	(100)
		result = gain or loss	nil

			£m
Year 7	Disposal:	UK plc disposes of $200m to bondholders when bonds are repaid (at the prevailing spot rate of US$1.5:£1, because no actual cash is received by UK plc)	133
	Cost:	UK plc acquires US$200m under swap at the day 1 spot contract rate of US$2:£1	(100)
		result = taxable gain	33

UK plc therefore suffers a non-allowable loss on its borrowing, but has made a taxable gain on the swap of £33m.

Forward rate agreement

4.24   UK plc requires sterling but borrows US$200m at 3% per annum and enters into a forward rate agreement to hedge its dollar interest and principal repayment exposure.

			$	£
Exchange rates:	Day 1	spot	2	1
		forward (1 yr)	1.9	1
		forward (2 yr)	1.8	1
		forward (5 yr)	1.6	1
	Year 1		2.4	1
	Year 2		1.8	1
	Year 5		1.5	1

Interest hedge (year 1)			£m	£m
Coupon cost ($6m) at year 1 spot of $2.4:£1				(2.5)
Capital loss on FRA:				
	Disposal of currency:	sale of £6m at imputed spot of $2.4:£1	2.5	
	Cost of currency:	acquisition of $6m under FRA at forward rate of $1.9:£1	(3.16)	(0.66)
	result =	net interest expense		(3.16)

Principal hedge (year 5)			£m
Disposal of currency:		UK plc repays $200m to bondholders at imputed spot of $1.5:£1	133
Cost of currency:		UK plc acquires $200m via FRA at 5 year forward rate of $1.6:£1	125
result =		taxable gain on FRA	8
Corresponding loss on bond			
	Debt revalued at redemption (at $1.5:£1)		133
	Actual cost of repayment at 5 year forward rate under FRA (at $1.6:£1)		125
result	= loss		8
BUT	because UK plc's debt obligation is not a chargeable asset, no loss can be offset		

3   THE FINANCE ACT 1993:
THE INLAND REVENUE'S SOLUTIONS

4.25   The relevant provisions of the Finance Act 1993 are as follows:

Section 60:	Certain interest not allowed as a deduction.
Sections 92–96:	Corporation tax: sterling and foreign currency accounting (including a minor amendment to the rules relating to the controlled foreign companies).
Sections 125–170:	Foreign exchange gains and losses. Many of these sections contain definitions or deal solely with principles of interpretation which are to be applied to the new legislation.
Schedules 15–18:	The alternative calculation of exchange gains and losses; transitional arrangements; amendments to the rules dealing with the taxation of chargeable gains; amendments to existing legislation.

Summary

4.26   The main elements of the new provisions are as follows.

(i)   Gains and losses arising in respect of a company's trading transactions as a result of currency fluctuations on certain assets and liabilities and certain foreign currency exchange contracts are to be taxed as trading receipts or allowable trading expenditure, as appropriate. Such gains and losses arising in respect of non-trading transactions will respectively be taxed as income (under Case VI of Schedule D) or relieved (broadly, as if they were management expenses).

Gains and losses on these assets arising otherwise than as a result of currency fluctuation continue to be dealt with under existing legislation as will gains and losses on assets and liabilities not included in the new regime (very broadly, non-monetary items).

(ii)   Gains will come into charge to tax, and losses will be relieved as they accrue over the life of the relevant asset, liability or foreign currency contract.

(iii)   The legislation applies to all companies (except authorised unit trusts and approved investment trusts), including banks and other financial traders as well as non-resident companies within the charge to income or corporation tax.

(iv)   There is a limited relief to defer unrealised currency gains in respect of long-term capital borrowings and advances.

(v)   There are also limited provisions for matching exchange differences on borrowings with exchange differences on certain non-monetary assets.

(vi)   Eligible companies will have a right to elect for their basic trading profits (broadly, profits before capital allowances) to be computed in a non-sterling currency in certain limited cases.

(vii)   Detailed anti-avoidance provisions disallow certain exchange losses and isolate (through a ring-fencing mechanism) certain exchange losses arising on non-arm's length transactions.

4.27 Much of the detail of a number of important aspects of the regime has not yet been published; for example, the provisions relating to 'matching' and the transitional provisions relating to assets and liabilities held or owed on the date on which a company becomes subject to new rules. Indeed, it is believed that, at the date of writing, none of the secondary legislation has even been drafted. Accordingly, the effect of the regime, taken as a whole, cannot adequately be evaluated. This has been the subject of considerable criticism by all the professional bodies making submissions in response to the draft clauses set out in the Consultative Document and was also the subject of considerable discussion by the House of Commons Standing Committee (see, in particular, the discussion of 18 May 1993). The Inland Revenue has, however, stated that a consultation procedure will also be followed in respect of the secondary legislation. Whilst this is to be welcomed, this will no doubt further delay full implementation of the new rules.

4.28 At present, no firm information is available from the Inland Revenue as to when the new rules will be brought into force. Some commentators have predicted that it is highly unlikely that they will come into effect before the end of 1994 at the very earliest. During the House of Commons Standing Committee debates on 18 and 19 May 1993, the Government indicated that the commencement date of the relevant sections of the Act would not be set until at least three months after the provisions of the regulations had been finalised, and stated that this would certainly not be before the end of 1993.

Definitions and interpretation

To whom will the new rules apply?

4.29 Any 'qualifying company' will be subject to the new regime. Section 152 provides that any company other than a company established for charitable purposes, the trustees of unit trusts and a company which is an approved investment trust is a qualifying company for these purposes.

4.30 The new regime will, therefore, not apply to non-corporate taxpayers at all; so, for example, individuals and partnerships fall outside the new rules and so will continue to be subject to the old rules. Note that where a partnership consists of corporate and non-corporate members, the corporate partners will be subject to the new rules (if they are qualifying companies).

To what will the new rules apply?

4.31 The new provisions apply to exchange gains and losses arising in respect of 'qualifying assets', 'qualifying liabilities' and rights to settlement and duties to settle under 'currency contracts' held or owed by a qualifying company.

4.32 A *qualifying asset* is defined in section 153 as, broadly, a monetary asset, being:

(i)   a right to settlement under a 'qualifying debt' (as to which, see further below (section 153(1)(a)));
(ii)   currency in the form of cash (section 153(1)(b)); or

(iii)   a share held in 'qualifying circumstances' (section 153(1)(c)). Such circumstances will exist where the share is held as trading stock (as will often be the case for banks and other financial traders) and the value of the share is, in effect, marked to market in the company's accounts under SSAP 20 (section 153(11)). Note that a number of banks hold preference and other share investments issued by their corporate customers in lieu of raising conventional debt finance. These are often held as so-called trade investments, not stock-in-trade, and are not marked to market.

4.33   There are two noteworthy exclusions from the definition of a qualifying asset. Firstly, rights to settlement under currency contracts are specifically excluded from being qualifying assets, as the method for calculating the accrued currency gain or loss in respect of such rights is dealt with separately from the rules governing the calculation in respect of qualifying assets. Secondly, rights to settlement in respect of convertible bonds (ie bonds which can be converted into or exchanged for shares) are also excluded, unless the relevant security is a deep gain security or the bond is held in qualifying circumstances (section 153(3) and (4)). The rationale behind this exclusion appears to be that the investor's currency gain, in the first instance, is already subject to income tax under Schedule 11 to the Finance Act 1989 and, in any case, would be expected to be picked up under the normal mark-to-market valuation methods.

4.34   A *qualifying liability* is defined as:

(i)   a duty to settle under a 'qualifying debt' (as to which, see further below (section 153(2)(a)));

(ii)   a contingent liability for which provision has been made in the qualifying company's accounts and which would, if it were to crystallise, constitute a duty to settle under a qualifying debt. In addition, the contingent liability must be such that, if it were to crystallise, it would be owed for the purposes of the company's trade, and the provision must be deductible on revenue account (ie in computing the profits or losses of the trade) (section 153(2)(b) and 153(7)); or

(iii)   an obligation to transfer shares or securities under a 'short sale' contract (ie where the transferor has entered into the sale contract before it has acquired the shares or securities in question) (section 153(2)(c) and (d)). These contractual obligations will not constitute qualifying liabilities unless the shares or securities in question would be qualifying assets in the hands of the company if it had already acquired them, rather than sold them short; so, again, this is probably only relevant to banks and financial traders (section 153(8) and (9)).

4.35   Just as with qualifying assets, a duty to settle under a currency contract is excluded, as is a duty to settle a convertible or exchangeable debt unless, again, the debt security is a deep gain security (section 153(5) and (6)).

4.36   A *qualifying debt* is a debt whose terms require settlement by the payment of money or by the transfer of another debt which must itself be settled by a payment of money (section 153(10)).

4.37   Normally, the face value of the debt, by reference to which the accruing currency gains will usually be measured, will be evident at the outset. However, the rules specifically provide that interest which has accrued on a debt and which may have been capitalised will not be treated as being part of the par value of that debt for the purposes of calculating the taxable exchange gain or loss (section 153(12)).

4.38   *Currency contracts* are identified by the application of section 126(1). Such a contract is defined as a contract under which a qualifying company:

'(a)   . . . becomes entitled to a right and subject to a duty to receive payment at a specified time of a specified amount of one currency (the first currency), and

(b)   . . . becomes entitled to a right and subject to a duty to pay in exchange at the same time a specified amount of another currency (the second currency).'

4.39   This definition is intended to encompass not only, for example, the exchange of currency under a forward rate agreement, but also any re-exchange of principal between two parties to a standard currency swap agreement (or one embedded in a typical cross-currency and interest rate swap) at its final maturity. It does not extend to (in the case of a currency swap) the recurrent fees payable during the term of that agreement. The Inland Revenue have stated that they intend that these fees should fall to be considered under the anticipated new legislation relating to financial instruments.

Lists of the most important instruments which fall within and of those which are outside the new rules are set out at 4.181 below.

4.40   A number of additional detailed rules which are to be applied to determine when a qualifying company is to be treated as being entitled or subject to a qualifying asset, qualifying liability or a currency contract are set out in sections 154 to 157. In particular:

(i)   the fact that the company may have pledged, mortgaged or otherwise transferred an asset by way of security is ignored in determining whether the company is entitled to that asset (section 154(2));

(ii)   where a company acquires or disposes of an asset or becomes or ceases to be subject to a liability under a contract, it is the time at which the contract relating to the acquisition or disposal of the asset or under which it becomes or ceases to be subject to the liability is entered into (or, in the case of a conditional contract, the time at which the contract becomes unconditional) rather than the time of any actual transfer of the asset or liability which is taken for the purposes of the legislation (sections 154(3)–(6) and 155(2)–(4));

(iii) in a number of instances, the accounting treatment adopted by the company is capable of overriding the rules that would otherwise apply (see, for example, sections 154(12), 154(13), 155(7), 155(11), 155(12), 156(2) and 156(4)); and

(iv)   any identification rules used for the purpose of preparing a company's accounts on normal accountancy principles are to be used to identify which particular shares or securities have been disposed of out of a particular holding (section 154(11)). Otherwise, they are to be identified on a 'first in, first out' basis (section 153(10)).

What benchmark currency should be used in the accruals calculations?

4.41   The principle governing the new regime remains that sterling is the main currency of account, in computing both a company's commercial and fiscal profit. Thus, the general rule, set out in section 149(1), which will apply in most circumstances, is that the local currency for the purposes of making the calculations required under sections 125–127 is to be sterling.

4.42   However, this rule can be rebutted in certain circumstances, thus permitting a non-sterling currency to be used to calculate currency gains and losses.

4.43   If, at any time in the period for which a calculation is made – an accrual period – an asset or contract is held or a liability or duty to settle is owed by a qualifying company for the purposes of a trade in circumstances where the local currency of that trade for the whole of that period is not sterling, then that local currency will apply to the calculation of the relevant exchange gain or loss (section 149(4)).

4.44   Where more than one local currency is involved, the calculations required by sections 125–128 are to be made by reference to each local currency. Any exchange gain or loss is to be ignored unless it is found to arise in the local currency of the trade for the relevant accounting period (section 149(5)).

4.45   In all other circumstances, section 149(6) provides that sections 125–128 are to be applied by reference to sterling, and sections 129–133 are to be applied to any non-trading exchange gains and loss. Sections 125–128 are then to be applied separately in respect of trading gains and losses by reference to each local currency involved. Any exchange gain or loss of a trade is to be disregarded unless it is found in the local currency of the trade for the relevant period.

4.46   In the Standing Committee debate of 19 May 1993, the Government indicated that sub-ss (5) and (6) would be of relevance where several local currencies were involved, because, for example, the relevant asset or contract was held, or liability owed, for the purposes of more than one trade or for a mixture of trading and non-trading purposes. In each case, exchange differences are to be initially calculated by the reference to each relevant currency, but then an apportionment between the different purposes is required. The exchange difference in each local currency is taken into account only to the extent of the relevant proportion.

When and over what period should exchange gains or losses be calculated?

4.47   Having identified the qualifying company's currency assets, liabilities or contracts, and having decided whether a sterling or other local benchmark currency is to be used to calculate exchange or losses within or between periods of account, it is necessary to decide when, and over what period, the currency movements on those assets, liabilities or contracts should be measured.

4.48   Section 158 identifies the times, defined in the legislation as *translation times*, at which qualifying assets, qualifying liabilities and currency contracts should be valued. In each case, there will be a translation time:

(i)   immediately after the company becomes entitled to the asset or contract or becomes subject to the liability (ie on acquisition);

(ii)   immediately before the company ceases to be entitled to the asset or contract or subject to the liability (ie on disposal); and

(iii)   at the end of each intermediate accounting period.

4.49 An *accrual period* is then defined as being the period between one translation time and the next. Thus, except for the periods in which acquisition and disposal fall, an accrual period will correspond to the company's accounting period. For example, when a qualifying company acquires a qualifying asset, the period beginning immediately after it has done so and ending immediately before the end of the accounting period during which the asset is acquired ends will be an accrual period. The next accrual period will be the company's next accounting period (unless the asset is disposed of before the end of that period).

Which exchange rates should be used when translating amounts or values?

4.50 An exchange rate is needed to find the local currency equivalent, at any translation time, of:

(i)   the *basic valuation* of an asset or liability;

(ii)   the *nominal amount* of a debt outstanding; or

(iii)   an *amount of currency*.

Each of these three values is dealt with below.

4.51 In most circumstances, the company should use the exchange rate employed in its accounts, provided it is an arm's length rate (as defined in section 150(3)). If it is not, the London 'spot rate' will normally be used (section 150).

4.52 Particular rules, set out in section 150(6)–(7) and (11), apply where a company has entered into a forward currency contract which is not reflected in accounts prepared under normal accounting practice. In these circumstances, a company is permitted to translate the currency underlying the contract using the rate of exchange specified in or implied by the terms of the contract (provided that rate is an arm's length rate).

4.53 The rules in section 150 are adapted in section 151 in order to determine, immediately after the time at which the nominal amount of a debt outstanding increases or decreases, the local currency equivalent of a debt whose nominal amount varies during the relevant accrual period. In these circumstances, the two currencies whose values are compared in the computation are the local currency of account and the settlement currency of the debt.

Basic valuation

4.54 Any calculation of a movement in value of an asset, liability or currency contract needs a starting-point by reference to which all future exchange rate movements can be measured in order to compute whether the value has indeed increased or decreased in accounting and tax terms. Hence, a starting-point, defined in section 159 as the *basic valuation*, is needed.

4.55 The basic valuation of an asset or liability will normally be the value actually attributed by the company to the asset or liability immediately after it has acquired or become subject to that asset or liability, or (if different) the value that the company would attribute to that asset or liability under normal accountancy practice (section 159(1)). If the asset or liability is valued in a currency other than the nominal currency of that asset or liability, the valuation must be converted into the nominal currency at the London spot rate prevailing on the relevant acquisition date (section 159(2)).

4.56 The basic valuation of a liability under a short sale of shares or securities is the consideration received by the company in return for accepting the liability to deliver the relevant stock (section 159(3)).

4.57 Special rules apply to determine the basic valuation of securities which are subject to the accrued income scheme and to adjust the price paid for such securities purchased cum or ex-div by the amount of accrued interest (section 159(5)–(9)).

Nominal currency of assets and liabilities

4.58 The rules for identifying the nominal currency of assets and liabilities are contained in section 153. In the case of currency in cash, the nominal currency is simply that currency. The nominal currency of a right of settlement under a qualifying debt, a duty to settle under a qualifying debt and a contingent liability is the settlement currency of the debt. The nominal currency of shares held in qualifying circumstances and of obligations to deliver securities or shares is the currency in which the relevant shares are denominated or the settlement currency of the debt (as appropriate).

Settlement currency of a debt

4.59 With certain exceptions, the settlement currency of a debt is the currency in which it is ultimately to be settled or, where final settlement is determined by reference to another currency, that other currency (section 161(1) and (2)). Where the settlement currency cannot be determined by applying these rules, the settlement currency is the currency that can reasonably be regarded as the most appropriate in the circumstances (section 161(4)).

Nominal amount of a debt

4.60 The nominal amount of a debt is, in most straightforward cases, the amount outstanding at the appropriate time, expressed in terms of its settlement currency (section 159(1)). However, the terms of the debt may provide for payment or repayment to be made in a currency other than the settlement currency. As a result, there may be an increase or decrease in the nominal amount of the debt outstanding; so, the amount of payment or repayment must be calculated by reference to the settlement currency (section 162(2)).

Local currency of a trade

4.61   In general, the local currency of a trade is sterling (section 163(1)). However, where the basic profits or losses of a trade are permitted to be computed and expressed in another local currency under regulations yet to be made under sections 93 or 94, that local currency may be used instead of sterling (see 4.124–4.135).

How are trading and non-trading exchange gains and losses taxed and relieved?

4.62   The relevant sections are sections 125–133 which, firstly, set out rules to identify whether there has been an exchange gain or an exchange loss in respect of any financial transaction falling within the new provisions, and, if so, rules to quantify the amount of that gain or loss, and secondly, dictate the tax consequences of both trading and non-trading exchange gains and losses which have been so identified.

Accrual of gains and losses: general

4.63   The rules identifying and quantifying exchange gains and losses falling within the provisions are contained in sections 125–127.

4.64   During the House of Commons Standing Committee debate, Mr Nelson underlined the Government view that the new rules reflected general accounting standards and, in particular, the application of SSAP 20. For example, he stated on 18 May 1993 that:

> '. . . [The new regime] should not require extensive changes in most companies' system of accounting . . . No adjustment will be necessary in the majority of cases involving translation. That is the legislation's intention and, we believe, its effect.'

Accrual on qualifying assets and liabilities

4.65   If a qualifying company holds a qualifying asset or is subject to a qualifying liability, section 125 directs that, unless section 127 applies, there should be a comparison between the local currency equivalent (which will usually, but not always, be the sterling equivalent) of the basic valuation of that asset or liability at the beginning and at the end of each accrual period. The comparison must be made at the end of each accrual period as well as immediately before a disposal of the asset or release of the liability in question.

4.66   If an exchange difference is identified, the rules go on to ascertain whether a taxable gain or a relievable loss has arisen. In the case of a qualifying asset, if there is an increase in the local currency equivalent over the accrual period, there is an 'initial exchange gain'. If there is a decrease, there is an 'initial exchange loss'. The amount of the gain or loss is the difference between the local currency equivalents at the beginning and end of the period. In the case of a qualifying liability, the opposite applies: an increase or decrease in the local currency equivalent over the accrual period produces, respectively, an initial exchange loss or an initial exchange gain.

4.67   Accordingly, where sterling (assumed to be the local currency equivalent) strengthens during an accrual period, there is an exchange gain on a qualifying liability (eg to repay a foreign currency loan) because a lesser amount of sterling will be required to repay that liability. However, there is an exchange loss on a qualifying asset (eg a currency loan receivable) because the currency repayment produces a lesser equivalent amount of sterling. The converse applies where sterling weakens during an accrual period.

EXAMPLE

(A) Qualifying liability	£m
Sterling value of borrowing of $2m on 1 January (the beginning of an accrual period)	1.4
Sterling value of same borrowing on 31 December (the end of that accrual period)	1.6
Difference in local currency equivalents	0.2

Since there is an 'increase' (in sterling terms) over the accrual period, this is treated as an 'initial exchange loss' (section 125(4)(b)).

(B) Qualifying asset	£m
Sterling value of loan of $1.5m made by company on 1 January	1.05
Sterling value of same loan on 31 December	1.2
Difference in local currency equivalents	0.15

Since this is an 'increase' (in sterling terms) over the accrual period, this is treated as an 'initial exchange gain' under section 125(2)(a).

Accrual on currency contracts

4.68   Equivalent provisions apply to forward contracts (including the re-exchange of principal at the end of a swap agreement) to buy and sell currency.

4.69   Exchange differences are calculated by comparing, at the end of successive accrual periods, the local currency equivalents of the foreign currency or currencies to be exchanged under the contract. In so far as the currency received (the first currency) is concerned, if there is an increase over the accrual period of the local currency equivalent, an initial exchange gain for the company is produced; in contrast, a decrease gives rise to an initial exchange loss (section 126(2) and (3)). Conversely, in relation to the currency paid (the second currency), if there is a decrease in the local currency equivalent over the accrual period of that second (final exchange) currency, an initial exchange gain accrues, while an increase produces an initial exchange loss.

EXAMPLE

A currency swap is entered into at the beginning of the accrual period. Under the swap, the qualifying company agrees, inter alia:

(a)   to pay the counterparty £1m in exchange for $2m; and

(b)   after five years, to re-exchange thos? principal amounts.

Applying section 126, the first currency in the above example is sterling. The second currency is dollars.

At the end of the first accrual period, $2m is in fact worth £800,000.

The tax consequences in respect of the exchange gains and losses are as follows:

(i)   there is no exchange difference in relation to the first currency; but

(ii)   there is an exchange difference in relation to the second currency, calculated as being:

	£m
Sterling equivalent of second currency at beginning of accrual period	1
Sterling equivalent of second currency at end of accounting period	0.8
Exchange difference	0.2

By virtue of sub-section (5)(a), the decrease over the period (of £0.2m) is treated as an initial exchange gain of the company.

Accrual on debts whose amounts vary

4.70   Separate rules (which are set out in section 127) apply to debts whose nominal amounts vary (either up or down) during an accrual period. Section 127 will, therefore, apply where part of a debt is repaid or additional moneys are advanced during an accrual period. Each increase and decrease in the local currency equivalent of the debt from the beginning of the accrual period must be separately identified and calculated; all increases are added to the initial base figure, and all decreases are then subtracted, producing an average figure reflecting the movements for the entire period (known as the 'first amount'). (This calculation mirrors the accounting treatment under which a company will keep a 'running balance' of its debt in any relevant currency.)

4.71   The first amount and the nominal amount at the end of the accrual period (which is identified as the 'second amount') are then compared to identify the amount of any net exchange difference. In the case of a right to settlement (ie where the qualifying company is a creditor), if the second amount exceeds the first amount, an initial exchange gain will arise; if it is less, an initial exchange loss will be suffered (section 127(3)). The opposite applies in the case of a duty to settle (ie where the qualifying company is the debtor).

4.72   The rules are modified to cover, inter alia, the situation where a company purchases a debt or securities (for example, if a company purchases, for a consideration of $800, a loan with a nominal value of $1,000). In that case, the basic valuation (in the above example, $800) rather than the nominal amount of the debt is taken into account in making the appropriate calculations.

Trading and non-trading gains and losses: general

4.73   Having identified whether an exchange difference has accrued in respect of a qualifying asset, a qualifying liability or a currency contract, and, if so, the amount of that difference, it is then necessary to apply sections 128–135 to ascertain the amount of the corresponding tax charge or relief.

4.74   The corresponding tax charge or relief will depend on whether the gain or loss has arisen while the relevant asset or contract was held, or liability owed, for the purposes of a trade (or part of a trade) carried on by a company or whether that asset, contract or liability was held or owed for non-trading purposes. No guidance is given in the provisions for determining whether a transaction relates to a trade or not, and so it would appear that general principles established in case law must be applied for these purposes.

Trading gains and losses

4.75   Where any qualifying asset, qualifying liability or currency contract is held or owed at any time during an accrual period for the purposes of a trade or part of a trade, the provisions of section 128 will apply regardless of whether the relevant asset, currency contract or relevant liability is held or owed on capital or revenue account. If section 128 applies, the provisions of section 74 of the Income and Corporation Taxes Act 1988 ('TA 1988') are overridden, and the common law and other statutory rules relating to deductions which are not allowable in computing trading profits are irrelevant (see section 128(10)(a) and (b)).

4.76   Where section 128 applies, the gain or loss identified by application of the rules set out in sections 125–127 (as appropriate) is statutorily deemed to be a taxable receipt or an allowable expense of the trade (as appropriate). The receipt or expense will be treated as arising in the relevant accounting period which either constitutes the accrual period (where there is no disposal or release within the accounting year) or in which the accrual period falls (where there is such a disposal or release). If the relevant asset or contract was not held, or the liability not owed, solely for trading purposes throughout the accrual period, the exchange gain or loss must, under section 128(3) and (7), be apportioned on a just and reasonable basis. A debt incurred for the general purposes of the company's trading and non-trading business is likely to fall within the apportionment rule; in these circumstances, time apportionment will not be appropriate.

4.77 Thus, as exchange gains and losses arising in the course of a trade will be treated as receipts and expenses of the trade, they will be taxed or relieved as they accrue under Case I of Schedule D.

4.78 The rules prevent exchange gains or losses which arise in respect of qualifying assets or liabilities or currency contracts from being taken into account in the computation of trading profits otherwise than in accordance with FA 1993, Pt II, Ch II; these provisions therefore represent an exclusive code in relation to this particular area (section 128(11) and (12)).

Non-trading gains and losses

4.79 Non-trading exchange gains and losses are, broadly, exchange differences arising in respect of all the investment transactions of qualifying companies (whether investment, trading or holding companies). Non-trading exchange gains fall to be charged to tax under section 130; relief for non-trading exchange losses will be available under section 131. Any exchange gain or loss in respect of a qualifying asset or liability or a currency contract which is not held or owed for the purposes of a trade falls to be dealt with under these rules. Where there is an apportionment between a trading-related and a non-trading exchange gain or loss under section 128, the non-trading exchange gain or loss will be dealt with under section 129.

4.80 The amount of a non-trading exchange gain or loss for the accrual period is, as for trading gains and losses, calculated by reference to the rules set out in sections 125–127. The exchange gain or loss is treated as being received or incurred in the accounting period which constitutes the accrual period or in which the accrual period falls.

4.81 First, the aggregate of relevant non-trading exchange gains and losses accruing to a company in any accounting period must be identified by application of the provisions of section 129. The total amount of the non-trading exchange gains of a company in such a period is described as 'amount A', while the total amount of such losses is described as 'amount B'.

4.82 Where there is no net non-trading exchange gain or loss (ie where amount A and amount B equal one another in an accounting period), the rules in sections 130–132 do not apply because the aggregated gains and losses are treated as cancelling each other out. Further, any non-trading exchange gain or loss will be treated as not accruing where that amount is chargeable as income or is deductible as a charge on income under existing law (section 129(7) and (8)). This is intended to prevent any 'double counting' of such gains or losses.

4.83 Where these provisions do, however, apply, the rules in TA 1988 s 396 relating to Case VI losses are disapplied.

4.84 Where a non-trading exchange gain has arisen in any accounting period a charge to tax arises under section 130 under Case VI of Schedule D. The charge to tax will be either on the full amount of the gain (where no non-trading exchange loss has arisen in that period) or on the amount by which amount A exceeds amount B (where such a loss has arisen but is less than the amount of the gain).

4.85 Relief is available in respect of non-trading losses under section 131. Although the rules in TA 1988 s 396 relating to Case VI losses are disapplied by section 129(9), section 131 provides relief in two cases:

(i)   where a qualifying company makes non-trading losses, but no non-trading gains, in any accounting period (section 131(1)); and

(ii) where the amount of non-trading losses exceeds the amount of its non-trading exchange gains in that period (section 131(2)).

4.86 Thus, if a company has only non-trading exchange losses, the full amount can be relieved. However, if the currency has accrued any non-trading exchange gains the total amount of those gains must first be taken from the aggregate amount of its non-trading exchange losses, leaving only the balance to be relieved.

4.87 Relief for such losses can be claimed in a number of ways:

(i)   all or part of the loss may be surrendered as group relief as if it were a trading loss (section 131(3));

(ii)   the loss may wholly or partly be set off against any profits of the same accounting period (section 131(4));

(iii) where no claim under the provisions described in (i) or (ii) has been made (or partial relief only has been obtained) the relevant loss may be carried back to be set against, broadly, non-trading exchange gains (after previous reliefs) of accounting periods falling wholly or partly in the previous three years. Relief will be given against earlier gains on a 'last in, first out' basis; or

(iv)   if unrelieved non-trading exchange losses still remain (either because no claim has been made under the preceding provisions or because the non-trading exchange losses in question exceed the relief available under them), the losses can be carried forward, in which case the company is treated as incurring a non-trading exchange loss equal to the unrelieved amount in the immediately succeeding accounting period. This results in a corresponding increase in amount B for that subsequent period.

4.88 Any claim for relief must be made within two years of the end of the relevant accounting period, unless the Board of Inland Revenue allows an extension.

4.89 Additional rules, contained in section 132, apply where non-trading exchange losses are carried forward to be relieved as mentioned in (iv) above. The losses carried forward (to increase amount B for that later year) are 'ring-fenced' so that the increase in amount B can only be set off against non-trading exchange gains. The amount carried forward is not available to be surrendered by way of group relief or to be set off against any other profits of the company in the same accounting period. The amount carried forward and the loss arising in the following year must, therefore, still be distinguished.

EXAMPLE

	£m
Year 1	
Non-trading exchange gain (amount A)	2
Non-trading exchange loss (amount B)	(10)
Available for relief under section 131	(8)
Relief available	5
Unrelieved amount to be carried forward	(3)
Year 2	
Non-trading exchange gain (amount A)	1
Non-trading exchange loss in that year (amount C) (£4m)	
Amount B (amount C plus amount B carried forward)	(7)
Available for relief under section 131	6
In year 2, amount C can be relieved under any of the provisions of section 131, but relief is available only as follows in respect of the amount carried forward:	
Relieved against non-trading exchange gain of year 2 (as shown above)	1
Available to be carried forward	(2)

The amount that is still unrelieved will then form part of the amount B of year 3, but will be 'ring-fenced' (as above).

4.90 There is a necessary interaction between the provisions of TA 1988 and this relief; therefore, section 133 sets out the way in which relief is obtained for excess non-trading losses.

4.91 Relief under section 131(4), where losses may be set against other profits of the same accounting period, takes priority over the provisions of TA 1988 s 393A(1), although no relief is available under section 131 against any ring-fence profits arising in respect of oil extraction activities.

4.92 However, relief under section 131(7), where losses may be carried back and set off against exchange gains of the preceding three years must be applied after any relief under TA 1988 s 393A(1) (section 133(3)). Additionally, relief will not be available under section 131(7) where it overlaps with relief in respect of charges on income paid by a trading or investment company.

Alternative tax treatments of certain exchange gains and losses

4.93 The legislation envisages two alternative means by which certain exchange gains and losses may be treated for tax purposes, each of which is considered below.

The deferral of unrealised gains

GENERAL

4.94   Broadly, under sections 139–143 companies will be able to defer tax on unrealised exchange gains on long-term capital borrowing and advances (ie those whose original term was 12 months or more) where those gains form a significant proportion of the company's taxable profit.

4.95   Essentially, the amount available for deferral is the excess of the net unrealised exchange gains on long-term capital borrowings and advances for the accounting period in question (or, if lower, the aggregate net realised and unrealised exchange gains on all borrowings, advances and forward currency contracts) over 10% of the company's taxable profit for the relevant accounting period. The excess (or such part of the excess for which the company claims relief) can be carried forward to the next accounting period leaving the balance to be taxed in the current year.

4.96   A gain or loss is unrealised if the accrual period concerned ends solely because the company's accounting period comes to an end (section 143(1)).

CONDITIONS FOR RELIEF

4.97   For an asset or liability to be of a long-term capital nature, the asset or liability must represent capital throughout the relevant accounting period, and the final settlement date of the debt under which the asset or liability subsists must be not less than one year from the date on which it was created. For these purposes, the final settlement date is assumed to be the earliest possible time at which settlement can be required by the creditor.

4.98   A claim for deferral may not be made in respect of any unrealised exchange gain which is attributable to repayment of all or part of a debt. Thus, if a portion of debt is redeemed by a company, section 139 cannot be used to defer any exchange gain arising in respect of that portion. For these purposes, the gain is to be apportioned on a just and reasonable basis. But for this rule, it might be possible for taxpayers to manipulate the rules to their advantage by varying the nominal amount of long-term debt outstanding at any time while purporting to defer an element of any exchange gain on, say, the corresponding liability which, because the full debt might be drawn down subsequently, would nevertheless remain fully on balance sheet and so eligible for deferral relief.

4.99   Regulations may subsequently be introduced to modify the effects of the provisions relating to deferral in certain circumstances. In particular, section 143 envisages that regulations may be introduced to deal with the situation where the debt under which a long-term capital asset or liability subsists is settled and is replaced by another such debt. The Inland Revenue stated in the Consultative Document that where a long-term borrowing, fixed in both term and amount, is replaced by a similar loan within the period of one month before and one month after settlement of the first loan, the regulations will treat the first loan as unrealised for the purposes of the deferral rules. Regulations may also provide for the amount of a company's profits for the purpose of calculating the amount of non-trading exchange gains (amount A) in section 141 which are to be reduced by, for example, any overseas income or chargeable gains to the extent that such income or gains are covered by foreign tax credits.

4.100 In order to make a claim to defer unrealised gains in respect of an accounting period, a number of conditions (set out in section 139) need to be met. Firstly, a company must have an unrealised exchange gain in an accrual period. Secondly, the unrealised exchange gain must arise in respect of a long-term capital asset or a long-term capital liability. Deferral is possible, however, both in respect of an unrealised trading exchange gain and an unrealised non-trading exchange gain (section 139(1)). Thirdly, the claim must, inter alia, set out the amounts in respect of which a claim is to be made, and the way in which the company wishes that claim to be treated. Only one claim may be made as regards an accounting period, but that claim can be made in respect of more than one gain.

4.101 Certain time limits and other constraints apply before a deferral claim will be allowed. A claim must, unless the Board of Inland Revenue decides otherwise, be made (or withdrawn) within six years from the end of the relevant accounting period. In addition, a claim may not be made or withdrawn once the company's corporation tax assessment has become final and conclusive (unless the claim is made or withdrawn within two years of the relevant accounting period).

4.102 The effect of a successful claim is that the gain in question is treated as not accruing in the accrual period in which it actually accrued (the first accrual period). If the relevant asset or liability is held or owed solely for the purposes of a trade throughout the next accrual period (the second accrual period), the exchange gain of the first accrual period will be treated as if it had accrued in that period, and will be taxed accordingly under the general rules in section 128(4); that is, under Case I of Schedule D as if the amount of the gain had been received by the company in that subsequent period.

4.103 If, however, the asset or liability is held or owed by the company solely for non-trading purposes throughout the second accrual period, a non-trading exchange gain will be deemed to accrue in the second accrual period, and will, accordingly, be taxed under the rules set out in sections 130–133 (see 4.79–4.92).

4.104 Where the asset or liability is held partly for trading and partly for non-trading purposes in the second accrual period, there must be a just and reasonable apportionment with a view to computing the appropriate amount of tax on the trading or non-trading portion of the exchange gain (see section 140(6)–(8)).

4.105 If a deferral claim is made and the asset or liability is held in 'exempt circumstances' (as defined in section 143) in the second accrual period, the deferred gain is deemed to be a non-trading gain and taxed accordingly. There will be an apportionment where the asset or liability is held in exempt circumstances for only part of the second accrual period, in which case, the gain will be treated partly as a trading and partly as a non-trading gain.

4.106 For so long as the asset or liability continues to be held or owed, a claim may be rolled over in each subsequent period in which it is so held or owed (section 140(11)).

CALCULATION OF RELIEF

4.107 Detailed rules to determine the maximum amount which can be deferred are set out in section 141.

4.108 The starting point is to calculate the amount of the company's profits for the accounting period on which corporation tax would be payable, disregarding any claim for deferral or group relief. 10% of this figure is then calculated: this amount is referred to as 'amount A'. Amount A is then compared with two other amounts, 'amount B' and 'amount C'.

4.109 Amount B is the company's net unrealised exchange gain or loss on long-term capital assets or liabilities.

4.110 Amount C is the company's net exchange gain or loss accruing on certain assets and liabilities (as defined in section 153) and on currency contracts (all of which are referred to collectively as 'relevant items').

4.111 The lower figure obtained from two further calculations – first, the deduction of amount A from amount B and second, the deduction of amount A from amount C – is the amount which is available for deferral relief under section 139.

4.112 The rules relating to the deferral of gains and losses are further complicated where the local currency is not sterling. The rules referred to in sections 93(6) or 94(11) (as appropriate) are to be used to ascertain the relevant sterling equivalent. Where a claim is made to defer an exchange gain of a trade whose local currency is not sterling, the sterling amount of the gain which is not deferred must be taken into account after the basic profits or losses of the trade for the accounting period are found in sterling. The amount of the gain which is deferred is treated as being the local currency equivalent of its amount expressed in sterling, calculated by reference to the London closing exchange rate for the two currencies concerned for the last day of the accrual period into which the gain has been deferred (section 142(6)).

The alternative calculation

4.113 Schedule 15 outlines the circumstances in which regulations may provide for the calculation of exchange gains and losses by means of the 'alternative method' referred to in paragraph 1. This method allows exchange differences to be left out of account to the extent that they arise on:

(i)   assets, liabilities held or owed in exempt circumstances (paragraph 2);
(ii)   debts or currency representing income that cannot be remitted to the United Kingdom (paragraph 3); or
(iii) liabilities which are matched to certain non-monetary assets under a matching election (paragraph 4).

4.114   Where the alternative method applies, the gain or loss on an asset, liability or contract for an accrual period is derived from the 'accrued amount' for each day in that period (paragraph 1 of Schedule 15).

EXEMPT CIRCUMSTANCES

4.115   Regulations to be made under paragraph 2 of Schedule 15 will identify the consequences of holding or owing assets, liabilities or currency contracts in 'exempt circumstances' (ie for the purposes of long-term or mutual insurance business; the occupation of commercial woodlands; by a housing association; or by a self-build society).

UNREMITTABLE INCOME

4.116   No details of the regulations relating to the application of the alternative method where the income represented by certain assets is unremittable were available at the date of writing.

MATCHED LIABILITIES

4.117   Regulations are to be introduced under paragraph 4 of Schedule 15 to allow a company to elect to 'match' certain non-monetary assets with borrowings in a specified foreign currency for the purposes of operating the alternative method of calculating any exchange and gain or loss, and deciding when exchange gains and losses on the borrowings are to be taken into account under the accruals regime. Such elections will only be permitted on a company-by-company basis. Although the ability to match is expected to be fairly restricted, it is anticipated that it will be of considerable importance in practice to many companies wishing to ensure that the tax treatment of foreign currency borrowings used to fund specific foreign assets follows their accounting and commercial treatment.

4.118   In summary, where a matching election is made, commercial profit or loss will be recognised for tax purposes only at the end of a particular transaction; thus the tax treatment of the transaction will follow its accounting treatment.

4.119   An election to match will be possible only in respect of certain prescribed liabilities (ie a duty to settle a qualifying debt). Again, although paragraph 4 provides certain information in respect of the conditions which must be satisfied before an election can be made, the detailed rules will be contained in regulations, which were not available at the date of writing.

4.120   Such general guidance as has already been provided by the Inland Revenue can be summarised as follows.

(i)   A matching election will be possible where:
    –   the asset consists of shares in an overseas subsidiary, a net investment in an overseas branch, or ships or aircraft; and
    –   borrowing in the specified currency could reasonably be expected to eliminate (or substantially reduce) the economic risk of holding those assets compared with what might have been the position if sterling had been borrowed to fund the relevant asset; and

— the borrowing and the asset are treated as matched in the company's accounts (ie exchange differences on both are computed on the translation basis and carried to reserves, in accordance with SSAP 20).

(ii) If a matching election is made, the company will need to compare the value of the relevant asset, as shown in the accounts, with its net liabilities in the specified currency; that is, the difference between eligible borrowings – any debts (other than short-term trade debts) that are qualifying liabilities – and qualifying assets in the same currency (other than shares held on trading account).

An asset will then be treated as matched with the company's net liability in the specified currency up to the value of the asset at the beginning of the accounting period (or, if later, when the election takes effect). A company will be able to elect in relation to part of an asset and to match in different currencies.

(iii) Matching will cease if:
— a company has no net liability in the specified currency (although minor interruptions of up to one month will be permitted to allow the company to replace any underlying funding); or
— the asset can no longer be regarded as hedged by a borrowing in that currency; or
— an asset is transferred to another United Kingdom group company (although any net gain or loss on the matched liability will pass to the transferee company and continue to be deferred provided, in the case of gains, that that company makes a matching election in respect of the asset).

(iv) A matching election (once accepted by an inspector) will be irrevocable and will usually take effect from the date of election.

(v) Where the alternative method of calculation is used, exchange differences will be deferred, and treated as realised at the date of disposal of the matched asset (or in certain circumstances, at an earlier date, eg if matching ceases). At that time, any resultant net exchange gain or loss will be treated as a chargeable gain or allowable loss, and so will fall to be taxed under the rules relating to corporation tax on chargeable gains.

Corporation tax on chargeable gains

4.121   Schedule 17 sets out the amendments required to be made to the application of the Taxation of Chargeable Gains Act 1992 ('TCGA' 1992) as a result of these new provisions.

4.122   Qualifying assets currently subject to the capital gains rules will cease to be so, to take account of the fact that exchange gains and losses will now be taxed as income. Chargeable gains and allowable losses which might otherwise have arisen may now, in certain circumstances, fall outside the charge to corporation tax on charge.

4.123   The amended rules provide the following.

(i) No chargeable gain or allowable loss will accrue on the disposal by a qualifying company of both non-sterling debts (which are not debts on a security) and (unless they are held in exempt circumstances) non-sterling debts on securities. From now on, such debt securities will be treated as qualifying corporate bonds.

To achieve this, the definition of 'qualifying corporate bond' in TCGA 1992 s 117 is amended for these purposes by removing the usual requirement that the debt be expressed in sterling and be neither convertible into (or redeemable in) any other currency, nor calculated by reference to the value of any other asset or currency. Moreover, in order to exclude the restrictions in Schedule 18 to TA 1988 on 'results dependent' return and premiums payable on redemption, the definition of 'normal commercial loan', an integral part of the meaning of qualifying corporate bond, will be amended to exclude those restrictions where the settlement currency of the debt on a security is not sterling.

Foreign currency debts on securities issued between United Kingdom (chargeable gains tax) group members by TCGA 1992 s 117(10) will now normally fall within the qualifying corporate bond definition.

The interaction of these rules appears to produce the slightly odd result that a debt on a security technically may be a qualifying asset and not a qualifying corporate bond, and thus within the scope of both the new accruals regime and the existing chargeable gains rules.

(ii) The amendments to TCGA 1992 s 117 set out in (i) above are similarly applied by paragraph 6 for the purpose of applying TCGA 1992 s 254 to any loan which is a debt on security made by a qualifying company, and the right to settlement under that debt is a qualifying asset. Thus, relief will still generally be available, where the conditions of section 254 (as amended here) are satisfied, on an amount which is calculated having regard to any exchange loss (whether incurred in the course of a trade or not).

The amount which would otherwise be allowed under section 254(6) (as amended for these purposes) is to be reduced by the aggregate of any exchange losses (ignoring exchange gains) previously allowed before the section operates (the relevant date). The non-exchange loss element of the loss is therefore allowed in the normal way.

Once a qualifying company comes within the new regime these rules are to apply to claims for relief in respect of any relevant debt on a security, regardless of when that debt arose.

(iii) No chargeable gain will accrue on the disposal of foreign currency which is held by a qualifying company in exempt circumstances, which match those circumstances referred to at 4.115.

The removal from the new regime of foreign currency held in exempt circumstances ensures that currency remains within the existing corporation tax framework (including, where appropriate, corporation tax on chargeable gains) until an alternative method of calculation is applied under regulations made under paragraph 2 of Schedule 15.

(iv) Paragraph 7 applies in respect of assets held for the purposes of long-term insurance business or for mutual insurance business purposes, or for both these purposes. Broadly, paragraph 7 disapplies TCGA 1992 s 139 (no gain/no loss on disposal on reconstruction or amalgamation involving the transfer of a business), s 171 (no gain/no loss on disposal intra-group) or s 172 (no gain/no loss on disposal on a transfer of a United Kingdom branch or agency) if there is a disposal or acquisition by a qualifying company of certain specified assets.

(v)   In applying TCGA 1992 s 103(7) (which restricts the availability of the indexation allowance in certain circumstances), the effects of paragraphs 2 and 4 of Schedule 7 are to be ignored (paragraph 8). Thus, the indexation allowance will not be restricted merely because exchange gains and losses are not subject to corporation tax on chargeable gains.

Local currency accounting

4.124   The new rules relating to the currency in which the profits and losses of a trade may be computed and expressed for corporation tax purposes are intended to meet many of the criticisms of the Inland Revenue's insistence that sterling is the only currency in which a taxpayer's commercial profit, and thus its liability to corporation tax, can be calculated.

4.125   The relevant provisions (in sections 92–95 and regulations to be published) have been subject to some criticism by commentators, particularly on the grounds that, first, they are too restrictive (for example, they do not permit a company to reflect the currency in which it draws up its statutory accounts or the 'base currency' in which it keeps its management or other non-statutory accounts), and second, that it would be preferable to make functional currency calculations taking capital allowances and trade charges into account.

4.126   The general rule referred to above, that the profits or losses of the trade of a company are to be computed and expressed in sterling, will still apply in most circumstances, but is now set out in statutory form (section 92).

4.127   Sections 93–95 then set out the consequences of a company making an election to use a currency other than sterling (including, for these purposes, the ECU) in calculating its 'basic profits or losses'. Regulations will in due course establish the circumstances in which an election to use a non-sterling functional currency may be made.

4.128   For these purposes, the basic profits or losses of a trade (eg a branch) or part of a trade are defined as being all of the profits and losses of that trade or part of that trade before taking account of capital allowances and any unrealised exchange gain which is deferred under section 142 (as described in 4.94–4.112).

4.129   Although the relevant regulations have not, at the date of writing, been published, some guidance, which is summarised below, has been given on the subject by the Inland Revenue.

The election to use a currency other than sterling

4.130   To make an election, a company must have reasonable grounds for believing that all the relevant conditions described below will be fulfilled throughout the first accounting period for which the election will apply. A successful election will normally be effective from the start of that accounting period.

4.131 When making an election, the company must specify whether its *trading* income is to be translated into sterling at the average or the closing rate of exchange for the account period. Whichever method is selected must then be used consistently.

4.132 An election will normally remain in force until the company revokes it; for example, where sterling has actually become the local currency, or where the company elects to adopt a different local currency. Where election is withdrawn or the local currency changes, sterling (or the new local currency) will be adopted from the beginning of the next succeeding accounting period.

Conditions

4.133 These depend largely on where, and the extent to which, the trade is carried on. In summary, they are as follows.

(i) For a trade carried on either wholly outside the United Kingdom or partially through an overseas branch:
   – the desired functional currency must be that of the primary economic environment in which the overseas trade or branch is operated and in which net cash flows are generated; and
   – the whole, or substantially the whole, of the expenses and receipts of the trade or branch must be generated in that currency; and
   – accounts must be either prepared in that currency or the company must incorporate the overseas trade or branch results into its accounts using the 'closing rate/net investment' method referred to in SSAP 20, or must elect (in a case where the temporal method is used to incorporate the results of the overseas trade or branch) to continue the existing tax treatment applied in the two years immediately preceding the date on which the legislation comes into force.
(ii) For a trade carried on wholly or partially within the United Kingdom, the same rules apply, save that:
   (a) in the case of a United Kingdom resident company:
      – accounts must be prepared in that currency in accordance with accepted United Kingdom accounting practice; and
      – the whole, or substantially the whole, of the company's aggregate share and loan capital must be denominated in that currency;
   (b) in the case of a United Kingdom branch of a non-resident company:
      – the branch accounting records must be maintained, and the branch accounts prepared, in that currency; and
      – the whole, or substantially the whole, of the aggregate liabilities of the branch, including amounts owed to the head office of the company, must be denominated in that currency.

The consequences of making an election

4.134 The basic profits and losses of a company (ie before taking account of capital allowances and deferred unrealised exchange gains) are to be treated, for corporation tax purposes, as their sterling equivalent, calculated in accordance with rules prescribed under section 93(6) setting out the appropriate rate of exchange, failing which the London closing rate for the last day of the relevant accounting period will be used. Any amounts which have been excluded in calculating the basic profits or losses (eg any capital allowances and any deferred unrealised gains) will be taken into account in calculating the profits and losses of the company for the relevant accounting period.

4.135   Similar rules apply to a company which either carries on part of a trade in the United Kingdom, and carries on a different part of the trade through an overseas branch (or different parts through different overseas branches) or carries on different parts of a trade through different overseas branches (section 94).

Anti-avoidance

4.136   The Inland Revenue has always prefaced its willingness to reform the tax treatment of exchange gains and losses by the caveat that adequate measures would need to be taken to avoid taxpayer manipulation of currency differentials and to avoid borrowings or assets being incurred or acquired with a view to taxpayers exploiting currency and interest rate discrepancies.

4.137   The Inland Revenue has, therefore, introduced a number of provisions dealing with specific or general avoidance and related issues. These are as follows:

(i)   section 135: main benefit test;
(ii)   sections 136–138: arm's length test;
(iii)   section 166: anti-avoidance: change of accounting period; and
(iv)   section 60: certain interest not allowed as a deduction.

Each of these is dealt with in turn below.

Main benefit test

4.138   Section 135 provides that, where an exchange loss (whether trading or non-trading) would accrue to a company in respect of a qualifying asset or qualifying liability, the nominal currency of which is chosen so that the main benefit or one of the main benefits that might be expected to arise out of the holding of the asset or the owing of the liability would be an exchange loss, that loss will be disregarded for tax purposes. This is aimed at ensuring that allowable losses cannot be created artificially by a company by choosing to borrow or lend in currencies chosen merely because it is anticipated that exchange rate fluctuations will be such as to give rise to an exchange loss.

4.139   The provision will apply only where the Board of the Inland Revenue so directs; if there is such a direction, the test to be applied is whether an exchange loss might be expected to be the 'main benefit or one of the main benefits' to the company holding or owing the asset or liability in question.

4.140   In the debate of the House of Commons Standing Committee on 19 May 1993, the Government asserted that the reasons behind the test set out in the section were as follows:

'This clause applies only when obtaining relief for an exchange loss is the main benefit of borrowing or lending in a particular transaction. If the loan is for commercial purposes and the accrual of an exchange loss is merely incidental, the clause will not apply . . . A sole or main benefit test might fail to counter an avoidance scheme because an ostensibly commercial purpose is attached to the transaction . . . the clause will be used only to counter objectionable schemes.'

4.141   While it is not yet known how the Inland Revenue will operate this test in practice, there must be at least a concern that this broadly-expressed test could catch transactions where no avoidance was intended. In the view of the authors, the fact that the test is not specifically restricted to require consideration of the circumstances at the time the transaction was entered into, so that the Inland Revenue could seek to apply the test with the benefit of hindsight, only serves to aggravate this concern.

Arm's length test

4.142   Sections 136–138 set out rules designed to ensure that exchange losses arising out of transactions which have been entered into otherwise than on arm's length terms will, where the Board of the Inland Revenue so directs, be 'ring-fenced', and so available for relief only against future gains arising on the same transaction rather than against other profits and gains. In each case, trading exchange losses can only be set against trading exchange gains, and non-trading exchange losses against non-trading exchange gains. Separate provisions apply to assets and liabilities, currency contracts and non-sterling trades.

ASSETS AND LIABILITIES

4.143   The provisions relating to assets and liabilities are set out in section 133, in which three basic situations are covered. In each case, the provisions will apply only where the Board of the Inland Revenue so directs.

4.144   The first, referred to in section 136(1), is where, as a result of a transaction, a qualifying company becomes a creditor or a debtor under a qualifying debt and, if they had been dealing at arm's length, the parties to the transaction would not have entered into the transaction at all, or would have done so only on different terms. In this case, section 136(2) deems no exchange loss whatsoever to accrue to the company for the relevant accrual period.

4.145   However, relief may not be denied altogether. If the relevant asset or liability continues to be held or owed by the company beyond the relevant accrual period, the exchange loss may be set against subsequent exchange gains arising, but only in respect of that asset or liability. The company must continue to hold the asset or be subject to the liability if relief is to remain available.

4.146   The second situation, envisaged in section 136(4), applies where, although the terms of the transaction would have been the same if the parties had been dealing at arm's length, the debt would have been smaller. Here, the allowable exchange loss will be reduced to the amount commensurate with the lower amount of debt. Carry-forward relief will still be available in respect of the amount by which the loss is reduced in similar circumstances to those described above.

4.147   The third case covered is where the company, being a loan creditor under a qualifying debt, would have charged interest at a higher rate than that actually paid on the debt. In other words, the company is receiving interest at less than a commercial rate. The restriction on loss relief in section 136(2) will not apply to the extent that the profits or losses of the company are adjusted on the entire loan through an imputation of interest at a commercial rate under the transfer-pricing rules in TA 1988 s 770. However, where interest is imputed in respect of part only of a loan, the restriction on loss relief will apply to the part not affected by section 770 (eg if the debtor and creditor are both UK-resident trading companies so that the transfer-pricing rules are specifically disapplied). Again, unrelieved losses may be carried forward in similar circumstances to those described above.

4.148   These provisions may be disapplied, however, where there is an intra-group transaction and where there is no overall benefit to the United Kingdom tax group (as that group is determined by application of the tests set out in TCGA 1992 s 170), because the benefits accruing to one company are matched by the obligations of the other. As a result, most intra-group loans are expected by the Inland Revenue to be excluded from the ring-fencing provisions.

4.149   Finally, it is worth noting that the relieving provisions in sub-sections (4)–(12) are disapplied in respect of variable debts. However, specific relieving provisions may be introduced by regulations (sub-section (14))

CURRENCY CONTRACTS

4.150   Where a currency contract is entered into by a company on terms such that (taking into account, inter alia, the factors mentioned in section 137(4)) the parties would not have entered into the contract at all, or would have done so on different terms, if they had been dealing at arm's length, any exchange loss which accrues will be disregarded for tax purposes in the accrual period in which it arises (section 134). However, as in respect of qualifying assets and liabilities, if the contract continues to be held by the company beyond the relevant accrual period, the loss may be carried forward to be set against future exchange gains relating to the relevant contract, the relief being available in the same way and subject to the similar conditions as mentioned above in relation to qualifying assets and liabilities.

NON-STERLING TRADES

4.151   Where a subsequent exchange gain of a trade (which has been calculated on the basis of one functional currency) is sought to be reduced by exchange losses carried forward (pursuant to section 136 or 137), but the gain and loss are each expressed in different currencies – for example, where there is a change in the local currency of the trade – section 135 provides that the loss must be expressed in the currency in which the gain is expressed in order to ascertain the available relief. The required currency conversion is to be made by reference to the London closing exchange rate for the two currencies for the first day of the company's accounting period constituting the relevant accrual period or in which that period falls.

Change of accounting period

4.152 If a company changes its accounting reference date in order to manipulate exchange gains or losses and the change is effected solely or partly for tax purposes, section 166 provides that the change of that date may be ignored by the Inland Revenue in determining the exchange gains and losses accruing to the company. Any adjustment will be made by the inspector to the company's corporation tax liability on a just and reasonable basis. The adjustment will have to take account of the position which would have obtained in the absence of a change of accounting reference date.

4.153 Subject to the restrictions in the Companies Acts, companies generally have a certain degree of flexibility over the length of their accounting periods. In the absence of this provision, it may have been possible for a company to take advantage of favourable rates of exchange by closing an accounting period and thereby triggering a 'translation time' which could affect the amount of tax it would have had to pay.

Interest on certain dual currency borrowings not allowed as a deduction

4.154 Section 60 applies to what are colloquially known as dual currency debts; namely, debts whose nominal currency of issue is different from the currency in which or by reference to which final repayment is to be made (the latter currency being known as the 'settlement currency').

4.155 Where the interest payable in respect of such a debt exceeds a commercial return – measured by reference to the settlement currency – the amount of excess interest paid by the company will be disallowed as a deduction from its total profits in computing its corporation tax for the accounting period in which the excess interest was paid.

4.156 This provision is aimed at the situation where a loan is advanced in one – usually weak – currency and is to be repaid in another – usually stronger – currency. Although the interest rate may be reasonable when reference is made to the nominal (weak) currency of the advance, it may be excessive by reference to the (strong) settlement currency underlying the loan. Viewed from a purely economic perspective, the high coupon deductions might often be sufficient – particularly if exchanged back into sterling-equivalent payments through a cross currency and interest rate swap – to give the borrower an effective deduction for the underlying capital, in addition to the running funding cost. The disallowance for the excessive interest is expected to eliminate this possible advantage.

Miscellaneous provisions

4.157   Of particular importance are the provisions considered below.

Irrecoverable debts

4.158   Sections 144 and 145 are intended to ensure that, where all or part of a qualifying debt will not be met, or if such a debt which is treated as irrecoverable subsequently becomes recoverable, the amount of any exchange gain or loss in respect of the irrecoverable amount, or the amount subsequently treated as recoverable (as appropriate), will be taken into account for the purposes of the accruals calculations under section 127 and so will be taxed or relieved accordingly. This situation would arise, for example, where a foreign currency loan made by a company became irrecoverable because exchange control or other laws in the borrower's jurisdiction made repayment of the loan illegal.

4.159   Relief in respect of all or part of an irrecoverable debt (whether owed to or by a qualifying company) is given in one of two ways: if the whole of the debt is irrecoverable, the company will be treated as if it had ceased to hold or owe the debt immediately before the end of the accounting period in which it became irrecoverable; if part of the debt is irrecoverable, relief is given by deeming the nominal amount of the outstanding debt to be reduced by the irrecoverable amount immediately after the beginning of the immediately succeeding accounting period. Relief will be available only where the creditor company's inspector is satisfied that all or part of the debt outstanding at the end of that accounting period could reasonably have been regarded as irrecoverable; it is not necessarily sufficient for the company to regard the debt as being irrecoverable. It should be noted that the test to be applied is a subjective one.

4.160   Section 145 will be applied if a company's inspector is subsequently satisfied that all or part of the outstanding debt, which was previously treated as irrecoverable, can reasonably be regarded as recoverable.

4.161   The amount that becomes recoverable is to be treated, from immediately after the time when the inspector is satisfied that a debt has become wholly or partly recoverable, as a new debt, or as an increase in the nominal amount of an existing debt (as appropriate). Thus, exchange gains and losses will be taken into account once again from the date on which the debt becomes recoverable.

Currency contracts: special cases

EARLY TERMINATION

4.162   Section 146 applies when there is an early termination of a currency contract but there is no acquisition by (or disposal to) the company of currency under the terms of the contract. Any net exchange gain or loss under the contract must nevertheless be ascertained. This is done by comparing the aggregate of the amounts which the company is treated as having received and the aggregate loss which it is treated as having incurred; if the amounts received exceed the amounts incurred, the company is treated as having a net contractual gain equal to the excess; if the opposite is found, the company is treated as having a net contractual loss.

4.163 If the company has a net contractual gain of a trade, it will be treated as incurring (in the period in which termination occurs) a loss of an amount equal to that gain. If it has a net contractual loss of a trade, it will be treated as receiving in that period, in respect of its trade, an amount equal to that loss. In other words, a balancing adjustment will be made to give or recover relief; the effect of the early termination will be that any gain or loss which has already been deemed to accrue will be reversed out.

4.164 Equivalent provisions apply in respect of net contractual non-trading gains and losses where an adjustment is to be made to amount A or amount B (as appropriate) for the purposes of the rules in section 129 (as described at 4.79–4.92).

4.165 Where a net contractual gain or loss is incurred in respect of a trade, but either that trade had ceased before the termination of the currency contract or the company carries on 'exempt activities' (which includes companies carrying on long-term and mutual insurance business and approved housing associations), immediately before the termination date, the net contractual gain or loss is treated as if it were a net contractual non-trading gain or loss of equal amount and so eligible for the relief under section 129.

4.166 Finally, it is worth noting that the Inland Revenue have indicated that it intends that any termination receipts or payments will be assessed under the proposed financial instruments legislation.

RECIPROCAL CURRENCY CONTRACTS

4.167 Where a currency contract is entered into, but is then 'closed out' by a company by entering into a second currency contract on reciprocal terms, no exchange gains or losses on either contract are recognised from the date on which the contract is closed out (section 147). At the time it is closed out, the first contract is treated as if it had terminated without the company making or receiving payment of any currency, and thus falls within the provisions of section 146, as described at 4.162–4.166. On the other hand, the second contract is ignored altogether.

4.168 This rules mirrors the commercial result of such a transaction. A currency contract will normally only be closed out to ensure commercial neutrality for the company, so that the company is left in the same situation as it would have been in if the first contract had been terminated.

Excess gains or losses

4.169 Regulations may be introduced under section 148 to provide relief in certain circumstances from tax on excess gains and losses. The regulations are intended to ensure that if a company makes a non-exchange loss on an asset or liability which is not otherwise relieved (for example, if a non-trading loan is written off by the company), relief will be available for an amount equal to the net exchange gain previously charged to tax in respect of that asset or liability. Equally, where a non-exchange gain would not otherwise be taxed, it will be brought into the charge to tax under the regulations. A balancing adjustment would, therefore, be made.

4.170   As the regulations have not been published at the date of writing, it is difficult to provide further guidance on the way in which the rules are intended to operate.

Insurance companies

4.171   Special rules are required in respect of insurance companies because of the special tax framework in which they operate and because of the long-term nature of much insurance business.

4.172   Regulations are, therefore, to be introduced under section 168 for varying the general corporation tax treatment of exchange differences arising in respect of assets and liabilities held or owed by insurance companies.

4.173   While the regulations have not been published at the date of writing, the Inland Revenue have indicated that the special rules will apply to deal with exchange differences on an insurance company's general insurance business provisions for liabilities in respect of unsettled claims, claims incurred but not reported (technical reserves) and investments held to support those reserves. These rules will only apply to a proprietary insurance company, not a mutual life company.

4.174   Deriving some guidance from Inland Revenue statements and from the Consultative Document, it would appear that these regulations will embody the following principles:

(i)   Technical reserves which are taken into account for corporation tax purposes will constitute qualifying liabilities (but see (v) below).

(ii)   Monetary investments (held to back liabilities under policies and technical reserves for possible future liabilities) will be qualifying assets (but see (v) below).

(iii) A proportion of foreign currency non-monetary investments (other than real property) will be treated as qualifying assets to the extent that the book value of total foreign currency monetary investments is less than that of total foreign currency technical reserves, at the accounts date. This should prevent distortion (for example exaggerated tax losses) where qualifying liabilities are backed with assets which would otherwise be outside the scope of the legislation.

(iv)   A proportion of unrealised exchange differences on non-monetary investments will also be taxed (this proportion is the amount by which total currency technical reserves exceeds total currency monetary investments expressed as a fraction of currency non-monetary investments (excluding real property). This proportion is stated to be designed only to avoid the necessity of complex asset and liability identification rules and so exchange differences recognised under these special rules prior to the actual disposal of a non-monetary asset will be reversed out (on a just and reasonable basis) on that actual disposal.

(v) Where investments are not accounted for on a translation basis (which is unusual), unrealised exchange gains and losses on currency technical reserves will not be recognised until the liability (for which the technical reserve was made) is due to be paid. Corresponding currency monetary investments (held to cover those technical reserves) will not be qualifying assets.

4.175 In addition to these principles, provision is to be made in Schedule 17 to exclude entirely from the new regime assets, liabilities and foreign currency contracts (which would otherwise qualify) which are held or owed for the purposes of long-term insurance business or mutual insurance business. These assets and liabilities will therefore be dealt with (if at all) under general tax principles as modified by the current special regime applicable to insurance companies. This continuity of treatment is subject to any new regulations made under paragraph 2 of Schedule 15.

Commencement of and transition to the new system

Commencement

4.176 The rules (set out in section 165) are, in addition, to be the subject of regulations, details of which are not available at the date of writing. Section 165 provides that the new rules relating to exchange gains and losses are to apply to all qualifying assets, qualifying liabilities and rights and duties under currency contracts to which a company becomes entitled or subject after it has become subject to the new regime. They also extend to such assets, liabilities and currency contracts held or owed on the day on which a company becomes subject to the new rules. This day is known as the company's 'commencement day'.

4.177 A company holding or owning assets and liabilities or which is a party to a currency contract on its commencement day will be treated as becoming entitled or subject to the asset or liability on that day. This rule may, however, be disapplied in respect of assets and liabilities of a prescribed description by transitional provisions to be contained in regulations, but these regulations may themselves permit a company to elect to disapply those regulations and so come back under the general provisions.

Transition

4.178 The rules relating to transitional arrangements are also to be contained in regulations. Schedule 16 provides for regulations to be made in respect of assets, liabilities and contracts which are held at the time that a company becomes subject to the new regime.

4.179 The Inland Revenue have already outlined the anticipated scope and operation of these transitional rules in the Consultative Document. Its proposals can be summarised as follows:

(i) Trading assets and liabilities on which exchange differences are currently recognised under SSAP 20:
- no change in treatment.

(ii) Trading assets and liabilities on which exchange differences are currently taxed under Case I:
- the relevant currency item will be deemed to be disposed of and reacquired at closing balance sheet values, giving rise to a normal Case I gain or loss which may be held over and set against future translation exchange gains or losses on the same asset or liability.

(iii) Assets currently subject to corporation tax on chargeable gains (eg debts on a security or foreign currency bank accounts):
- will generally be deemed to be disposed of and reacquired at market value on the commencement date.

(iv) Assets and liabilities on which exchange differences are not recognised under the current tax rules (eg debts (other than debts on a security) and borrowings):
- debts and borrowings of fixed amount and term will be brought into the new regime immediately, but will be subject to a 'kink test', which will prevent the exchange differences taken into account under the new scheme from exceeding the exchange differences which have actually accrued over the life of the asset or liability; and
- other 'fluctuating' debts and borrowings are expected to be excluded from the scheme for a period of six years, although companies may elect that these items should be brought into the scheme on the commencement date.

(v) Assets subject to corporation tax on chargeable gains disposed of prior to commencement date:
- a company will be able to elect, prior to commencement, for realised and allowable losses on monetary assets to be set against future exchange gains on the same class of assets (ie monetary assets formerly subject to corporation tax on chargeable gains).

4 PLANNING

4.180 As has been stressed throughout this report, full details of the new regime relating to the taxation of exchange gains and losses are not yet available, because details of the extensive regulations to be made in respect of certain aspects of it have not been published by the Inland Revenue. This means that, despite the guidance provided by the Inland Revenue in the Consultative Document, there is still a good deal of uncertainty relating to a number of areas.

4.181 It is, therefore, not possible to set out extensive guidance in respect of the way in which it may be possible to plan for the introduction of the new rules. Nevertheless, the following points may provide some food for thought.

(i) Set out below are two lists showing, in the first column, details of the main derivative instruments to which the new regime will apply, and, in the second, details of those which will fall outside its scope. These lists assume that sterling is the relevant local currency.

Instruments to which the new provisions will apply	*Instruments falling outside the new provisions*
foreign currency loans (whether or not marketable debt securities)	sterling loans
all non-sterling cash	sterling cash
currency swaps (final exchange only)	interest rate and cross-currency interest rate swaps
currency futures	interest rate futures
currency forward rate agreements	stock index futures
	option dated forwards
	commodity forward rate agreements
	interest forward rate agreements
	currency and other financial options
	synthetic currency positions (whether long or short puts or calls)
	currency warrants
	repurchase agreements (repos)

(ii)   Current hedging and other financial engineering arrangements which will still be in place at the end of 1993, and so may fall within the new regime, or within the transitional arrangements, should be considered carefully to decide (in so far as it is possible to do so) whether they will remain viable or will be adversely affected by the new rules. For many companies, there may be no advantage to be gained in settling liabilities or disposing of assets, because of the transitional reliefs (and also the anti-avoidance provisions) forming part of the new regime. However, some transactions, such as those which currently benefit from being 'tax nothings' (such as, for example, soft currency borrowings or currency bonds trading at a discount, in each case, on capital account) may cease to be attractive, and so it may be worth bringing these transactions to an end if the cost of doing so is not unacceptable. A further example of funding arrangements which should be reviewed with care are foreign currency bonds. An indexation allowance is available in respect of these bonds at present, but they will, if they are qualifying assets, be treated as qualifying corporate bonds under the new provisions, so that the indexation allowance no longer applies. It may be preferable, therefore, to consider alternative investments.

(iii) The effect of the new rules on offshore financing subsidiaries should be looked at carefully. For example, if financing subsidiaries have large exchange exposures which are currently treated as being on capital account, the treatment of those exposures for United Kingdom tax purposes will become very different under the new rules.

(iv) Only qualifying companies will fall within the new regime, although the Government has indicated that consideration is being given to whether similar provisions should extend to partnerships.

(v) Many groups, particularly large multinationals, manage their currency exposure on a group basis – either within the United Kingdom or on a worldwide basis. Hedging transactions should be reviewed and, if necessary, relocated within the group, so that an election to match can be made if appropriate. The Inland Revenue's proposals envisage that matching will only be possible on a company-by-company basis, and, therefore, it may be necessary for many treasury departments to give considerable thought as to arrangements that need to be put in place to ensure that matching elections are accepted by the Inland Revenue.

(vi) Similarly, the transactions in respect of which a claim for the deferral of tax will be available should be identified.

(vii) It is vital to realise that the new rules will require detailed records of all transactions, and of hedging and other similar arrangements to be kept. The Government stressed during the House of Commons Standing Committee debates that it did not believe that any additional administrative burden would be placed on companies by the new rules, as the relevant information was already required for, in particular, its accounting records. However, although this may be true in respect of a substantial amount of the information that will be required, the record-keeping and information-gathering requirements of the new rules will almost certainly require additional administration, to ensure that sufficient detail is available at all times. For example, precise details of the purposes for which an asset is intended to be (or was) held must be available where an apportionment or an election to match may be appropriate.

(viii) Where a company wishes to make elections (eg to match, or to compute and express its trading profits or losses in a currency other than sterling), it will be required to do so within the time limits to be set out in the relevant regulations. The time limits which have been proposed by the Inland Revenue have been criticised by many commentators, firstly, as being rather short, and, secondly, because they do not correlate with accounting periods. For example, if a company wishes matching to take effect in respect of assets which it holds at the date on which the legislation comes into force, it has been suggested that the election must be made within six months of that date (or, if later, three months after the start of the first accounting period beginning on or after the day on which the legislation comes into force). Where a company wishes an asset to be matched from the date of its acquisition, it is proposed that the election must be made within three months of acquisition. It is proposed that there will be a similar 'three month' rule in respect of an election to compute trading profits in a currency other than sterling. In that case, it is proposed that if a company makes an election within three months of the beginning of the first accounting period for which the new rules apply, the election may take effect from the start of that accounting period, and that if a company makes an election within three months of the date of coming within the charge to corporation tax, the election may take effect from that date. Companies will need to take great care to ensure that all relevant elections are identified and made within the requisite period.

(ix) Where transactions are currently on revenue account, the tax treatment of exchange gains and losses will remain largely unchanged. For example, for banks and other financial institutions, most medium- and long-term debt transactions are currently treated as being revenue transactions; in many cases, those transactions will have been 'marked to market'. However, when the new rules come into effect, it is those new rules which must be followed, and not any existing arrangements which are in place. Existing methods of calculating exchange gains and losses must, therefore, be reviewed, to ensure that the new rules will be satisfied when they come into force.

(x) Even when the regulations become available, there will still be uncertainty surrounding the operation of the new regime for some time to come. The new rules are complicated, and every aspect of how they are to take effect in practice will probably not be immediately apparent. It is uncertain how flexible the Inland Revenue will be, particularly at the time at which the new regime comes into effect, (for example, when applying the subjective tests set out in sections 144 and 145). Not least because there is no advance rulings procedure, under which the tax treatment of individual potential transactions could have been ascertained (such as that available under TA 1988 707 in respect of transactions in securities), it appears that this uncertainty will remain for some time to come.

CHAPTER 5

Benefits in kind

1 PREFACE

5.1 In this chapter we examine the effect of the Finance Act 1993 provisions on employee benefits: company cars and vans, outplacement counselling and the provision of sporting and recreational facilities. The new provisions regarding relocation expenses are reviewed separately in Chapter 6.

2 COMPANY CARS

Introduction

5.2 Company cars are one of the most standard benefits included in any remuneration package designed to attract and retain high quality staff. Now that the Finance Act 1993 has been published, we take stock of the present position.

5.3 Although this note is intended to take an overall look at car provision, we also take the opportunity to explain and analyse the new rules and, in particular, to provide guidance on the surprise in the Finance Act 1993 (about employee contributions to capital cost) and on the difficult case of the treatment of accessories.

5.4 Company cars used to provide a very tax-efficient way of remunerating employees. Since 6 April 1988, the advantages have been gradually reducing as successive Chancellors have let it be known that they want the tax payable to reflect the true benefit received. The wide-ranging changes, starting on 6 April 1994, announced in the recent budget, have gone a long way to removing tax-driven distortions, thus giving employers an opportunity to review their car schemes and ensure that they are meeting their requirements.

The impetus for change

5.5 Many employers feel and have felt for some time that they should be doing something about their car schemes. In our view, the change in the tax regime does not itself justify a change.

5.6   The impetus for change is more likely to be that of containing the costs of running car fleets, helped now more than ever by the likelihood that some employees will be more prepared to give up their cars entirely or trade down the model ranges.

5.7   A few companies have taken the major step of closing down their schemes altogether – but buying out employees from existing schemes can involve incurring additional costs, or having to provide additional benefits, and not savings. The advantage therefore to those companies is in the release of management time and the potential to control costs in the longer term.

5.8   Whether a complete buy-out of a scheme is appropriate will depend much on the characteristics and culture of the organisation – how critical the car is for getting business, and how critical a car is in the perception of the individual employees.

5.9   Some companies are concerned that if an employee who uses his car extensively for his work is required to provide his own transport he will tend to buy a cheaper and older thus less reliable car for himself. A less obvious but often greater concern on the part of the employee is the financial responsibility, and risk, associated with car ownership. For such companies fleet management facilities may be a feasible alternative. As far as employees are concerned these are relatively new services which may take away some of the concerns of employees moving from a wholly managed scheme.

Categories of company cars

5.10   Company cars generally fit into the following categories:

(a)   the need or essential user car – this would cover cars supplied for operational or business reasons; and

(b)   the status or perk car – such cars are normally provided as a reward to the employee.

Most cars fit to some extent into both categories: the essential user car represents a significant benefit for the employee and many status cars are driven extensively on business.

5.11   For perk cars, employers and employees have more flexibility. The primary concern of both parties is normally to maintain the value of an employee's package, though the employer may also be seeking to reduce costs or at least control them and the employee may be seeking a reduction in the tax burden.

5.12   For cars supplied for operational reasons, costs take on different perspectives as they must be seen in the context of the car being a tool of the trade which the employee needs to perform his duties effectively. However, this does not mean such an employee must have a company car, it just means that he must have a car, whether supplied by the employer or owned personally. The fact that it is essential to have access to a car should not preclude the employer from finding the most cost-efficient way of providing this access.

Controlling car scheme costs

5.13   Where an employer decides to do away with its car scheme altogether transition costs can be extremely high. They will typically include administration costs, legal fees, penalties for early termination of lease agreements, the costs of amending staff handbooks and contracts of employment, and the costs of deciding on and introducing alternative forms of remuneration. Furthermore, such a decision could have an undesirable impact on morale and motivation and result in a deterioration in employee relations.

5.14   For these reasons such a course of action is unlikely to be attractive to most employers. Many will prefer to offer a company car and cash alternative and allow the employee to choose whichever suits him better. We address the issue of the cash versus company car option in greater depth at 5.17ff.

5.15   There is much merit in looking first at ways of reducing the cost of the car fleet to the company. Many companies anyway have been gradually increasing the life of the company car before it is due for renewal, from the previous norm of three years to four. With increasing reliability in most standard cars this can be further reviewed.

5.16   Savings can be found in the range of cars made available – and in the subsequent financing of them. Depending on the usage of the different employees within the scheme it is often appropriate to have a mixed financing package for larger fleets – spread between leasing, hire purchase and outright purchase. The decisions will vary from one organisation to another and be driven by the funds available, the culture of the company as well as what the car is used for. Taxation allowances and disallowances play a large part in this decision-making.

The cash versus company car option

5.17   As mentioned above the company car has become one of the most standard benefits in kind. Despite this practice, in recent years many employers have modified their schemes to enable their employees to choose a cash option instead of a company car. The take-up of such schemes tends to be low: few employers who have offered a cash alternative have seen a higher take-up of the cash alternative of more than 20% of the employees eligible and most have seen much lower figures. However, offering the cash alternative can be attractive for both the employer and the employee.

5.18   From the employer's viewpoint, offering a cash alternative demonstrates care for employees by allowing them to determine the shape of the package. The cash alternative may also be cheaper for the employer: it can be varied more frequently and by reference to what the employer can afford, not by movements in car prices. Setting a cash alternative therefore brings greater control over employee costs.

5.19   However, the employer must consider operational issues as well as financial issues. Where the employee requires the use of a car for business purposes, having a company car may be the most effective method of providing him with one. The employer can then control the model of the car and hence its quality and reliability. He can also make pool car facilities available should the company car break down. In cases where the employee needs a specially adapted car for his work, eg to transport goods, then by operating a company car scheme the employer can ensure that he is provided with a suitable car. If a cash alternative is offered, the employee may be unable or unwilling to purchase a specially adapted car and hence his ability to do his job may suffer.

5.20 The image of the employer should also be considered. By operating a company car scheme, an employer has considerable control over appearance and can therefore influence the image of the company. If a cash alternative is offered to employees who then provide their own cars, many will select or will only be able to afford a less expensive model. Employers who wish to maintain the company image will have to bear this in mind when deciding whether to offer the cash alternative and when setting the cash amount, and may even consider refusing to pay the full cash alternative to individuals who do not have a car of appropriate quality, reliability and appearance.

5.21 From the employee's viewpoint, the cash alternative may be attractive because it gives greater freedom of choice and may enable the employee to choose a car which really suits him or which he particularly wants. This option may also be cheaper particularly where the employee has an expensive company car and low business mileage.

5.22 The effect on employee morale should also be taken into account where an employer is considering modifying his car scheme. For many years now, the company car has been regarded as the norm for managerial grades and for many employees who need to be mobile in doing their jobs. Yet, as mentioned above, in recent years more and more employers have decided to offer their employees a cash alternative to the company car and some have even taken the step of withdrawing their car schemes altogether, at least for some grades of employee. These decisions may be influenced by financial considerations as the cost of running a car scheme continues to escalate, but they also have far-reaching implications with regard to employee aspirations and motivation.

5.23 Company cars traditionally have been seen by employees as a desirable emblem of status and image, and they have been used as a motivational tool by employers. If an employer withdraws company cars completely for its employees, demotivation is bound to occur and will probably be followed by difficulties in retaining staff. For this reason employers have often decided to bring in car scheme changes gradually, perhaps letting existing employees retain their company cars but not offering them to new recruits. However, this approach in itself can lead to problems – new recruits may feel that they are being unfairly discriminated against.

5.24 Many employees regard the company car as an essential part of their remuneration package and employers who do not offer this may experience difficulties in recruiting high quality staff. On the other hand, the introduction of a cash or company car alternative is welcomed by many employees who see it as giving them more flexibility over their remuneration packages. Therefore, many employers now feel obliged to offer the cash alternative in order to remain competitive in the recruitment market.

5.25   These matters represent a hidden cost of car scheme decisions and the effect on the business may be considerable but difficult, if not impossible, to quantify. Furthermore, the effects of the car scheme changes will not be seen overnight – the timescale may be several years for the full effects to feed through.

Setting the cash alternative

5.26   The approach taken in assessing the opportunities for substituting cash for company cars will differ between employers but, in the main, will be aimed at ensuring that employees do not suffer financially from such arrangements and that the employer does not incur any greater costs than those associated with the provision of a car. Other issues such as employee morale and recruitment are of equal importance.

5.27   The process of identifying a cash substitute usually involves a full analysis of the current costs of the cars already provided. This should include costs such as the output VAT charge on fuel for private motoring and the opportunity costs of the funding method for the fleet, together with corporation tax and employer's National Insurance Contributions (NIC) where appropriate. These costs can then be compared with those that an employee would incur in providing himself with a similar car, taking account of differences in matters such as purchase discount levels, interest rates and insurance which may be significant.

5.28   The employee's likely costs should themselves be analysed according to the alternative funding mechanisms likely to be available to the employee, such as a commercial loan or a loan from the employer (on either commercial or 'soft' terms). It is important to be thorough in this analysis, as matters such as comparative personal and corporation tax reliefs, together with VAT, can have a significant bearing on the results of the analysis.

5.29   Finally, the calculations must take account of the employee's liability to income tax and NIC. For example, the employee might enjoy a saving of tax and possibly NIC when provided with cash instead of a car (due, say, to a high scale charge for the type of car or the employee's ability to make a large claim for tax relief on business travel) or, conversely, he may suffer a higher liability.

5.30   It is then possible to compare the cost to employer and employee of continuing the car scheme in its present form with the cost of replacing it by a cash alternative. With this information, if it is decided to withdraw the car, it will be possible to calculate the extra salary which needs to be paid to compensate the employee for the lost benefit. This figure may not necessarily coincide with the cash amount finally offered but it is important to quantify it at the outset (see below).

5.31   The exact level of benefit will differ for each employee due to different circumstances, eg business and private mileage, insurance risks, methods of funding. On an on-going basis it is probably not practicable to offer employees of the same grade different amounts of cash and it is usual for employers to offer employees of the same grade the same amount.

5.32   Most organisations do not make an adjustment for administration costs on the grounds that, even though there is a higher administrative cost associated with cars than there is with cash, those costs are relatively fixed unless the fleet is substantially reduced.

5.33   The level of cash allowance offered is likely to differ depending on whether a choice is being offered between cars or cash or a car scheme is being fully replaced with cash allowances. It is generally cheaper both in financial terms and in terms of employee satisfaction to offer a choice. A full buy-out of the car scheme could be much more expensive, not just because of the penalties of terminating existing commitments but also because if a choice is offered the employer can set the cash figure at any level he likes (within reason) as the value of the remuneration package is maintained by virtue of the fact that the employee may still opt for the car. However, if employees are compulsorily required to give up their cars, the cash allowance needs to be high enough to ensure that no employee is worse off and the allowance is high enough to attract new recruits.

5.34   The employer should also consider how to deal with business mileage. If the cash alternative covers the full cost of the company car, it would be double-counting to pay a full reimbursement for business mileage: a small premium over the petrol costs would be more appropriate. This is, however, costly in terms of NIC (Class 1 NIC would be payable on the extra salary) and individuals would obtain income tax relief only by making a rather complex claim in their tax returns. The alternative of paying a lower additional cash allowance but higher mileage rates is more efficient but may make it more difficult to achieve equity between different employees.

Avoiding the tax traps

5.35   A properly constructed scheme under which employees have the right to take cash allowances in lieu of cars should not give rise to any untoward tax consequences. That is to say, those who take company cars will be taxed merely by reference to the cars which they take and those who take cash alternatives will be taxed by reference to the cash alternative which they take. In addition, those taking company cars will give rise to Class 1A NIC contributions in the hands of the company, but not Class 1 contributions, and those taking cash will give rise to Class 1 contributions only.

5.36   There are limits to how frequently the choice can be exercised by an individual. If he is in receipt of a company car, the Inland Revenue will, probably correctly, argue that he is taxable on the higher of the scale charge and the cash alternative which he could have taken if he is allowed to change his selection more often than once a year. It is normal practice with many employers for cars to be allocated to employees for longer periods, normally three or four years, and as long as that remains the rule there should be no problem.

5.37   There is no tax difficulty if an employer allows those who have opted for the cash alternative to change their minds at any given time. As a matter of administrative convenience, the employer will presumably wish to limit the number of occasions on which they can opt for a car, but there are no tax issues to take into account.

5.38   The employer should also be sure that the contractual arrangements with the employees are dealt with carefully. The danger that needs to be avoided is that, if individuals have a high salary, part of which they can apply in payment for a car, there will be VAT on the amount used to take the car, there will be income tax and Class 1 NIC on the higher salary, there will be a scale charge and Class 1A NIC on the car and, quite possibly, no relief for the amount which the individuals are applying in order to take the car.

5.39   What must be avoided, therefore, is individuals having a contractual right to a relatively high salary which they are entitled to apply in part to taking a company car. It is perfectly acceptable if they have a lower salary with the right to either a car or a cash supplement in addition. The commercial difference between the two may be small but the tax difference is substantial. The probability of Inland Revenue attack can be reduced by ensuring that the contractual documentation, whether in contracts of employment, letters announcing salary changes, staff handbooks or payslips is all in line with the contractual situation which the employer is attempting to establish, and is properly worded for tax purposes.

5.40   The employer should also consider the relationship between the cash allowance, which would be paid to people not taking a car, and salary-related benefits. The employer must decide and make it clear in the documentation whether the cash allowance is or is not eligible to be taken into account as salary for the purposes of the company's pension scheme and any other salary-related benefits such as bonuses, overtime or share schemes. It is also necessary to cross-check the rules of the related benefit plans, such as the pension scheme or share scheme, to ensure that consistency is achieved.

5.41   If it is decided that the cash allowance should be taken into account in fixing certain salary-related benefits, the level of allowance payable could be reduced accordingly. Most employers take the view that cars are ignored in calculating salary-related benefits and that the cash allowance should similarly be ignored.

5.42   The employer should consider what would happen to the cash allowance in cases of long-term sickness and of maternity leave. Presumably the allowance would remain payable if a car would be available during such periods but not otherwise.

5.43   It is also necessary for the employer to decide how often an individual's cash allowance will be revised. It could be annually. This makes sense: he or she can choose annually whether to retain the cash allowance or take a car. On the other hand, an annual revision could in the second and subsequent years mean that the salary alternative was more than the cost of the car the employee could have taken in the first year. Many of a car's costs are effectively fixed at the time of acquisition. A cheaper alternative, and a more convenient one from an administration point of view, would be to review the allowance at the same time as the car which the individual could have taken would come up for renewal. There is also the issue of how to deal with promotions (which might tie in with the employer's rules about whether individuals change car on promotion or whether they wait for the car's normal replacement date).

The current position with regard to cash v company cars

5.44   In Diagram 1 and Diagram 2 are set out some of the typical cars made available to employees and compare in very simple terms of the cost to the company of running the car with the equivalent cost that the employee would face. In most cases the company will have to pay more to buy the employee out than it is paying to run the car at present if it wishes to leave the employee in a 'benefit neutral' position. The cash equivalent is the benefit neutral line representing the gross amount that the company must pay the employee to enable him to retain his current level of benefits at no extra cost to him. The cost neutral line shows how much the company can pay to an employee as an allowance without changing its overall cost.

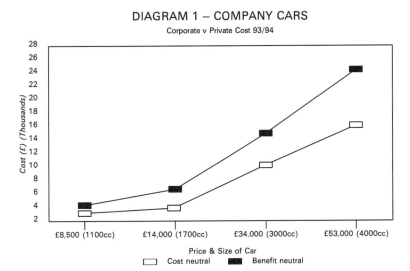

DIAGRAM 1 – COMPANY CARS

Corporate v Private Cost 93/94

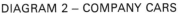

DIAGRAM 2 – COMPANY CARS

Corporate v Private Cost 94/95

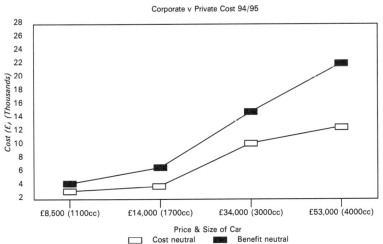

5.45   These figures are based on a series of assumptions, which will vary from company to company and user to user. The difference between the cost neutral line and the benefit neutral line is being eroded. This has occurred because, with the general increase in taxation of company cars since 1988, the tax effectiveness of a company car rather than salary is decreasing. Therefore, the costs of providing a company car and of paying extra cash to enable the employee personally to acquire a car of a similar standard are converging.

5.46   The main cause of variances in the figures is any change in business mileage. (Other important variables include depreciation, private mileage, insurance and finance costs.) Diagram 3 illustrates the effect on the figures of changing annual business mileage. It also demonstrates that the question of whether an employee should elect for cash or car is a very difficult decision which will vary from employee to employee.

DIAGRAM 3

Vauxhall Cavalier 1.6i

Cost of car	£10,265
Cylinder capacity	1,598cc
Residual value after 3 years	£4,209
Employee's marginal tax rate	40%

Petrol consumption	33.2mpg at £2.30 per gallon

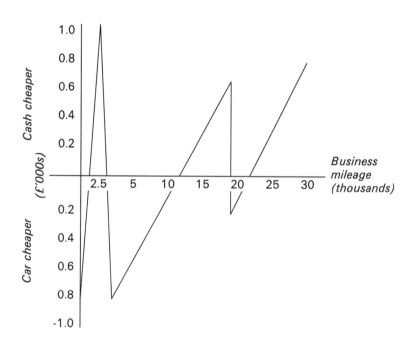

The current system of taxing company cars

5.47   The new system of taxing company cars will not come into effect until 6 April 1994. For 1993/94 the scale charges for cars increased by 8%.

The scale charges for 1993/94 are as follows (1992/93 figures in brackets):

Cylinder capacity	Original market value	Age of car at 5 April 1994	
		Under 4 Years	4 Years or More
Up to 1,400cc	Up to £19,250	£2,310 (£2,140)	£1,580 (£1,460)
1,401–2,000cc	Up to £19,250	£2,990 (£2,770)	£2,030 (£1,880)
Over 2,000cc	Up to £19,250	£4,800 (£4,440)	£3,220 (£2,980)
Any	£19,251–£29,000	£6,210 (£5,750)	£4,180 (£3,870)
Any	Over £29,000	£10,040 (£9,300)	£6,660 (£6,170)

(a)   50% (50%) increase in the charge if car is driven no more than 2,500 (2,500) business miles per annum and for second cars.
(b)   50% (50%) decrease if car is driven 18,000 (18,000) business miles or more per annum.

The employer is required to account for Class 1A National Insurance Contributions at 10.4% on the income tax scale charge.

5.48   Two changes affecting the provision of private fuel in a company car have been introduced and have taken effect from 6 April 1993:

(a)   the scale charges are to be increased by 20%;
(b)   the 50% reduction in the fuel scale charge where business mileage is at an annual rate of 18,000 or more will be abolished: the reasoning behind this being the fact that a high business mileage does not mean the benefit of private fuel is any less, therefore there is no logic in charging less tax.

5.49   For the purposes of the employee's income tax, the fixed scale charge continues to apply when any quantity of fuel is provided for private motoring in a car which is taxed as a company car (ie by reference to the scale charges), unless the employee is required to make good the whole of the cost of providing the private fuel and does so. If the employee has the use of the car throughout the year, a full year's fuel charge applies even if fuel is provided for only part of the year.

5.50   The proposed fuel scale charges for 1993/94 are as follows (1992/93 in brackets):

Cylinder capacity	Petrol		Diesel	
1400cc or less	£600	(£500)	£550	(£460)
1401–2000cc	£760	(£630)	£550	(£460)
Over 2000cc	£1,130	(£940)	£710	(£590)

The change will also affect the position of the employer in the following two ways.

The employer is required to account for output VAT on an amount based on the fuel scale charge. The rule whereby the fuel scale is reduced by 50% where business mileage during the VAT accounting period is at the rate of 18,000 or more per year is to be abolished. For prescribed VAT accounting periods beginning after 5 April 1993, the amounts of the VAT-inclusive deemed supply of fuel, and the VAT payable, are set out below. These amounts apply for each VAT prescribed accounting period irrespective of the amount of fuel provided and whether the fuel was provided throughout the period.

THREE-MONTH ACCOUNTING PERIOD

	Petrol		Diesel	
Cubic capacity	*Scale charge*	*VAT due per car*	*Scale charge*	*VAT due per car*
1400cc or less	£150	£22.34	£138	£20.55
1401–2000cc	£190	£28.30	£138	£20.55
Over 2000cc	£283	£42.15	£178	£26.51

ONE-MONTH ACCOUNTING PERIOD

	Petrol		Diesel	
1400cc or less	£50	£7.45	£46	£6.85
1401–2000cc	£63	£9.38	£46	£6.85
Over 2000cc	£94	£14.00	£59	£8.79

The employer is required to account for Class 1A National Insurance Contributions at 10.4% on broadly the income tax fuel scale charge. Again, the rule whereby the fuel scale is reduced by 50% where there are 18,000 or more business miles in a year is to be abolished for this purpose.

5.51 As a result of these proposed changes it may be worthwhile for employers to reconsider whether fuel for private motoring should continue to be provided to employees. It may be possible to offer an amount of cash compensation for not providing private fuel which would leave the company better off.

5.52 However, for many employees, provision by the employer of fuel for private motoring may still be tax efficient. For example, if a 40% taxpayer has a company car in the 1,401–2,000cc range for 1993/94 (say a 1,600cc car with consumption of 32 mpg) and is provided with petrol for private use, private mileage must be at least 4,325 miles to derive a tax benefit: the tax charge of 40% of £760 corresponds to 4,324 miles at 32 mpg. Since the national average for private mileage remains of the order of 10,000 miles pa the tax system is still biased in favour of providing private fuel.

The new rules (1994/95 onwards)

5.53 The new rules for 1994/95 onwards aim to provide a fairer system of taxation of the benefit of having a company car, that is, to arrive at a system whereby the tax paid by an individual reflects the benefit of the car provided to him rather than taxing him on an arbitrary basis.

5.54 From 6 April 1994 company cars will be taxed by reference to list price rather than cylinder capacity. The benefit is calculated as follows:

(a) take 35% of the list price of the car, subject to a deduction of up to £5,000 for the employee's capital contribution; a list price in excess of £80,000 is taken as a list price of exactly £80,000;
(b) discount the result by one-third if the employee drives more than 2,500 business miles in a year, or two-thirds if the employee drives 18,000 or more business miles;
(c) reduce that result by a further one-third if the car is more than four years old at the end of the tax year;
(d) reduce the result, as now, for periods before or after the car was made available or for periods when the car is off the road for at least 30 days;
(e) finally, deduct, as now, private use charges (which are still defined as extending only to charges which 'the employee is required, as a condition of the car being available for his private use, to pay . . . for that use').

For individuals with two company cars simultaneously, the first discount is available only for the car used for the higher business mileage.

List price

5.55 The list price on which the benefit is based is deemed to be the manufacturer's list price of the car and of extras. This is the list price of the car on the day before its first registration, regardless of how old it is when the employee first has the use of it. It is the list price of the car itself.

5.56 The term 'list price' means the price 'published by the car's manufacturer, importer or distributor (as the case may be) as the inclusive price appropriate for a car of that kind if sold in the United Kingdom singly in a retail sale in the open market'. If there is no published list price, it is necessary to work out the published list price that 'might reasonably have been expected to be its list price' if there had been one. Whether or not there is a published list price it is not permitted to deduct the cash discounts which a retail buyer may obtain nor to deduct the bulk discounts or rebates available to large fleets.

5.57 For the first time, there is tax relief for an employee's capital contribution. In establishing the list price on which the 35% is calculated, one deducts any capital sum which the employee contributed, at the time when the car was first made available to him, for the car or for accessories taken into account in fixing the list price. This deduction has a ceiling of £5,000.

5.58 The term 'list price' embraces delivery charges, car tax (if the car attracted the car tax which has now been abolished) and VAT. It presumably does not include vehicle excise duty, petrol provided with the car on delivery or, probably, the cost of number plates (whether or not these items were separately charged).

5.59 The term also extends to accessories 'attached to the car (whether or not permanently)'. The following can be ignored:

(a)   accessories which are not fixed to the car (such as travelling rugs);
(b)   accessories which were both ordered and fitted on or after the date when the car was first made available to the employee and before 1 August 1993;
(c)   accessories fitted for business purposes only (for example, tool racks);
(d)   mobile telephones (which attract their own tax charge).

5.60 Manufacturers will have to consider in some detail what list prices to publish. Some manufacturers publish list prices which allow for substantial reductions in the amount a customer will pay. In other cases there is only a small discrepancy between what the customer will pay and the list price. The rules are likely to mean that list prices, as a general rule, will fall more in line with the actual selling price (although bulk purchase discounts will probably not be included). For cars already in use which will still be in use in 1994/95, employees may suffer if the list price was high in relation to the selling price.

5.61 There will be special rules for classic cars, that is, cars at least 15 years old and worth more than £15,000 at the end of the tax year or, if earlier, the last day on which the car is available to the employee. In these circumstances, market value will be substituted for list price. Many classic cars can be bought for under £15,000 so as a perk such cars might still be worth considering.

The employer's position

5.62 Tax allowances available to employers who provide company cars are still subject to limitations where the car costs in excess of £12,000. Employers will still have to pay Class 1A National Insurance Contributions in respect of company cars and private fuel provided. The Class 1A charges will change in line with the new income tax rules. There has been no change in the disallowance of the VAT on the purchase price of the car and full recovery on running costs (for organisations not partly exempt for VAT purposes) and no VAT arising as a result of a cash alternative being offered.

Winners and losers under the new rules

5.63 The following table gives examples of employees who might benefit or lose out after 6 April 1994.

Example make of car	Existing measure of benefit – cc of car or original market value if over £19,250	List price	% Tax increase/ (decrease) in 1994/95 (compared to 1993/94 figures)
Peugeot 106 XN 1.0	Up to 1,400	6,142	(38)
Vauxhall Cavalier 1.6 4dr	1,401–2,000	10,575	(17)
Mercedes-Benz 190E Auto	1,401–2,000	16,672	30
Mercedes-Benz 300E Auto	Over £29,000	30,590	(23)
Mercedes-Benz 400 SEL	Over £29,000	53,320	34

Note: all cars under four years old

5.64 The following break-even points will enable employees to establish at a glance if they will be winners or losers in 1994/95. 1993/94 figures are compared with 1994/95 figures.

Exisiting measure of benefit – cc or original market value if over £19,250	List price Break-even point
Up to 1,400cc	£9,900
1,401–2,000cc	£12,814
Over 2,000cc	£20,571
£19,251–£29,000 (any cc)	£26,614
Over £29,000 (any cc)	£43,029

5.65 To interpret the figures an employee should establish, by looking at the first column above, the benefit category for 1993/94. If the break-even list price for the appropriate category is higher than the list price of his car, he will pay less tax in 1994/95. Conversely, if the break-even list price is lower than the list price of his car, he will pay more tax in 1994/95. When reviewing the table it is important to appreciate that the £19,250 and £29,000 figures are based not on list price but on the original market value, that is the retail price the purchaser could expect to pay immediately before the date of first registration. Unlike list price, this takes account of retail and cash discounts.

5.66   The over 2,000cc original market value £19,250 or less category throws out the most interesting results. Virtually everyone whose car is in this category will pay less tax in 1994/95.

New rules – new issues

5.67   Inevitably, a new system means new anomalies, albeit less serious anomalies than those which arise under the current system.

(a)   A major change in the new system of taxing company cars is the decision to tax by reference to the list price. This approach is at variance with the general principle that the cash equivalent of a benefit is set by reference to the cost to the employer.

(b)   Under the current system employees are used to annual increases (in recent years of more than inflation) in the amount of tax they pay (unless the car reaches its fourth anniversary in the tax year). Under the new rules the tax to be paid will be fixed for the life of the car (subject to any change in actual tax rates and again the reduction after four years). Employees may face very steep rises when cars are replaced, depending on how fast the car prices have risen.

(c)   There are no transitional measures: from 6 April 1994 all cars will be taxed under the new rules including cars acquired before the budget in March 1993. Given that contracts of employment frequently contain the condition that once an employee has accepted a particular company car he cannot opt for a different model or for a cash alternative before a period of time has elapsed (typically three years) the absence of transitional arrangements could be seen as inequitable.

(d)   Because the scale charge is now based on list price, second-hand cars could now have extremely high-scale charges in comparison to the cost to the employer.

(e)   Under the current system, the employer's reporting obligation required him to provide details of company cars on form P11D after the year end. Employers will now, from 6 April 1994, additionally be required to inform the Tax Office on a quarterly basis of new company cars provided to employees, and adjustments will be made through the Pay As You Earn codes where appropriate.

(f)   With the removal of banding, the tax that employees will pay will be linked to the price of the car provided. When a company car is off the road for any length of time many employers offer a 'pool' car. Employees may be reluctant to accept a temporary replacement car attracting a higher tax charge. This could cause additional administration problems when running a car scheme.

Compliance costs

5.68   The new regime for taxing company cars is bound to increase the compliance burden and therefore the cost for employers. The initial exercise of providing the Inland Revenue with all the appropriate details may well be very time-consuming. Information which was previously not required and therefore not recorded will now have to be provided to the Inland Revenue: for example, in some cases list prices of cars may not be readily available and these will have to be established or a suitable compromise negotiated with the Inland Revenue.

Action

5.69 Employers should consider now what action they should take. They should undertake a review of their current car scheme and analyse carefully the cost and financing. They should establish what both the employer and the employee want and need and consider whether a cash alternative should be offered. In particular they should think carefully before any new cars are acquired during 1993/94. If they decide to assess the alternatives available to the car scheme they may also want to find out what the costs would be for fleet management services for employees to contract directly with the providers.

3 COMPANY VANS

Introduction

5.70 Changes in the method of taxing company vans which are made available by employers for the private use of their employees have also been introduced. The changes are set out in FA 1993 s 73 and Sch 4 and took effect from 6 April 1993.

5.71 The issue of company vans has been the subject of much media interest in recent years and these changes have been made in response to intense lobbying by employers and representative bodies who have been pressing for the previous cumbersome system to be replaced by a simpler one which would reduce the administrative burden on both employers and employees and clarify the tax treatment.

5.72 The new rules apply to all vans, ie vehicles built primarily to carry goods or other loads and with a gross vehicle weight of 3,500 kilograms or less. Any benefits from heavier vans will be exempt from tax unless the van is used wholly or mainly for the employee's private purposes. The new rules do not apply to the private use by employees of vehicles built primarily to carry people, eg minibuses.

The old system

5.73 Prior to 6 April 1993 the benefit arising from the private use of company vans, unlike company cars, was not the subject of a special income tax regime. Instead, vans were assessed under the general charging provisions where the employee is regarded as having the use of an asset by reason of his employment and is assessable on the cash equivalent of that asset less any contribution he makes towards it.

5.74   For company vans available for private use by an employee, the cash equivalent was deemed to be the sum of 20% of the market value (or 10% if the van was bought before 6 April 1980) of actual cost, and the additional running expenses incurred by the employer which related directly to the employee's private use. These were usually calculated by apportioning expenses in the ratio of private mileage to total mileage.

Private use

5.75   The main difficulty lay in establishing what constituted private use. The legislation and case law did not give clear guidance and there was no consistency in the Inland Revenue's interpretation. Rough and ready bases were used which frequently did not bear relation to the actual benefit received. The Finance Act 1993 does not amplify or clarify the meaning of private use.

5.76   It merely defines it as being that use which does not fall within the definition of business use. No further guidance is given on this matter and the confusion and ambiguity look set to continue.

5.77   An employee can only claim that travel is for business purposes and therefore not taxable where he can demonstrate that he was necessarily obliged to undertake the journey and where the journey was done in the performance of his duties of employment. The first condition is not usually difficult to satisfy – if the journey is for business reasons that is usually sufficient. The fact that the employee could have taken an alternative means of transport is not relevant.

5.78   The more difficult test to prove is that travelling was done in the performance of the duties of employment. This is particularly the case with home-to-work travel. In the past, in some cases, the Inland Revenue regarded the practice where employees drove company vans home, kept them there overnight and then drove them to work the following morning as involving only business use. In other cases a more aggressive approach was adopted and this particular practice was regarded as private use. It was excluded from business travel on the grounds that it merely put the employee in a position to do his duties and was not incurred on doing the job itself. However, where an employee can demonstrate that in getting into his company van he immediately commences his duties of employment, it can be argued that there is no private use of the van so no tax charge should arise.

5.79   This approach has been successfully argued where employees who keep company vans at their homes when actually on duty are required to contact their employer and register for work as soon as they are called out, eg by logging on via a terminal in their vans, and so are at work and performing their duties of employment from that time, and are paid from that point in time. A further condition that employees must then proceed directly to the location required by their employer also applies.

5.80   Clearly, there is scope for planning here. Employees should review their instructions to their employees who keep vans at their homes and should consider whether a change in working practice and terms of employment would result in a similar exemption from taxation. Where such a change in working practice is not feasible, both employees and employers may wish to dispense with any use of a van which could be deemed to be private use. This may have adverse effects on the business: an employee who previously drove a company van home in the evening and from there drove it to work in the morning, thus being immediately effective, will now be required to find other means of getting to and from his workplace in order to pick up a company van.

The new system (1993/94 onwards)

5.81   FA 1993 s 73 and Sch 4 inserts Sch 6A to TA 1988 which takes the taxation of the private use of company vans out of the general charging provisions and taxes them separately under special rules. Under the new rules the benefit is calculated as follows:

(a)   a standard charge of £500 in 1993/94 is imposed if there is private use of the van;
(b)   the charge is reduced to £350 if the van is more than four years old at the end of the year of assessment;
(c)   any contribution made by the employee to the employer for the use of the van is deducted from the standard charge.

5.82   A van will be deemed to be available for private use unless the terms on which it is made available prohibit such use and no such use is made of the van in the year of assessment. The burden of proof is therefore on the employee and employer to show that the employee was prohibited from using the van for private purposes and the employer would therefore be advised to revise staff handbooks and contracts of employment where necessary to include such express prohibitions and to ensure that they are adhered to in practice.

5.83   The charge on the employee is reduced where the van was only available for his private use for part of the year or was not available throughout a period of 30 days or more.

5.84   Where an employee has more than one van available for his private use at the same time, he is liable to pay income tax on the standard amount of each van.

5.85   Where an employer pays for fuel for an employee's private use of a company van, no additional charge to tax arises. Nor will any charge arise on fuel provided for vans with a gross vehicle weight of more than 3,500 kilograms. Employers should therefore consider whether they should pay for some or all of the employees' fuel for private use of a company van where the employees will be taxed on private usage of the van.

Shared vans

5.86   It is common practice for a single van to be available to a number of employees in the year – a shared van – and in the past there was no specific guidance as to the calculation of the taxable benefit arising to each employee. This issue is addressed in FA 1993 s 73 and Sch 4 inserting Sch 6A to TA 1988. Under the new rules a shared van is a van that is available to more than one employee of the same employer although there is no requirement that it is available on the same terms to the employees.

5.87   However, where a van is made available to a single employee for a period of more than 30 days, it will not count as a shared van for that period.

5.88   The charge to tax for shared vans is calculated by adding together the standard charges for all the employer's vans which were shared at some time during the year – there is no requirement for the vans to have been shared throughout the entire year. This total is then divided equally among all those employees who used a shared van for private purposes in the year irrespective of whether they had equal usage of the van in the year.

5.89   However, where this apportionment gives a figure in excess of £500 for any employee, the amount on which the employee is taxed is restricted to a standard amount of £500.

5.90   Clearly, these provisions could tax employees who have only very limited private usage of shared vans on an amount which is disproportionately high in relation to the benefit actually received and they are therefore entitled to claim instead an alternative daily rate on which they will be assessed to tax. This daily rate has been set at £5 for 1993/94 for each day the employee uses a shared van for private purposes. In order to make a claim under this provision the employee will be required to keep detailed records during the year and to submit these together with a claim after the year end to his tax office.

Pooled vans

5.91   FA 1993 s 73 and Sch 4 inserting s 159AB to TA 1988 introduces the notion of a pooled van that is a van which is shared and is not normally kept overnight at or near the homes of the employees who use it; any private use which is incidental to the business use will not give rise to a tax charge. These provisions are analogous to those relating to pooled cars and presumably the interpretation of 'incidental' and 'not normally kept at or near the homes' will follow that relating to pooled cars.

5.92   There is scope for tax planning, but employers and employees should note that the conditions for pooled vans will be applied strictly and it is advisable to keep private use of such vans to the absolute minimum, and to forbid the garaging of the van at an employee's home other than, exceptionally, the night before a long business journey which necessitates an early start so that the van is not disqualified from the above exemption from tax.

5.93   As in the case of pooled cars where vans are used by several employees without meeting the above conditions, the van would not be a pooled van. As a result, all employees who use the van privately would be subject to tax under the shared van provisions.

Administration

5.94   Although one of the Chancellor's stated aims in introducing a new method of taxing company vans was to simplify the system, the provisions relating to shared vans would appear to place a major administrative burden on both employers and employees.

5.95 Records for each van will have to be maintained showing which employees used the van, whether private use was involved and the number of days the van was available to each employee. Clearly, for employers who have large fleets of company vans the amount of administration will be considerable. Furthermore, a single vehicle could fall into the definitions of van available for private use, a shared van, and a pooled van within the same year, so the calculation of each employee's taxable benefit could be complicated and time-consuming.

4 OUTPLACEMENT COUNSELLING

5.96 Outplacement services provided to employees who lose their jobs are now exempt from income tax (FA 1993 s 108 inserting ss 589A and 589B to TA 1988). The exemption applies where 'qualifying counselling services' are provided to an employee in connection with the termination of an office or employment. Thus it appears that counselling in connection with a change of duties or of location within the employer's organisation will not qualify for the exemption, since the employment is not being terminated (s 589A(1), (2)).

5.97 The exemption takes effect for employees whose employment terminates on or after 16 March 1993 or, for employees whose employment terminated before then, for services bought by the employer on or after 16 March 1993 (s 589A(1), (2)). Employers paying for these services are given an automatic tax deduction (s 589A(8)–(10)), which would not previously have been available if, for example, the expenditure was incurred as part of the cost of closing down a business.

5.98 The main purpose of the counselling services must be to enable the employee to adjust to the loss of his job or to find other gainful work (including self-employment), or to do both (s 589B(2)(a)). Qualifying services fall within the categories of giving advice and guidance; imparting or improving skills; and providing or making available the use of office equipment or similar facilities (s 589B(2)(b)). Many forms of therapy in which the counsellor takes a more passive role than giving advice and guidance would appear to fall outside this definition, and it is to be hoped that the Inland Revenue will not interpret it too literally. Rather surprisingly, no limit is set for the period of time over which counselling services may be provided. At first sight it would appear that an employer could provide office facilities from which a redundant employee could carry on a self-employed business for an unlimited period and still fall within the exemption.

Counselling services will only qualify for the exemption if all the following conditions are met:

(a) the employees receiving the services have been employed full-time for a period of at least two years;

(b)   the services are available to all an employer's staff or to a particular class of staff; and

(c)   the services are provided in the United Kingdom (s 589B(2)(c)–(e)).

5.99   Thus, where counselling services are made available to employees on a selective individual basis, rather than being made generally available to that class of staff, the exemption will not apply. Where services are provided partly in and partly outside the United Kingdom, there is provision for just and reasonable apportionment (s 589B(3)).

5.100   For counselling services which do not fall within the new exemption, there is no change to the existing tax treatment. Outplacement counselling is taxed (at the date of termination of employment) under the regime of TA 1988 s 148 ('payments on retirement or removal from office or employment'). By virtue of TA 1988 s 188(4), the first £30,000 of a redundancy package, including the counselling services provided, is free of tax and only the excess over £30,000 is taxable.

5.101   This much seems clear, but it may be more difficult to determine the quantum of the taxable amount in respect of outplacement counselling in circumstances where the new exemption does not apply. Where a specific payment is made by an employer on behalf of an employee, that payment is the taxable amount (s 148(3)). If the employer is invoiced a stated amount by the counsellor with reference to each individual employee, the Inland Revenue take the view that there are payments 'on behalf of' the employee, giving specific and identifiable amounts which are liable to income tax. However, where the fee issued by the counsellor is not allocated to individual employees, it appears arguable that the taxable amount under s 148(3) is the 'valuable consideration' which is treated 'as a payment of money equal to the value of that consideration at the date when it is given'. The rules in s 156 for calculating the cash equivalent of a benefit in kind have no relevance to s 148. On basic Schedule E principles for arriving at amounts taxable under s 19 (the main charging provision), the valuable consideration would be the value which can be derived by conversion into money's worth. Given that where a service is being provided there is no asset which can be converted into money's worth, there is no valuable consideration which can be taxed.

5.102   The Revenue, however, take the view that s 148 stands on its own and that the concept of 'money's worth' cannot be used in interpreting it. This seems dubious: s 148 is an extension of the Schedule E charge, but there is no clear-cut evidence why the valuation methods which the courts have held to apply to s 19 should not also apply to s 148. Meanwhile the Revenue take the view that the taxable amount under s 148 requires an objective view of what the facility is worth when it is given as part of the redundancy package. They suggest that apportioning the cost to the employer of the outplacement counselling among the group of employees to whom it is given is the most practical way of achieving this.

5.103   It remains to be seen how vigorous the Revenue will be in pursuing this argument in respect of unsettled cases prior to 16 March 1993. In cases where the new exemption in s 589A does not give automatic relief (for example, because the employee has worked for less than two years), it may be sensible for employers to agree with outplacement counsellors for a global bill to be issued by the counsellors which is not apportioned between individual employees. There is a requirement for employers who pay for counselling services which do not fall within the new exemption to report details of such payments to the Inspector within 30 days of the end of the tax year (s 148(7)).

5   SPORTING AND RECREATIONAL FACILITIES

5.104   The Inland Revenue's Budget Press Release of 16 March 1993 announced that employees were not to be subject to tax on the benefit of in-house sports and recreational facilities provided by employers for use by their staff generally. This takes effect from 6 April 1993.

5.105   The cost to the Exchequer of the new measure is estimated by the Revenue to be negligible: this confirms that such benefits have not, in practice, been taxed in the past. The Inland Revenue appears to have accepted that employer-subsidised sports facilities and social clubs have generally fallen within the effective scope of the de minimis rule, so that no taxable benefit arose. This position was borne out by a statement made by John Moore, the Financial Secretary to the Treasury, during the course of the debate on the Finance Bill 1985 (9 July 1985). Further help is given by the decision in the case of *Pepper v Hart* [1992] STC 898, confirming that the taxable benefit arising from in-house benefits is based on the marginal cost to the employer. This supports the conclusion that any benefit arising in earlier years will normally escape tax on the de minimis principle.

5.106   The Revenue has always previously sought a tax charge where there is an easily identifiable external sports facility benefit, such as membership of a golf club. The director or employee will not then be able to make a claim under TA 1988 s 198 ('relief for necessary expenses'): see, for example, *Brown v Bullock* (1961) 40 TC 1, CA. Subject to this, demands from the Revenue for tax in respect of past benefits should normally be strongly resisted.

5.107   The detailed new legislation is found in TA 1988 s 197G ('sporting and recreational facilities'), inserted by FA 1993 s 75. Like much of the Act, s 75 is extremely long-winded, but key points include the following.

(a)   The new exemption applies to the provision of sporting or recreational facilities which are available generally to employees or their families: thus facilities for individuals or limited groups of employees will not be covered by the exemption. The facilities may be provided by way of non-cash voucher (s 197G(1), (2)).

(b)   A facility which is used mainly by members of the public or by those whose opportunity to use it does not derive from their employment does not qualify (s 197G(3)(d), (e)).

5.108   It is clear from this that subscriptions paid for employees to belong to sports clubs will not be exempt. It is not entirely clear what further significance this provision may have. If an employer books part of a local sports hall for his staff for an evening, does the facility in question relate to the use of the sports hall, in which case it is available to the public generally so that the exemption is not available? Or does it relate to the specific use of the rooms booked in the hall between, say, 7pm and 11pm on a Tuesday evening exclusively for the use of that employer's employees, in which case the exemption is available? The former interpretation seems to be at least arguable, but the Revenue do not seem to have had this type of situation in mind when the legislation was drafted, and it is interesting to note that the Budget Press Release refers specifically to 'in-house sports facilities'.

(a)   Sporting facilities with overnight accommodation or on domestic premises do not qualify for the exemption (s 197G(3)(b), (c)).

(b)   Provided that the other conditions are met, facilities provided by two employers jointly will qualify for the exemption, as will facilities which are run by an outside firm for an employer's staff generally; this was confirmed by the Revenue in the Budget Press Release.

CHAPTER 6

Relocation expenses

1 INTRODUCTION

6.1 Until the Finance Act 1993, removal expenses and benefits paid or provided to employees were taxable by statute, as Schedule E emoluments. Relief from taxation was provided in broad terms by two Extra Statutory Concessions, A5 and A67. In practice the detail was filled in by negotiations between individual taxpayers and the Revenue, usually at district level.

6.2 The Finance Act 1993 Schedule 5 replaces the previous concessionary treatment with statutory relief. Removal expenses and benefits are now exempt from tax, subject to an £8,000 ceiling.

6.3 The new legislation goes beyond the standardising and codification of previous practice, and marks a significant departure from the previous tax position.

Key changes

6.4 Significant differences between the previous concessional treatment and the new rules are as follows:

(a) the introduction of an £8,000 ceiling on tax-free relocation payments paid or benefits provided to employees (6.104–6.106);
(b) bridging loan interest (6.47–6.70) and tax-free disturbance allowances (6.110–6.112) are included within the £8,000 limit;
(c) the costs of international relocations are largely excluded from the new legislation (6.153–6.159);
(d) the withdrawal of Extra Statutory Concession A67, which allowed tax relief for additional expenses incurred on relocations to higher cost housing areas (6.125–6.130);
(e) the Inland Revenue have announced that tax relief on compensation payments made to employees for losses on sale of their old homes will no longer be available (6.139–6.141);
(f) employees are no longer required to sell their old home to qualify for tax relief on relocation expenses and benefits (6.89–6.98);
(g) all qualifying relocation payments and benefits must be paid or provided by the end of the tax year following the relocation, unless an extended time limit is negotiated with the Inspector of Taxes (6.99–6.103).

Effect of changes

6.5 The effects of the changes are threefold: higher tax costs, reduced employee mobility and increased legislative complexity.

Costs

6.6 A recent survey commissioned by UK relocation companies suggested that the average cost of a relocation is currently £25,000. A tax-free allowance of only £8,000 means that part of the cost of many relocations will now be taxable.

6.7 If the tax cost is met by the employer, the original sum must be grossed up at the taxpayer's marginal rate of tax, and the total is then subject to National Insurance Contributions (NIC). A £1,000 payment to a 40% taxpayer will thus cost the employer a further £840 in grossed-up tax and NIC.

6.8 The Inland Revenue have estimated that yield to the Treasury, and thus the cost to taxpayers, is £200m a year, rising to £250m as the withdrawal of Concession A67 becomes fully effective.

6.9 In addition, compliance costs will increase because of the new reporting requirements and the detailed nature of the legislation (6.12–6.15).

Employee mobility

6.10 Previously, the Inland Revenue accepted that compensation and guaranteed price payments made to relocating employees could be paid tax-free. Compensation payments allowed employees to move who otherwise would have been trapped by the negative equity in their property. Guaranteed price schemes enabled individuals to make a cash purchase in their new location, rather than waiting, perhaps for a year or more, for someone to buy their old property.

6.11 The Inland Revenue have now announced that all such payments in respect of relocations occurring after 6 April 1993 will be regarded as taxable. Assuming a flat housing market, the mobility of the UK workforce will be reduced. This will in its turn further depress the housing market.

Complexity and compliance

6.12 With the exception of the rules for bridging loans and higher cost housing allowances, the Inland Revenue have until now accepted that relocation payments and benefits were allowable if 'reasonable and controlled' (Concession A5).

6.13 The replacement of the concessionary basis by legislation means that all taxpayers will now be dealt with on the same basis, rather than according to individual interpretations and agreements with local Inspectors of Taxes.

6.14 However, the taxpayer is now faced with 14 pages of very specific and detailed legislation. It needs to be read carefully, as there are some unexpected surprises. The relief for duplicate expenses, for example, is now restricted to domestic goods (6.71–6.72) where it was previously available for a wide range of expenses; payments for temporary accommodation can now only cover the employee, not his family or household.

6.15 The employer has also to monitor the cut-off point and ensure that, at each tax year end, any allowable payments in excess of £8,000 per relocation are reported. Failure to apply the legislation may result in expensive penalties for submitting incorrect PAYE or P11D returns.

Inland Revenue powers of amendment

6.16 The itemising of specific allowable expenses means that the legislation will need constant updating as circumstances change. The lists of allowable expenses and benefits can be added to by statutory instrument, as can the £8,000 limit.

6.17 The £8,000 limit cannot however be reduced, or an item removed from the list of eligible removal expenses/benefits except by legislation (FA 1993 Sch 5, para 2 (15)(1),(23)(1) and (24)(10). The principle behind this was well explained by Mr Watts in the Committee stage of the Finance Bill:

'It is not a sound principle that benefits that have been granted under primary legislation should be capable of being removed under secondary legislation.'

6.18 However, power is also given to make regulations which include:

'such supplementary, incidental or consequential provisions as appear to the Treasury to be necessary or expedient; and such provisions may be made by way of amendment to other Parts of this Schedule, or otherwise.'

(FA 1993 Sch 5, para 2(15)(2) and (23)(2))

6.19 These are sweeping powers. While taxpayers may hope that Mr Watts' words, which were made in the context of deletions from the listing, will be remembered if use of powers is ever threatened, the fact remains that the powers are enshrined in legislation and Mr Watts' words only in Hansard.

General charging provision

6.20 Benefits in kind are charged to tax under TA 1988 s 154. However, for this section to apply, there must be a benefit to the employee. Where an employer requires the employee to move, and there is no gain to the employee, it is arguable that there is no benefit.

6.21 Where, however, expenses are reimbursed rather than benefits provided, 'any sums paid' to the employee 'in respect of expenses' are taxable (TA 1988 s 153).

6.22 However in this context it is interesting to note that when Concession A67, covering payments to employees moving to higher cost housing areas, was originally introduced in 1985, Simon's Tax Intelligence added the following note to its publication of the Concession:

> 'The Board of the Inland Revenue was advised some years ago that the taxability of such payments was uncertain in law and has in practice not sought to tax them.'

Simon's Tax Intelligence 1985 p26

This view was perhaps based on the possibility that employees could claim a deduction for the expenses under TA 1988 s 198 (6.165–6.167).

6.23   The Inland Revenue's current view is clearly, however, that relocation costs paid or provided by the employer are taxable, subject to the new reliefs. This view has therefore been taken as the basis for the discussion of the legislation which follows.

Scope of the new relief (FA 1993 Sch 5 para 2 (1–4))

6.24   The new relocation tax relief covers qualifying removal expenses paid or benefits provided to an employee which would, apart from this legislation, be taxable as emoluments under Schedule E.

6.25   Schedule E emoluments include cash payments to all employees (TA 1988 s 131) and benefits in kind provided to all directors and to employees earning more than £8,500 (TA 1988 s 167(1)). In practice, a company is unlikely to go to the expense of relocating an employee who earns less than £8,500.

6.26   Amounts paid or benefits provided directly to the employee, his family or household (6.76–6.80) or on his behalf to a third party are also included in the relief.

6.27   In order to be a qualifying removal expense or benefit three conditions must be satisfied:

(a)   the expense/benefit must fall within the definition of eligible removal expenses/benefits (6.28–6.80); and

(b)   it must be reasonably incurred in connection with a change of the employee's residence (6.81–6.98); and

(c)   it must be reasonably incurred within the time limits set out in the legislation (6.99–6.103).

2   ELIGIBLE REMOVAL EXPENSES/BENEFITS (FA 1993 SCH 5 PARA 2(7) AND (16))

Definition of eligible removal expenses/benefits

6.28   To be eligible a removal expense/benefit must fall into one of the following categories :

a) disposal expenses/benefits (6.29–6.38);
b) acquisition expenses/benefits (6.39–6.41);
c) abortive acquisition expenses/benefits (6.42–6.43);
d) expenses/benefits of transporting belongings (6.44);
e) travelling and subsistence expenses/benefits (6.45–6.46);
f) bridging loan expenses/benefits (6.47–6.70);
g) duplicate expenses and benefits in respect of the new residence (6.71–6.72).

Disposal expenses/benefits (FA 1993 Sch 5 para 2(8) and (17))

6.29 In order for disposal expenses or benefits to fall within the legislation, the relocating employee and/or his family or household (6.76–6.80) must have an interest in the property; it must be this interest which is disposed of; and the expenses must be eligible disposal expenses or benefits.

Eligible disposal expenses and benefits

6.30 The specific disposal expenses and benefits which are listed in the legislation are as follows.

a) Legal expenses/benefits, including those connected with the redemption of any loan relating to the residence.[1]
b) Estate agent's or auctioneer's fees. This is assumed to include valuation costs.
c) Advertising costs.
d) Public utility disconnection charges. This would cover items such as telephones, washing machines and gas fires and fittings. It does not include any disconnection costs which may apply to services other than public utilities, such as cable TV. However the costs of this may be covered under the relief for transporting belongings (6.44).
e) Redemption penalties on any loan related to the residence. This covers both loans raised to buy the property and loans secured on the property.[1]
f) Maintaining, insuring and preserving the security of the property while unoccupied. This would include, for example, cleaning and gardening expenses and the cost of any repairs.
g) Any rent payable on the property while unoccupied. This is eligible only as an expense, not as a benefit. Thus, if rent is billed directly to the employer, or (where the property is owned by the employer), the rent is waived, it is not allowable. This appears to be an anomaly.

There is no requirement that the loan must have been raised by the employee and/or his family or household. It is therefore less restrictive than the similar clause on acquisition expenses (FA 1993 Sch 5 para 9(3); 6.40(b)).

Council tax

6.31 Council tax payable on the property being disposed of is not an eligible relocation expense, either under this paragraph or under the 'duplicate goods' category (6.71–6.72). For its position under the transitional reliefs see 6.123.

6.32   This is in contrast to the previous position on rates and community charge. Rates on the old property would have been allowed as a reasonable expense, if payment was also being made in respect of a new property.

6.33   Following the abolition of domestic rates, the Revenue clarified the position on poll tax.[1] Standard community charge paid or reimbursed by the employer was allowable since it was a tax on the property; personal community charge was not, as it was a personal liability.

6.34   The basis for including rates and standard community charge as reasonable relocation expenses in the past was logical; it is not clear why council tax has been excluded from the new rules.

6.35   The DSS appears to share this uncertainty: the National Insurance Contributions for Employers Manual from 6 April 1993 (Grenn Book) (Section 15 para 74) states, 'If you make any payment towards a relocated employee's council tax, please contact your local Social Security office for advice.'

1   Inland Revenue Press Release 10 November 1989; TR795 – Guidance Note to the Institute of Chartered Accountants, June 1990.

Intended disposals

6.36   Expenses and benefits are also eligible if the disposal is only 'intended'. 'Intended' is not defined in the legislation, but is assumed to be a disposal which was planned but does not actually occur. In other words the cost of an abortive attempt to sell a property will also be covered.

6.37   This may occur for example if a sale falls through, or if the employee attempts to sell the property but later changes his mind. Retaining the property is now no bar to relocation expenses being allowable for tax (6.90–6.94).

6.38   Unlike abortive acquisition costs (6.47–6.48), there is no requirement that there be 'reasonable grounds' for a change of intention.

Acquisition expenses/benefits (FA 1993 Sch 5, para 2(9–10), (18–19))

6.39   For acquisition expenses or benefits to fall with the legislation, it must be the relocating employee and/or his family or household (6.76–6.80) who acquire the interest in the property and the expenses/benefits must be 'eligible'.

Eligible acquisition expenses/benefits

6.40   The specific acquisition expenses/benefits allowed by the legislation are as follows.

(a)   Legal expenses/benefits, including legal expenses or services connected with any loan to acquire the interest.
(b)   Costs of obtaining a loan to acquire the property. This would include the costs of obtaining a valuation of the property for mortgage purposes.

Where this service has been provided gratis or at reduced cost, the waiving or reducing of the cost is an eligible benefit.

The loan may be raised by the employee and/or a member of his family or household (6.76–6.80).

However, where the previous property had been used as security for a loan, rather than the loan being acquired to buy the property, there is no provision for any relief for the costs of transferring the security to a new property. This contrasts with the position on disposal expenses (6.30(e)), which allows relief for 'any penalty for redeeming, for the purpose of the disposal or intended disposal, any loan related to the residence' (FA 1993 para 2(8)(2)(e)).

It is to be hoped that the Revenue will interpret the clause on disposal expenses as also covering the costs of transferring the security to the new property.

(c) Survey fees, land registry fees and stamp duty.
(d) Public utility connection costs (see 6.30(d)).
(e) Mortgage indemnity premiums.

Expenses/benefits not included

6.41 The expenses of obtaining a NHBC guarantee, and the costs of cleaning the property after acquisition, both of which were accepted as 'reasonable' under Concession A5, are not included.

Abortive acquisition expenses/benefits (FA 1993 Sch 5 para 2(10) and (19))

6.42 Abortive acquisition expenses are covered, providing that the purchase was not proceeded with, either for reasons outside the purchaser's control, or because the purchaser had reasonable grounds for not proceeding.

6.43 Reasonable grounds could, for example, include structural defects brought to light by a survey, a change in the date of vacant possession, or an increase in price.

Expenses/benefits of transporting belongings (FA 1993 Sch 5 para 2(11) and (20))

6.44 Included under this heading are the costs of packing, unpacking, transporting, insuring and the temporary storage of domestic belongings. The removal, adaptation and installation costs of domestic fittings are also covered.

The use of the word 'domestic' here suggests that the removal costs of items such as boats or horses would not be allowable.

Travelling and subsistence expenses/benefits (FA 1993 Sch 5 para 2(12) and (21))

6.45 These are again defined in great detail. Allowable costs are as follows.

(a) Costs of the employee, his family or household (6.76–6.80) visiting the new location for purposes connected with the relocation. Allowable expenditure includes the cost of food, drink and temporary accommodation during these visits.[1]

(b)   The employee's home to work travel costs from his old residence to his new place of work.[1]

(c)   The employee's travel costs between his new residence and his original place of work. This would be relevant where the individual relocated in advance of the job move. It is only available where a relocated individual is an existing employee; employees relocated on appointment are not included.

(d)   Subsistence costs of the employee (other than on temporary visits, which is covered in (a)). This would cover, for example, the cost of hotel meals at the new relocation. Again, this only applies to existing employees. It also only covers the relocated employee, not his family or household.

(e)   Temporary accommodation expenses for the employee (but again not his family or household). This may be a drafting error as temporary accommodation would clearly be needed for the family/household if, for example, the original home was sold before the new one was acquired. The only exception appears to be for children in education (6.39(f)).

(f)   Costs of the employee, his family and household, travelling from the old to the new residence for reasons connected with the relocation.[1]

(g)   The food, accommodation and travelling costs[1] incurred where a child remains at the old location in order to receive continuity of education. The child must be under 19 years old at the beginning of the tax year in which the relocation takes place and be a member of the family or household. It therefore excludes relief for the costs of older children in full-time education (6.76–6.80).

   Relief is also available, subject to the same conditions, for a child who moves to the new area for educational reasons before the new residence has been acquired.

   Under Concession A5, a contribution towards a child's board and lodging costs could be made by an employer if the child was within two years of GCSEs or A-levels. Relief was also available if the child had special educational needs.

6.46   The legislation was amended in Committee to exclude from its scope any travel or subsistence expenses which could be claimed as allowable under the foreign travel rules (TA 1988 ss 193-195); (6.153-6.159)

1   Allowable travelling costs include the provision of a company car or van, providing that the car is used only for travelling connected with the relocation, and there is no other private use apart from this (FA 1993 Sch 5 para 2(21)(2)).

Bridging loan expenses/beneficial loans (FA 1993 Sch 5 para 2 (13))

6.47   Bridging loans were the only area covered in some detail by Concession A5 and the new legislation mirrors the Concession in many ways.

6.48   The Finance Bill did not extend relief for bridging loan interest to beneficial loans, ie the provision by the employer to the employee if a cheap or interest-free loan for bridging purposes. Beneficial loans remained chargeable under TA 1988 s 160 as a benefit to the employee, even if they were granted as part of a relocation. However, this was amended in Committee and a new section 191B was added to TA 1988 (6.58).

6.49 There are, however, significant differences between the relief for loan interest paid and the new legislation on loans provided by the employer. The restrictions on the use of loan proceeds (6.52) and the market value limitation (6.55–6.56) are not included in the beneficial loan provisions. There is also a prescribed method (6.60–6.68) for the calculation of the relocation relief available on a beneficial bridging loan.

Timing of loan

6.50 Bridging loan interest paid by the employee is an eligible removal expense if the reason, or one of the reasons, for needing a bridging loan is that there is a gap between the time that expenditure is incurred on the new property and receiving the proceeds of the old property. The same conditions apply to a loan provided by the employer.

6.51 The wording is similar to that in Concession A5:

'"Removal expenses" ... includes the reimbursement of interest payable on a bridging loan . . . The loan must be used only to bridge an unavoidable gap between the date expenditure is incurred on the purchase of the new property and the date on which the sale proceeds of the old property are received.'

The omission of the words 'purchase' and 'unavoidable' from the new definition and the inclusion of 'one of the reasons' allows some flexibility with respect to loan interest which could perhaps be used to advantage in individual cases; subject of course to compliance with the other conditions in the legislation.

Use of loan proceeds

6.52 Bridging loan interest paid by the employee is only an eligible removal expense if the proceeds of the loan are used either to pay off the mortgage on the old property and/or to acquire the new one. If any part of the loan is used for other purposes, the related interest will be ineligible for relief.

6.53 This is again similar to Concession A5:

'The loan must be used only to pay off the mortgage on the old property, to fund the purchase of a new property or to meet immediately related incidental expenditure (eg legal or survey fees).'

The final phrase, 'immediately related incidental expenditure', does not occur in the new rules. Its inclusion in Concession A5 was a practical point, as fees are often included in loan payments or redemptions. It will therefore be necessary to ensure that the bridging loan is used only to cover the actual mortgage.

6.54 This restriction on the use of loan proceeds is not included in the legislation on beneficial loans. Again, this may provide for flexibility in individual cases.

Market value limitation

6.55   If the bridging loan exceeds the market value of the old property, interest on the excess is not eligible for relief. In this context, the market value is defined as being 'taken at the time his interest in the new residence is acquired'. This will require the old residence to be valued contemporaneously with the employee's acquisition of the new property.

6.56   This requirement is not included in the legislation on beneficial loans. It is therefore possible for interest on a beneficial bridging loan to be included in the relocation relief even if the loan is for an amount greater than the market value of the old property.

Ownership

6.57   The old and new properties can be owned by either the employee and/or by a member of his family or household. Similar provisions apply to the bridging loan.

Beneficial loans (TA 1988 s 191(B))

6.58   Relocation relief has been extended to cover the deemed interest on cheap or interest free loans provided by an employer on the relocation of an employee, providing the employee satisfies the change of residence rules (6.90-6.98).

6.59   The section only applies where the benefit would otherwise be taxable under TA 1988 s 160(1). In other words, exceptions to the beneficial loans rules continue to apply. These exceptions include de minimis interest (TA 1988 s 161(1)) (6.69-6.70) and loans which would otherwise be subject to MIRAS relief (TA 1988 s 160(4)).

6.60   Relocation relief for interest on beneficial loans is only available if the tax free limit of £8,000 has not been fully utilised by other eligible expenses or benefits (TA 1988 s 191B(5)). It therefore forms the top slice of eligible costs.

6.61   This unused relocation relief is then used to determine for how long a period the beneficial loan can be outstanding before it becomes taxable under TA 1988 s 160(1).

6.62   The calculation is:

$$\frac{A \times B}{C \times D} = \text{number of 'tax free' days}$$

Where:
A is the unused relocation relief;
B is 365;
C is the maximum amount of the loan outstanding between the date the loan was made and the end of the tax year following the relocation;
D is the official rate of interest (TA 1988 s 160(5)).

The answer is rounded up to the nearest whole number.

6.63

EXAMPLE

A relocated employee has eligible expenses of £6,000, and an interest free bridging loan of £60,000 provided by her employer. The official rate of interest is 7%.

A = 2000
B = 365
C = 60,000
D = 7%

$$\frac{A \times B}{C \times D} = \frac{2000 \times 365}{60,000 \times 0.07} = 174 \text{ days}$$

The loan can thus remain outstanding for 174 days before it becomes chargeable under TA 1988 s 160(1).

6.64 The calculation is unaffected if the loan balance is reduced below the maximum during the period or if the official rate of interest moves during the period.

6.65 If the loan is repaid before the end of the period then there is clearly no beneficial loan and TA 1988 s 160(1) is ignored.

6.66 The calculation can only be performed once all other relocation costs or benefits are identified. If these other amounts exceed £8,000, the bridging loan will be taxable in full under s 160(1). When a relocation crosses a tax year and costs remain to be ascertained it will be unclear whether the interest is taxable.

6.67 Where this is the case it is advisable to report the bridging loan as a beneficial loan on the employee's P11D unless there is certainty that total eligible relocation costs and benefits will not exceed £8,000. This is because, if the benefit does crystallise, omission of the benefit from a P11D return in a tax year may result in penalties being levied on the company.

6.68 Where an employee has been assessed in this way on a beneficial loan, which later proves to fall within the allowable relocation reliefs, a claim should be made by the individual and the Revenue will adjust the assessments (TA 1988 s 191B(13).

De minimis limits

6.69 The de minimis limits in TA 1988 s 161(1) mean that a benefit only arises for Schedule E purposes if the loan interest is more than £300 in a tax year. The current low interest rates mean that interest on a short-term bridging loan may not be taxable. If the loan falls across a tax year the employee can thus make use of the de minimis relief in both years.

6.70 It is of course important to remember that:

(a) if the total interest paid in the year is more than £300, the whole amount is a Schedule E benefit. The de minimis amount is not a relief on the first £300; and

(b)   in calculating the beneficial loan interest for the purposes of the de minimis relief, account must be taken of the deemed interest on all beneficial loans granted to the employee.

Duplicate goods and benefits in respect of a new residence (FA 1993 Sch 5 para 2 (14) and (22))

6.71   Relief is extended to the costs of purchasing domestic goods (or the provision of such goods by the employer) which replace similar items used in the employee's old residence but which are not suitable for the new residence. Items such as carpets and curtains could be included here. Any proceeds received from disposing of the old items must be deducted to produce a net cost to the employee.

6.72   This relief is restricted to domestic items and is thus more limited than the treatment under Concession A5. Previously, relief could be obtained for a range of duplicate costs, including the cost of new school uniforms, British Rail season ticket costs, club subscriptions, and day school fees.

Relocation management companies

6.73   Many employers use the services of relocation management companies in order to facilitate relocations. The provision of these services is not included as an allowable relocation expense or benefit, although some of the elements in their fee, for example, legal fees and stamp duty, would be covered.

6.74   As currently drafted, therefore, an amount paid to a relocation management company to cover their own administration and services is not an eligible cost/benefit. Its provision to the employee is therefore fully taxable, subject to the general benefit rule (6.20–6.23).

6.75   Representations have been made to the Revenue on this point and it may be reconsidered.

Definition of 'family or household'

6.76   The phrase 'family or household' is used throughout the Schedule and is defined as including the employee's spouse, son, daughter, parent, servant, dependant, guest or the spouse of the employee's son or daughter. The same definition is used for the general benefits legislation at TA 1988 Chapter 2 (TA 1988 s 168(4)).

6.77   However, if the employee is not married to his partner, and that partner is not financially dependent on the employee, it would appear that the definition operates to exclude the partner. Similarly, if the employee is not financially supporting the children of the partner, for example, because maintenance is being provided by the child's other parent, the children would also be excluded.

6.78   There are many households in the UK which contain two adults who are not married to each other, far more in number than households which include a servant who is willing to relocate as part of the household.

6.79   The exclusion is significant where it is the partner who owns the interest in the old property: the interaction of the sections operates to deny the employee all relief for disposal expenses. Similarly, where the individuals own the property as tenants in common rather than as joint tenants, only a proportionate part of the expenses will be allowable. Equally, if the new property is acquired by the partner, relief for acquisition expenses is excluded.

6.80   The Revenue are currently reviewing this issue. For the present the solution is for the employer to pay or make available the relevant part of the relocation expense or benefit directly to the partner. In this case the payment or benefit is, by virtue of the same definition, not taxable on the employee.

3   CHANGE OF RESIDENCE (FA 1993 SCH 5 PARA 2 (5))

Introduction

6.81   For relocation relief to apply, the employee must change his residence in order to take up either a new employment or a new position within his employer's organisation.

6.82   The phrase 'change his residence' was used in both of the relevant Extra Statutory Concessions, A5 and A67. It was not defined in either concession, and has not been defined in the new legislation. Prior to the Finance Act 1993, its interpretation was subject to dispute; since the publication of the Finance Bill in March 1993 the Revenue have issued a Press Release (14 April 1993; 6.90–6.94) setting out current interpretation.

The position before 6 April 1993

6.83   Until 1987 there appears to have been no dispute about the meaning of the phrase 'change his residence'. In that year the Inland Revenue stated that they interpreted it as meaning that the employee had to dispose of his old residence before he could be said to have changed it. It was not enough for the old property to be no longer available for use, for example by being rented out, or because it was outside the UK.

Effect on employees from overseas

6.84   Individuals coming to work in the UK often wish to retain a residence in their country of origin, perhaps for social or legal reasons, or to be protected against upward movements in the home country property market.

6.85   Where the overseas home had been retained, the Revenue denied all relief for relocation expenses other than travelling (6.155). This had a penal effect on employers who moved staff into the country from abroad. This was recognised in the introduction to the Budget Press Release of 16 March 1993, which stated that the Chancellor's intention was in part to 'remove a disincentive for companies to bring foreign nationals to work in the United Kingdom'.

The Revenue's proposed settlement

6.86   A number of taxpayers challenged the Revenue's interpretation of the phrase 'change of residence', and the position on these open cases was addressed in the Budget Press Release of 16 March 1993:

> 'Ministers have decided not to change the conditions on which concessional relief is available for the current and past years. The Inland Revenue will now seek to collect tax in a number of cases held open because their interpretation of the phrase "change his residence" . . . has been disputed. The Board of the Inland Revenue has decided that tax should be pursued for the tax years 1987–88 onwards only in those cases where the employer, or an agent acting specifically on behalf of the employer, was told by the Revenue that they interpreted the phrase to mean that an employee must dispose of his or her old home to qualify for relief.'

6.87   This is curious. It means that some taxpayers, who were made aware of the Revenue's interpretation, are to pay tax; others will not. At what point does the taxpayer need to have been told of the Revenue's view for liability to arise? After all, every taxpayer currently debating this issue with the Revenue must have been told of the interpretation at some point, or they would not be in dispute!

6.88   There are also taxpayers who conceded the point once they were made aware of the Revenue's view. Their cases are therefore not 'held open because [the Revenue's] interpretation . . . has been disputed'. Because of this, they are not to expect any repayment.

A decision by the Revenue to seek tax in this unequal fashion would appear to be contrary to the Taxpayers' Charter.

6.89   In this context it is particularly interesting that, although there is also no definition of the phrase in the new legislation, the Inland Revenue's own interpretation (6.90–6.94) is now the same as that held by the taxpayers in dispute: namely that there can be a change of residence without a disposal of the original property.

The current position

6.90   Although under the new legislation there is no definition of 'change his residence', the Revenue have stated that there is no longer a requirement for the employee to sell his old home (Budget Press Release 16 March 1993). However:

(a)   the old residence must be the sole or main residence of the taxpayer – this prevents an individual with more than one property from claiming relocation expenses relating to the disposal of a property other than his main residence; and

(b)   the new property must become his sole or main residence (FA 1993 Sch 5 para 2(23).

6.91   'Main residence' is further explained in the Revenue Press Release of 14 April 1993:

> 'Where an employee moves with his/her family to the new property and rents out the old home or visits it at weekends, the new home would become the main residence. So relief would be available on the costs of buying the new home and for other removal expenses and benefits. Where an employee comes to work in the UK from abroad we would expect his/ her home here to be the main residence for the purposes of this relief, even if the family remained in the country of origin. On the other hand where the employee relocating within the UK rents or buys accommodation near his/ her new office, but his/her family stay behind in the old home, it is unlikely that the new accommodation would become the employee's main residence. But it will depend on the facts. Exactly what constitutes a main residence in each case will have to be agreed with the Inspector of Taxes.'

6.92   From penalising overseas relocatees, the Revenue has thus now moved to a position where the 'main residence' test to be applied to overseas individuals will be less strict than that used for employees relocating within the UK.

6.93   The definition of 'main residence' in the Press Release is not harmonised with either of the other occasions in which the phrase appears in the legislation – the Capital Gains Tax and mortgage interest relief provisions (CGTA 1992 s 222; TA 1988 s 355(1)(a)).

It would thus be possible to have three properties, each regarded as an individual's main residence for tax purposes, depending on which section of the tax legislation is being considered.

6.94   Because he can now retain his old residence, the relocating taxpayer may take advantage of the tax reliefs relating to let property. Mortgage interest relief can be set against rental income with no restriction as to amount and at the taxpayer's highest rate of tax; CGT reliefs are significant for a let property which has been a principal private residence.

Reasons for change of residence

6.95   The change of residence must result from:

(a)   the employee taking up a new job; or
(b)   changing the duties of his existing job; or
(c)   moving his normal place of work, but with the same employer and the same duties.

6.96   These rules are essentially the same as the wording of Concession A5:

> 'no assessment is made in respect of removal expenses borne by the employer where the employee has to change residence in order to take up a new employment, or as the result of a transfer to another post within an employer's organisation.'

6.97   For tax relief to be available under (b) above it would be necessary to show that the employee's old home was not 'within a reasonable daily travelling distance' of his work in the light of the demands placed on him in his new position. For example, an individual may now be on call, be required to attend late meetings, or to be available to customers at short notice.

6.98   All three types of allowable relocation are subject to the overriding condition that the change was made wholly or mainly to allow the employee to have his residence within a reasonable daily travelling distance of the new place of work.

4   LIMITATIONS OF TIME AND COST

Time limits (FA 1993 Sch 5 para 2 (6))

6.99   Eligible relocation costs/benefits must be paid or provided before the end of the tax year following the date on which the individual takes up his new position. This time limit can be extended by the Inland Revenue in individual cases if there are reasonable grounds for so doing.

6.100   Under the old basis there was no fixed time within which a relocation had to be complete and all payments made. The key word was 'reasonable'. If the relocation had not taken place within a reasonable time after the individual started his new job, the need for the move could be questioned: for example, if an individual could commute for two years, was it really necessary for him to move house?

6.101   The only area for which there was a time limit under the old rules was interest relief on bridging loans. Relief was available under Concession A5 for 12 months, but the recession in the property market caused it to be extended to three years. A further extension was available by agreement with the Inspector of Taxes if there were good reasons why the original property had not been sold.

6.102   This was convenient for companies, since it meant they only had to inform the Revenue after three years that a relocation was taking longer than expected to complete.

6.103   The new rule will increase the number of cases for which time extensions need to be sought from the Revenue – unless of course the property market makes a significant recovery.

The £8,000 limit (FA 1993 Sch 5 para 2 (24))

6.104 Tax relief on qualifying removal benefits has been set at £8,000 for each change of residence. Although the Treasury has power to increase the limit by statutory instrument, there is no provision in the legislation for the relief to be indexed.

6.105 Where the individual is not reimbursed in cash, but rather receiving benefits from the employer, the value of any such benefits is to be calculated according to the normal Schedule E benefit provisions contained in TA 1988, Pt V, Ch II.

6.106 Relief for overseas relocation expenses is not taken into account when calculating the £8,000 limit (6.153–6.160).

6.107 The Finance Bill, as originally drafted, provided that where accommodation was provided as a benefit, it was to be valued according to TA 1988 s 145, rather than, if applicable, the expensive living accommodation rules of TA 1988 s 146.

6.108 This would have been a significant relief, as it would have been more tax efficient for the employer to pay for the accommodation directly than for the individual to be reimbursed, as the benefit calculation would have produced a lower value than the actual rent.

6.109 However, this was changed in Committee, and accommodation costs paid by the employer are now taxable under TA 1988 s 145 and, if appropriate, s 146 (new sub-para 5 inserted by FA 1993 Sch 5 para 2 (24)).

Flat rate allowances

6.110 The previous concessional rules allowed the payment of a round sum disturbance allowance to a relocating employee. This was tax-free up to civil service limits, which from 1 April 1992 were as follows:

Married householder	£2,655
Single householder	£1,615
Single non-householder	£ 625

The administrative simplicity of paying allowances rather than reimbursing a large number of small, specific expenses made this an attractive option for many companies.

6.111 Although the original legislation did not permit the payment of round sum allowances, after representations the Revenue included the following in their Press Release of 14 April 1993:

'Some employers may wish to pay their employees flat rate allowances rather than reimbursing expenditure on an item by item basis. Strictly such allowances should be subject to PAYE. But if the Inspector of Taxes is satisfied that such allowances do no more than reimburse employees' eligible expenses, then they may be paid gross, and should be reported on the return of employees' benefits (form P9D or form P11D) at the end of the year if the payments are not exempt under the new relief.'

In other words, a flat rate allowance will not be taxed if, taken together with other payments or benefits provided, the £8,000 ceiling is not exceeded, and the local Inspector of Taxes agrees that the payment is only sufficient to reimburse the employee's eligible expenses.

6.112   Agreement with the local Inspector can be expected to be on the same basis as other Inland Revenue dispensations, namely that the payments are reasonable in amount and properly controlled.

Secondments

6.113   Where an employee is on secondment, the Inland Revenue do not seek to tax the payment or provision of subsistence, temporary accommodation, standard community charge and/or travelling costs if the secondment is not expected to last for more than 12 months (Revenue Statement of Practice 16/80).

6.114   This concession can assist with some of the difficulties which may arise under the new relocation rules. For example, an employee could be sent on secondment for up to a year to fill a particular role. This may enable him to train a more junior employee to take on the role and thus avoid the need for a relocation, or the secondee may bridge a gap until a suitable local recruit is found.

6.115   A decision could be made at the end of the 12-month period to relocate the secondee. The new relocation rules would then come into operation.

6.116   It is a question of fact in any given case as to whether the individual is on secondment or is simply preparing for a relocation. Abuse of the concession may result in a further tightening of the rules. However, its judicious use could help to mitigate some of the consequences of the new legislation.

5   RELOCATIONS BEFORE 6 APRIL 1993 AND TRANSITIONAL RELIEFS

Relocations before 6 April 1993

6.117   Any employee who started a job in a new location before 6 April 1993 will continue to be covered by the concessional reliefs A5 and A67, providing the conditions set out in those concessions have been adhered to.

6.118   However, as the Inland Revenue make clear in their Press Release of 14 April 1993 (at paragraph 11):

'Under the old concessionary tax treatment of payments and benefits provided as part of a relocation package, employers were still obliged to report all such tax-free payments after the year end unless they had a dispensation from their Inspector of Taxes.'

Most employers had a corporate relocation package, which they submitted to their Inspector of Taxes for approval. On the basis of this agreed package, they obtained a dispensation so that relocation expenses and benefits falling within the package did not need to be reported on the employees' forms P11D.

6.119 The Inland Revenue announced in the same Press Release that all such dispensations were revoked with effect from 14 April 1993. The effect of this is that although the payments and benefits made to employees relocating under the old rules (or the transitional rules (6.122–6.124) will not be *taxable* if they fall within the Concessions, the employer must nevertheless *report* all such payments and benefits made after 15 April 1993 on the employees' P11D forms.

6.120 This appears to be a change of view from the earlier Budget Press Release (16 March 1993 at para 11) which said that payments made under the transitional arrangements would not have to be reported on form P11D.

6.121 It is to be hoped that the Inland Revenue will review this blanket withdrawal of the dispensations, and allow them to continue in force for employees relocating under the old rules. To do otherwise will involve employers in considerable administrative complexity. Relocation payments made under the dispensation will have to be identified and separated from payments made subsequently; in many cases a knowledge of the earlier payments will be necessary in order to understand the position. If this is the Inland Revenue's approach, it amounts in practice to a review of all relocations in process as at 14 April 1993.

Transitional reliefs

6.122 Payments made and benefits provided on or after 6 April 1993 continue to qualify for the previous concessionary tax relief provided the employee satisfies the following conditions.

(a)   Before 6 April 1993 the employee entered into a firm commitment to move. The Inland Revenue will require evidence that before 6 April either the employer gave formal notification of the job transfer or that the employee had committed to accepting the transfer.
(b)   Before 2 August 1993 the employee begins the job at the new location (Inland Revenue Press Release dated 16 April 1993).

The original end date for a relocation under the transitional provisions of 1 August was amended in Committee to 2 August.

The Revenue have indicated that, where the employee was on leave or sick on 2 August, the transitional provisions would still apply providing that it was intended that the individual would take up the post by 2 August.

It is worth noting that the relocation does not have to be complete by 1 August, merely that the new job must have commenced by that date.

6.123   Concessional treatment therefore continues to be available to all employees who satisfy (a) and (b) above. Additional housing cost payments are included in this concessional treatment, although with a restriction (6.125–6.130).

6.124   The same reporting requirement applies as for existing relocations (6.117–6.121).

Additional housing cost payments

6.125   Extra Statutory Concession A67 exempted from tax certain payments towards the additional housing costs (eg increased mortgage interest or rent) of employees relocated to more expensive housing areas.

6.126   Tax relief was available if the payments were made for a limited period, reduced year by year, and did not in total exceed a prescribed maximum. The maximum varied from time to time in line with changes to the amount payable to civil servants under their Additional Housing Costs Allowance. Since 1 February 1993, the maximum has been £13,440.

6.127   Concession A67 will continue to apply to employees who began a job in a new location before 5 April 1993. Any changes to the Civil Service maximum will increase the amount which they can receive tax-free.

6.128   Employees who relocate under the transitional arrangements (6.122–6.124) will have the tax-free amount frozen at the current £13,440.

6.129   The Inland Revenue Budget Press Release (16 March 1993) allowed an employee qualifying for the additional housing costs allowance under the transitional rules to include extra council tax paid in his calculations of the extra costs.

6.130   For all other employee relocations, the Concession has been withdrawn. The NIC position is discussed at 6.172–6.177.

6   COMPENSATION PAYMENTS FOR LOSSES ON SALE OF PROPERTY

Guaranteed price schemes

6.131   Under these schemes an employee received a guaranteed price for his home, either directly from his employer, or indirectly from a relocation management company. The price was generally the market value at the date the employee agreed to relocate.

6.132 The cash received could then be used to purchase a home in the new area. From the company's point of view this speeded up his relocation; it also protected the employee from a further drop in the value of his property after the relocation had been agreed.

Any loss on the eventual sale of the property was borne by the employer.

Compensation payments

6.133 Some employers were prepared to make good not only the difference between the market value of the property at the date of the relocation and the eventual sale, but all or part of the drop in value since the employee originally purchased the property. This enabled employees to move house despite having negative equity in their property.

The *Hochstrasser* case

6.134 In the cases of *Hochstrasser v Mayes* and *Jennings v Kinder* (1959) 38 TC 673, HL, the Inland Revenue unsuccessfully attacked the receipt of such compensation payments as taxable benefits. Lord Radcliffe, concluding for the taxpayer, said:

> 'what was paid to him was paid to him in respect of his personal situation as a house-owner . . . In my opinion such a payment is no more taxable than would be a payment out of a provident or distress fund set up by an employer for the benefit of employees whose personal circumstances might justify assistance.'[1]

Lord Denning concurred:

> 'If Mr Mayes had been injured at work and received money compensation for his injuries, no one would suggest that it was profit from his employment. Nor so here where all he receives is compensation for his loss.'[2]

6.135 However, the Schedule E provisions which were then in force (TA 1952 Sch 9 para 1) provided that:

> 'Tax under Schedule E shall be annually charged on every person having or exercising an office or employment of profit mentioned in Schedule E . . . in respect of all salaries, fees, wages, perquisites or profits whatsoever therefrom.'[3]

The word 'therefrom' was an important factor in the judgments given. Lord Denning's final words were:

> 'So tested the question simply is: was the £350 received by Mr Mayes a "profit" from his employment? I think not, for the simple reason that it was not a remuneration or reward for his services in any sense of the word.'[4]

6.136 The current Schedule E rules do not use the word 'therefrom'. Instead, TA 1988 Chapter 2 is to be interpreted as follows:

'For the purposes of this Chapter all sums paid to an employee by his employer in respect of expenses . . . are deemed to be paid to him . . . by reason of his employment' (TA 1988 s 168(3)).

The Revenue's view is that the deeming provision of TA 1988 s 168 (3) means that the decision in *Hochstrasser* is no longer valid, and there is no need for specific legislation. The new legislative provisions on relocations, therefore, do not include any mention of guaranteed price schemes.

6.137   However the *Hochstrasser* decision contained more than one line of argument, and the case remains good authority for the proposition that just because 'there is a link between the payment to the employee and the employment, and the payment would never have been made but for the employment, [this] is not sufficient to render the payment taxable.'[5]

6.138   The *Hochstrasser* case was quoted in *Hamblett v Godfrey* (1987) STC 60 and the decision in that case was distinguished from *Hochstrasser*. Since *Hamblett v Godfrey* was heard after the introduction of the deeming provision,[6] it would appear that the House of Lords consider that *Hochstrasser* is still good law.

1   *Hochstrasser v Mayes* and *Jennings v Kinder* (1959) 38 TC 673 at 707–708, HL.
2   Ibid at 711.
3   Ibid at 708.
4   Ibid at 711.
5   *Simon's Taxes* (3rd edn) at E4.422.
6   The 'deeming' provision was introduced by FA 1976 s 72(3).

Inland Revenue Concession

6.139   The Inland Revenue's view is that compensation payments made to cover a financial loss suffered by a relocated employee on the sale of his old residence were not previously taxed because they were regarded as falling within Concession A5.

6.140   The Revenue defined a loss in these circumstances as:

(a)   the actual loss when the original cost of the residence is compared with the selling price; or

(b)   the notional loss which arises when an employee is forced to sell for less than the normal market value because of the urgency of his move.[1]

6.141   The concession was extended to cover 'guaranteed price' schemes. Such schemes were generally submitted to the Revenue for approval in advance of being operated. They were generally accepted as being within Concession A5 subject to the following conditions.

(a)   The guaranteed price was based on fair market value at the time the house was put on the market. This market value should have been arrived at by reference to the average of at least two valuations by qualified independent experts. If these two valuations differed widely (and the guidelines here were by more than 5–10%) a third valuation had to be obtained.

(b) Active steps had to be taken to market the property and any such marketing was to be controlled, ie not simply left to the employee.[1]

1 Unpublished Inland Revenue guidelines on the operation of Concession A5.

The current position

6.142   The removal of this concession was announced by the Revenue in its Budget Press Release on 16 March 1993. Employers were instructed that any payments made after 6 April 1993 should be subjected to PAYE, with the exception of payments under the old or transitional rules (6.117–6.130).

Tax planning

6.143   The falling property market has meant that significant sums have been paid to compensate employees for losses on relocation property sales, or under guaranteed price schemes. In cases where the relocating individual had negative equity in his property, the relocation would not have been possible but for the compensation payment.

6.144   The need for such payments remains, and although it is by no means certain that the Inland Revenue's interpretation of the *Hochstrasser* case is correct (6.134–6.137), most taxpayers cannot wait for a challenge in the courts.

6.145   A similar result to a guaranteed price scheme can be obtained if the company purchases the property from the employee. This protects the employee from a further fall in prices and allows him to make a cash purchase in his new location.

Employee's tax position
6.146   Assuming the company's purchase was at market value, no taxable benefit should arise to the employee. Independent valuations will be needed to ascertain market value.

6.147   If, on the company's sale of the property, a gain is passed through to the employee (as it may have been under the old guaranteed price agreements, which simply ensured that the individual received a minimum price), it will of course be taxable as extra remuneration.

6.148   The purchase of the property at market value only protects the individual from further falls in value: the negative equity problem remains. This will have to be addressed by taxable cash payments, or by loans, which fall within the provisions of TA 1988 s 160.

Corporate tax position
6.149   Acquiring properties from relocating employees enables the better functioning of the company's business, and is therefore in general part and parcel of its normal trade or business.

6.150 The company would hold the property in its books as a fixed asset and account for any sale proceeds under the capital gains tax legislation. Any loss arising will thus only be deductible against other gains made by the company, and any gain will be taxed in the normal way.

6.151 A second option, if there were a number of such sales, is to argue that the company was buying and selling properties as a separate trade. Losses would then be on trading account, and could be offset against profits on the core business. Not surprisingly the Revenue could be expected to resist this approach.

6.152 Indeed the Revenue could use a similar argument, holding that a company which only or mainly bought properties in a falling market and sold them at a loss was not trading with a view to profit. If they were successful, any relief for losses would be denied.

7 INTERNATIONAL RELOCATIONS (FA 1993 SCH 5 PARA 2 (12)(4) AND (21)(7)–(8))

6.153 Where the travel and subsistence costs of an overseas relocation are met by an employer, they are excluded from tax by Statute rather than by Concession (TA 1988 ss 193-4). Relief also exists for the travel costs of non-UK domiciled individuals who are relocated to the UK (TA 1988 s 195).

6.154 The Finance Act 1993 was amended in Committee to make clear that these reliefs for international relocations remain in place and are not subject to the restrictions and conditions introduced by the new legislation, for example, there is no £8,000 limit.

Overseas relocations

6.155 If a UK resident employee is relocated overseas by his employer, no taxable benefit arises where the employer pays for or provides any of the following (TA 1988 ss 193-4):

(a) travel to the overseas destination to take up a post;
(b) return travel to any place in the UK on termination of the overseas employment;
(c) any other journey between the UK and the overseas location in the course of that employment, providing the inward journey is made wholly and exclusively for the purpose of the employment;
(d) board and lodging 'for the purpose of enabling the employee to perform the duties of overseas employment'. If it is partly for the purpose and partly 'for another purpose' apportionment is required;
(e) the travel costs of his spouse and/or children. This is limited to two return journeys for each person in a tax year. A 'child' for these purposes includes stepchildren and illegitimate children but excludes any child over 18 at the beginning of the outward journey.

6.156 These reliefs also cover individuals who have been recruited by a UK employer for an overseas post; there is no requirement that the employee has previously worked in the UK for that employer.

6.157 In many cases, overseas relocatees are not taxable in the UK, as they satisfy either the rules set out in IR20 para 18, by being overseas for a complete tax year, or TA 1988 s 193(1) since they are overseas for 365 days. However, some relocatees return unexpectedly, or unwittingly fall foul of the detailed provisions of TA 1988 Sch 12. In such cases, these reliefs for overseas relocations are particularly helpful.

Inward relocations of employees not domiciled in the UK (TA 1988 s 195)

6.158 Relief is available on the inward relocation of non-UK domiciled employees. The relief covers any employee who:

(a) is not domiciled in the UK; and
(b) was not resident in the UK in the two years of assessment preceding the year of his arrival in the UK; or
(c) was not in the UK for 'any purpose at any time' for the 24 months immediately preceding his arrival in the UK; and
(d) has his 'usual place of abode' outside the UK.

6.159 The relief allows an employer to pay for or provide travel for a five year period without there being an assessable benefit on the employee. The specific reliefs cover:

(a) the costs of any journey from the usual place of abode to the UK, in order to perform any duties of his office or employment in the UK, and his return journey;
(b) journeys by his spouse and/or children to the UK. This is limited to two journeys for each person in a tax year. A 'child' for these purposes includes a stepchild and an illegitimate child, but excludes any child over 18 at the beginning of the journey to the UK.

Reporting

6.160 It should be noted that it is the employee who has to claim these reliefs. An employer must therefore comply with the normal PAYE and P11D reporting requirements unless he has a dispensation from the Revenue. Clearance should also be sought from the DSS that the amounts fall within their definition of allowable relocation payments (6.172-6.177).

8 PAYE AND P11D PROCEDURES

Qualifying removal expenses and benefits

6.161 There is no requirement to deduct tax from any payment of a qualifying removal expense or benefit. This is the case even where the total amount exceeds the £8,000 statutory limit (Revenue Press Release 14 April 1993). The excess over £8,000 should instead be reported on the employee's P11D return at the year end.

6.162   There is no reporting requirement for payments of qualifying removal expenses, or provision of qualifying benefits, which have a total value of less than £8,000. This also applies to payments made in the period between 6 April 1993 and Royal Assent to the Finance Bill 1993, although strictly such payments should have been subject to PAYE (Inland Revenue Press Release 14 April 1993).

Other payments and benefits

6.163   Payments and benefits which fall outside of the new legislation and are not covered by the former concessionary basis or the transitional rules (6.117–6.130) are subject to PAYE or P11D procedures as appropriate.

6.164   The now draconian penalties for incorrect submission of P11D forms (for example, up to £3,000 for each incorrect return (TMA 1970 s 98(5)) mean that a careful review of all payments to ensure compliance with the legislation is essential.

Claims by employees under TA 1988 s 198

6.165   TA 1988 s 198 allows employees to claim that expenses reimbursed to them and otherwise taxable under the benefits legislation, should be exempt from tax. This section applies where the employees' expenses are incurred 'wholly, exclusively and necessarily in the performance of' the duties of his office or employment.

6.166   A relocation which is required by an employer is likely to satisfy the requirements that the payments are 'wholly, exclusively and necessarily' incurred in respect of the employment. The Revenue are, however, likely to argue that the expenses are not 'in the performance of' the duties, but simply put the employee in a position to carry out those duties (*Nolder v Walters* 15 TC 380; *Bhadra v Ellam* (1988) STC 239, 60 TC 466).

6.167   However, it is interesting to note that the Revenue concession for travel, accommodation and subsistence costs paid or provided in connection with a secondment is based on the view that the payments 'qualify for a deduction under the Schedule E expenses rule'.[1] Presumably, the seconded employee is considered to be acting 'in the performance of' his duties while he is away from his normal place of work. The line between this and an employee relocating at the behest of his employer is very thin. (See also 6.20–6.23.)

1 TR 795: Guidance Note to the Institute of Chartered Accountants, June 1990.

9 OTHER TAXES

Corporation tax

6.168 Relocation costs are deductible as revenue expenses in the company's corporation tax return as incurred wholly and exclusively for the purposes of the business.

6.169 The exception would be the costs of purchasing the employees' properties (6.143–6.152) and any associated expenses. These would all be capital transactions.

VAT

6.170 VAT can only be recovered on goods or services used by the company in making taxable supplies of goods or services. In general input tax on relocation expenses cannot be recovered, as the goods or services have been supplied to the employee rather than to the company.

6.171 However, recovery of the VAT on relocation costs such as estate agents' fees, removal costs and legal and survey fees, where the company does not buy the property, will generally be allowed if billed to the company rather than the individual, providing the relocation is genuinely for business reasons. This is, of course, subject to the normal VAT rules on input tax recovery and partial exemption.

It is recommended that the VAT recovery position be discussed with the local Customs and Excise office before claims are made.

National Insurance Contributions

6.172 National Insurance Contributions are payable on 'earnings', which include reimbursed expenses, but exclude payments in kind. There is thus no NIC liability on any benefits provided as part of a relocation package. Such benefits could include beneficial loans, legal services, accommodation or transport provided by the employer.

6.173 Reimbursed expenses which are 'absolutely necessary (for example a solicitor's bill, estate agent's commission or removal expenses)'[1] are not included in gross pay for NIC purposes. For the DSS's comments on Council Tax, see 6.35.

6.174 Round sum allowances are included in gross pay and subject to NIC, unless they are either 'payments to cover specific additional expenses incurred as the result of the move, such as a higher mortgage or rent'[1] or based on:

'an estimate of costs likely to be incurred, providing that:
- your scheme has no profit element
- payments are based on an accurate survey of the costs involved

    –   the scheme is designed to allow for movements in prices

    –   the payments are reasonable in relation to the employment involved.'[1]

6.175   Despite the withdrawal of the tax concession (6.125–6.130), payments for moves to a higher cost housing area continue to be exempt from NIC providing the payment 'accurately reflects any additional cost'.[1]

6.176   All relocation packages should be negotiated and agreed with the DSS in advance of payment. The Green Book warns:

> 'If the scheme is not supported by written evidence, or the scheme is not considered sound, NICs will be charged on all payments made under your scheme.'[1]

6.177   Where NIC is payable, it will generally be employer's contributions which are relevant, as most relocated employees are above the NIC threshold.

1   National Insurance Contributions for Employers Manual from 6 April 1993 (Green Book) at Chapter 15 para 74.

10   COMPLIANCE AND TAX PLANNING CHECKLISTS

Compliance checklist

6.178

1   Have all expenses/ benefits which are not eligible under the legislation been subjected to PAYE or included on the employee's P11D form as appropriate? These include:

– Council tax	6.31–6.35
– NHBC Guarantees	6.41
– Guaranteed price payments	6.142
– Transporting and installation costs of non-domestic items	6.44
– Temporary accommodation for the employee's family/household	6.45(e)
– Duplicate costs of any items which are not 'domestic'	6.72
– Bridging loan incidental expenditure	6.54
– Higher cost housing payments	6.125–6.130
– Some of the expenses of relocation management companies	6.73–6.75

2   Has the £8,000 limit on eligible expenses been exceeded in the tax year? Has the amount spent on an employee's relocation in the previous tax year been carried forward in calculating whether the £8,000 limit has been exceeded?   6.15

3   Have the time limits on paying or providing eligible relocation expenses/benefits been adhered to? If expenses

	have been paid after the time limit, has permission been sought from the local Inspector to extend the limit?	6.99–6.103
4	Have the main residence rules been adhered to, both in respect of the employee's old and new residence?	6.90–6.94
5	Has the payment of any flat rate allowances as part of the £8,000 limit been agreed in advance with the local Inspector of Taxes?	6.110–6.112
6	Have all payments made or benefits provided after 6 April 1993 to employees who relocated *before* that date been reported on their P11Ds?	6.117–6.121
7	Likewise, have payments made or benefits provided after 6 April 1993 to any employees who relocated under the transitional rules been reported on their P11Ds?	6.117–6.121
8	Have the transitional rules been complied with?	6.122–6.124
9	Have the DSS and Customs and Excise agreed to the company's treatment of relocation payments?	6.170–6.177
10	Have any beneficial loans for bridging purposes been correctly calculated and reported?	6.58–6.68
11	Have the rules for international relocations been correctly applied?	6.160

Tax planning checklist

6.179

1	Has the company considered replacing a guaranteed price scheme with a property purchase scheme?	6.143–6.152
2	Does the company or the employee wish to challenge the taxability of benefits and/or expenses?	6.20-6.23
3	Can advantage be taken of the de minimis limit for beneficial loans?	6.69–6.70
4	Is the company in dispute with the Inland Revenue over the interpretation of 'change of residence'. Or did the company previously concede the point?	6.86–6.89
5	Has the company agreed a flat-rate relocation allowance with the Inspector of Taxes to save administration costs?	6.110–112
6	Can company cars be provided to relocating employees within the terms of the tax-free relocation package?	6.45, note 1
7	Can the company make more use of the continuing Inland Revenue concession on secondments?	6.113 6.116
8	Can the employee make use of the mortgage relief and CGT provisions on let property now that there is no requirement to dispose of the old residence?	6.94
9	Has the company excluded NIC from its payments of higher cost housing allowances?	6.175
10	Is the company taking full advantage of the reliefs for international relocations?	6.153–6.159
11	Is the employee entitled to make a claim to recover tax where a beneficial loan was reported on a provisional basis?	6.68
12	Has the employee considered a claim under TA 1988 s 198?	6.165–6.167

CHAPTER 7

VAT

1 INPUT TAX

7.1 In his Budget speech and related press releases the Chancellor announced several changes relating to input tax, and linked changes to the provisions covering business gifts. The changes directly concerned with input tax are:

(a) a provision to prevent certain input tax appeals from being allowed unless it can be shown that the Commissioners have acted unreasonably; and
(b) an amendment to the general regulations to prevent the deduction of input tax which does not relate to the making of supplies.

7.2 The latter provision was introduced by the VAT (General) (Amendment) (No 5) Regulations 1993 (SI 1993/1623), to have effect from 1 August 1993.

Input tax appeals

7.3 The provision on input tax appeals is contained in section 46 of the Finance Act 1993, which inserts a new subsection (3ZA) into VATA 1983 s 40. The Clause as originally drafted covered a wide range of input tax appeals, and went far wider than the cases at which it was alleged to be aimed. The scope of the provision was narrowed by a Government amendment at the Committee stage.

Declared purpose

7.4 The stated aim of the restriction on input tax appeals can readily be deduced from the heading of Press Notice 28/93, issued on Budget day – 'VAT: New rules to prevent the recovery of VAT on goods and services bought for private consumption'. The Press Release went on to say:

> 'The Chancellor's intention is to ensure that private expenditure does not qualify for tax recovery. In practice anomalies have arisen following varying interpretations of the law by VAT Tribunals and the courts. As a result some businesses have recovered VAT on purchases which would normally be seen as being for private use. In future the link which must exist between expenditure and the making of actual supplies in the course of business will be more clearly defined. General business overheads are unaffected, as they are used for the purpose of making the business's supplies.

There will also be a new provision relating to appeals. From now on it will be up to traders to demonstrate that Customs and Excise have behaved unreasonably in refusing tax recovery.'

7.5 Budget Notice 106/93 gives the target as being to prevent the recovery of input tax on 'a wide range of goods having only a faint business characteristic and which on any reasonable basis would be seen as for private use'.

7.6 The cases which appear to be of most concern to the Commissioners are those dealing with input tax on such costs as horse racing, where traders have successfully claimed that the inputs were used in promoting the taxable business.

7.7 Chief among these is the case of *Ian Flockton Developments Ltd v CCE* [1987] STC 394. This case concerned a manufacturing company which claimed input tax recovery on costs relating to a racehorse. The VAT Tribunal had found as a fact that the sole object of the company's director (and hence of the company) in authorising this expenditure was the promotion of the company's business, but had nevertheless disallowed the input tax. The Tribunal found that the test to be applied was a subjective one, that it was necessary to look into the company's mind (or, rather, the minds of those controlling it) and determine its purpose in respect of the expenditure. However, it considered that in doing this it should not only approach with scepticism mere assertions as to purpose, but should also ask itself what would have been the decision of an average businessman. Applying this test it found that the company and its director 'ought not to have had any commercial belief that the purchase and running of a racehorse could have been for the purpose of its business'.

7.8 The court overturned the Tribunal's decision holding that, once it had determined what was in fact the company's purpose, it had no business in substituting some other purpose based on its finding as to what an average businessman might have thought.

7.9 Since the *Flockton* case there have been a number of decisions against the Commissioners on matters of business use. However, the claims that these are cases where the inputs have 'only a faint business characteristic' or 'on any reasonable basis would be seen as for private use' seem somewhat excessive. The cases of concern to the Commissioners must be those which they have lost, as no change is necessary to give them victory in those which they have already won. By definition these are cases where the Tribunals have found, on the evidence, that the purpose behind the expenditure was a genuine business motive. It would be wrong to presume that the Tribunals are made up of fools, and they are well able to discount the evidence of those who they consider are being economical with the truth. The propriety of this amendment is therefore questionable.

Types of appeal covered

7.10 As originally drafted, Clause 46 would have affected many more appeals than those held up as justification for it. It was expressed as applying to any appeal which relates, in whole or in part, to a determination by the Commissioners:

(a)   that any of the purposes for which any goods or services were or were to be used were not purposes of a business carried on, or to be carried on, by the trader; or,
(b)   that the matters to which any input tax was attributable were or included matters other than the making of UK taxable supplies (or other matters, such as taxable supplies outside the UK, in respect of which input tax is allowable.

7.11   The only input tax appeals which might have escaped these tests are those concerned with the question whether tax was properly chargeable on the inputs concerned (eg whether the inputs are treated as not being supplies under the provisions for the transfer of a business as a going concern), those concerned with purely procedural matters (such as whether proper evidence is held in support of the claim), and those concerned with the attribution of residual input tax after the basic decision (that the inputs are used both in making taxable supplies and for other purposes) has been reached.

7.12   Following a storm of protest, the provision was amended so that it only has effect where the input tax concerned is incurred on something 'in the nature of a luxury amusement or entertainment'. This classification is borrowed from Article 17(5) of the EEC Sixth Directive on VAT, in an apparent attempt to give the provision some semblance of validity under European law. This is likely, of course, to give rise to a number of disputes on what constitutes a 'luxury amusement or entertainment'.

Reasonableness test

7.13   Where section 46 applies (or VATA 1983 s 40(3ZA)), a new constraint is applied to the Tribunal's powers. The Tribunal is not permitted to allow the appeal (or that part of the appeal covered by s 40(3ZA)) unless it considers that the Commissioners could not reasonably have made the relevant determination as to business use or attribution to taxable supplies.

7.14   The effect of this is bizarre. It amounts to a provision that, the Appellant having been proved right and the Tribunal having held that the inputs were used for business purposes or, as the case may be, that they were used in making taxable supplies, the Tribunal is not permitted to give effect to its finding if the Commissioners could reasonably have taken the position which they did. It is not even a question of whether or not the Commissioners did act unreasonably. If they acted unreasonably but could reasonably have reached the same decision, the appeal cannot be allowed.

7.14A   In considering the reasonableness or otherwise of the determination, the Tribunal can take account of information made available later, but only if it could not have been made available to the Commissioners at the time of the determination.

Commencement

7.15   The new provision is expressed as applying to input tax appeals in relation to prescribed accounting periods beginning on or after the date of Royal Assent.

Effectiveness – UK position

7.16 Now that section 46 has been enacted, we must ask ourselves what will be its practical effect, and whether there is scope for minimising its effect in particular cases.

7.17 It seems unlikely that the Tribunals will take kindly to such a blatant restraint on their powers and the lack of confidence in their abilities which is implied by it. They have previously demonstrated their dislike of the restraints placed on reasonable excuse cases, in ruling out certain factors as potential excuses, and have demonstrated a welcome capacity to circumvent the cruder applications of these provisions which have been put forward by the Commissioners.

7.18 It can be expected, therefore, that the Tribunals will make use of whatever routes are legitimately available to them to apply their own findings, notwithstanding the existence of these restraints. Having said this, the toolbox available to the Tribunals is not well stocked. The question of what is reasonable generally arises in cases concerned with the powers of the courts to review the exercise of discretionary powers by Government authorities, the leading case being that of *Associated Picture Houses v Wednesbury Corporation* [1948] 1 KB 223.

7.19 The key point emerging from this is that, if the authority has taken into account those matters which it should do, and not taken account of matters which it should not, and has not misdirected itself in law, the courts will not usually interfere with the exercise of the discretion unless the decision reached by the authority is manifestly absurd. In particular, it is not for the court to substitute its own judgment for that of the authority.

7.20 The scope for the Tribunals to allow these appeals is therefore limited. Perhaps if the Tribunal can find that, on the facts, there is not a scintilla of doubt as to the allowability of the input tax, it can go on to find that the Commissioners could not reasonably have found otherwise. This would not work, though, in the kinds of cases where the Tribunal indicates that the question is a difficult one, and finely balanced, and that having heard the evidence it has with difficulty come down on the side of the Appellant. Perhaps, at the margin, some decisions will be more robustly expressed than they might have been in the past, which would not be a welcome outcome for the Commissioners.

7.21 There is also the question whether the reasonableness test is to be applied to the initial decision by the Commissioners, on the evidence before them at that time, or whether it should also be applied to a subsequent decision to maintain their position including, on occasion, their continuing to maintain it in the light of facts which only become apparent at Tribunal. There have been some indications from Customs that they must review the decision in the light of subsequent information if they are to claim at Tribunal not to have been unreasonable. However, it is difficult to derive such an interpretation from the legislation as enacted.

7.22 For traders and their advisers it becomes doubly important to document the decisions underlying transactions, and the implementation of those decisions, to provide as much external contemporaneous evidence as possible, and avoid the need to rely on mere assertions. If a Tribunal reaches a conclusion primarily because it considers X to be a witness of truth, it will have difficulty in saying that the Commissioners acted unreasonably in disagreeing with it as to X's reliability. The position will be more hopeful if there is additional evidence and it can be shown that this was made available to the Commissioners at the outset. Anyone hoping that the Tribunal will make bricks must at least ensure an adequate supply of straw for the purpose.

7.23   Another practical effect will be that the restraint on the actions of the Tribunals will act as a disincentive to discussing transactions with the Commissioners in advance. If a course of action remains commercially desirable whether or not related input tax can be recovered, there will be good reason to go ahead with it without seeking a ruling and hope that it is never questioned, rather than run the risk of an adverse, but incorrect ruling (possibly one encouraged by the officer's belief that the decision cannot be challenged at Tribunal). This does not encourage compliance.

Effectiveness – EEC position

7.24   In considering the effects of section 46 it should be remembered that the right to deduct input tax does not stem, in the first instance, from VATA 1983 ss 14 and 15. These are merely implementing, in the UK, Articles 17 to 20 of the EEC Sixth Directive on VAT (Directive 77/388/EEC).

7.25   The Directive confers an absolute right for a taxable person to deduct input tax where the goods or services concerned are used for the purposes of its taxable business activities, and lays down a scheme of apportionment for those who are partially exempt. It does not then trammel this right except to insist, in Article 18, that appropriate formalities are complied with, such as the possession of a tax invoice.

7.26   Nowhere in the Directive is there any power for member states to impose further restrictions (unlike other parts of the Directive, where member states may make conditions to ensure 'the correct and straightforward' application of the tax or to prevent 'any possible evasion, avoidance or abuse'). In the absence of any such enabling provision it is difficult to see how the proposed restriction can be maintained against the rights conferred by the Directive.

7.27   The Directive provides that tax on 'expenditure which is not strictly business expenditure, such as that on luxuries, amusements or entertainment' is not deductible (Article 17(5)). However, this is a provision which needs to be implemented in setting the criteria for deduction, not by rigging the proceedings before the Tribunal. It seems unlikely that this provision can give adequate *vires* to the UK provision in a case where the Tribunal has found that the national conditions have, in principle, been met.

7.28   This matter of European law can be raised before the Tribunal, which is entitled to consider it and reach a decision on it. Alternatively, the Tribunal can refer a question to the European Court of Justice. It would be interesting to see a case where a question on the following lines was considered by the Tribunal, or referred to the ECJ:

'In a case where the national court has decided that the conditions for deduction of input tax as set out in Title XI of Directive 77/388/EEC have been met, can a national provision prevent the taxable person from deducting that tax merely on the grounds that the tax authorities could reasonably have reached a contrary conclusion?'

The right to the deduction of input tax is fundamental to the operation of value added tax, not an optional extra to be adopted, or not, according to the whim of the tax authorities. This is likely to be recognised by the courts in the UK as well as the European Court.

Practical implications

7.29   A provision which tilts the odds in an appeal hearing so far in favour of the Commissioners may well encourage officers to assess 'from the hip'. By the same token, it is likely to militate against frankness on the part of traders and, particularly, to discourage them from raising input tax matters with the Commissioners in advance.

7.30   Businesses faced with input tax assessments will have to balance more carefully than ever the costs of an appeal and the prospects of success, bearing in mind that these prospects are diminished by section 46 while the costs are increased by the need to overcome a further hurdle.

7.31   As indicated above, the Tribunals are unlikely to apply the reason-ableness test as stringently as the Commissioners might hope, and there is scope for debate on what is a luxury, etc. There is also the prospect of having the entire provision overridden on the ground that it is inconsistent with the absolute right of deduction conferred by the EEC Sixth Directive.

7.32   It seems likely that someone with substantial amounts of input tax at stake will take a case on this latter point sooner rather than later. Once this is done, the choices become more straightforward for those with lesser amounts at stake (and have a case worth taking on its intrinsic merits). There is much to be said for filing an appeal and applying for it to be stood over until such time as such a test case has been decided.

Amendment to general regulations

7.33   The amendment to the VAT (General) Regulations 1985 (SI 1985/886) is contained in the VAT (General) (Amendment) (No 5) Regulations 1993 (SI 1993/1623).

7.34   The stated intention (BN106/93) is to amend the Regulations to confirm that 'input tax which does not relate to the making of supplies is not recoverable'. However, 'general business overheads are unaffected, as they will be used for the business of making supplies'.

7.35   The authority for the deduction of input tax stems from Article 17 of the EEC Sixth Directive (Directive 77/388/EEC) which allows a deduction 'insofar as the goods and services are used for the purposes of his taxable transactions'.

7.36   The existing Regulations (reg 30(2)) provide for:

(a)   full deduction of input tax on inputs used 'exclusively in making taxable supplies';

(b)   non-deduction of input tax on inputs used 'exclusively in making exempt supplies, or in carrying on any activity other than the making of taxable supplies'; and,

(c)   partial recovery of input tax on inputs used partly in making taxable supplies and partly for other purposes.

7.37   The amendment inserts a new reg 29A in the VAT (General) Regulations 1985 (SI 1985/886) which specifies that nothing in the Regulations is to be construed as allowing deduction of input tax in respect of goods and services not used or to be used in making supplies in the course of a business. It is difficult to see what this adds to the existing provisions.

2   CIVIL PENALTIES

7.38   Section 49 and Schedule 2 of the Finance Act 1993 embody the results of the recent review of the operations of the civil penalty system. They implement changes to the incidence of misdeclaration penalties and default surcharge, the introduction of mitigation for misdeclaration penalties, civil fraud penalties and belated notification, and the capping of default interest.

3   SERIOUS MISDECLARATION PENALTY

7.39   The changes to the serious misdeclaration penalty (SMP) system are to take effect for prescribed accounting periods commencing on or after a date to be set by statutory instrument. Periods commencing before that date will continue to be dealt with under the existing rules.

The changes consist of:

(a)   a change in the money and percentage thresholds used to determine whether a misdeclaration is potentially liable to SMP; and,

(b)   a change in the base to which the percentage threshold is applied for this purpose.

Money and percentage thresholds

7.40   In future a misdeclaration (or, rather, the aggregate of misdeclarations for a period not protected by reasonable excuse etc) will be sufficient to trigger an SMP if they exceed the lesser of:

(a)   £1m; or,

(b)   30% of the 'relevant amount' for the period.

7.41   The effects of these changes (subject to the change in the base for the calculations, covered below) is illustrated in the following table.

Relevant amount (RA)	Threshold (old rules)	Threshold (new rules)	Lowest threshold
0–£33,333	30% of RA (0–£10k)	30% of RA (0–£10k)	N/A
£33,334–£200k	£10,000 (£10k)	30% of RA (£10k–£60k)	Old
£200k– £3,333,333	5% of RA (£10k–£166,666)	30% of RA (£60k–£1m)	Old
£3,333,334– £20m	5% of RA (£166,667–£1m)	£1m (£1m)	Old
£20m+	5% of RA (£1m+)	£1m (£1m)	New

It will be seen that, even ignoring the change in fixing the relevant amount, the new thresholds will benefit all traders except those who, under the old rules, had a 'true amount of tax' of £20m per period or more. For many of those with a true amount of tax below this level the actual benefit, with re-basing, will be rather more than the table suggests.

Base for percentage threshold

7.42   The base to which the percentage threshold is applied under the new rules varies depending on whether the misdeclaration under consideration results from an assessment which understates a person's liability for a period, this understatement not being notified to the Commissioners within 30 days (FA 1985 s 14(1)(b)) or arises from an understatement of liability in a return (FA 1985 s 14(1)(a)).

ASSESSMENT UNDERSTATING LIABILITY

7.43   If an assessment understates a person's liability for a period and this is not drawn to the attention of the Commissioners within 30 days, the relevant amount for determining possible liability to SMP is the 'true amount of tax' for the period (ie the net amount of tax properly due). This is the same basis as previously although, as explained above, the percentage applied to it changes under the new rules.

RETURN UNDERSTATING LIABILITY

7.44   If a return understates a person's liability for a period, the relevant amount for determining possible liability to SMP under the new rules will be the 'gross amount of tax' for the period. This is the aggregate of the output tax and input tax which should have been shown on the return for the period. This should give a worthwhile increase in the penalty threshold for most traders. The Commissioners estimate that the gross amount of tax will, on average, be four to five times larger than the true amount of tax (BN59/93).

EXAMPLE

Smith's return for a period should have shown the following:

	£
Output tax	23,500.75
Input tax	12,750.50

The true amount of tax for the period is £10,750.25 (the difference between output tax and input tax) while the gross amount of tax is £36,251.25 (the sum of the two).

In determining the gross amount of tax, other refunds etc which should be included on the return (such as bad debt relief) are treated as if they were input tax.

7.45   Where errors are corrected under the procedure provided for in the VAT (Accounting and Records) Regulations 1989 (SI 1989/2248), reg 5, the amounts concerned are treated, in determining the true amount of tax or the gross amount of tax, as proper to the period of correction. Whether those errors remain potentially liable to penalty is a moot point. It is understood to be the Commissioners' policy not to seek penalties in such circumstances, although this is at variance with the High Court decision in the case of *Peninsular and Oriental Steam Navigation Co v C&E Comrs* (1992) STI 872. It seems a pity that this point could not have been clarified in the course of amending the legislation.

4   PERSISTENT MISDECLARATION PENALTY

7.46   The thresholds for determining whether an error is a 'material inaccuracy' for the purposes of the persistent misdeclaration penalty (PMP) are to be altered on similar lines to the SMP changes. Also, the procedure for the issuing of penalty liability notices, and the subsequent imposition of penalties, is to be amended. These changes will apply for periods beginning on or after a day to be fixed by statutory instrument, and the existing PMP system (including any penalty liability notices then in force) will lapse from that date.

Money and percentage thresholds and base for percentage threshold

7.47   The trigger for a material inaccuracy under the new system is that the under-declaration equals or exceeds the lesser of £500,000 or 10% of the gross amount of tax for the period concerned.

The previous trigger was the greater of £100 or 1% of the true amount of tax.

The new PMP limits are therefore more favourable for all traders except some (but not all) of those with a true amount of tax below £1,000, and any with a true amount of tax in excess of £500m.

Penalty liability notices and the imposition of penalties

7.48   A persistent misdeclaration penalty cannot be imposed unless a penalty liability notice (PLN) has first been issued, and further material inaccuracies arise for periods falling within the currency of the PLN.

ISSUE OF PLN

7.49   Under the new system, one material inaccuracy is sufficient to enable the Commissioners to issue a PLN. However, the PLN must be issued before the end of five consecutive prescribed accounting periods commencing with the period in respect of which the material inaccuracy arose.

This means that the Commissioners' entitlement to issue a PLN will vary depending on whether the trader makes monthly or quarterly (or annual) returns.

EXAMPLE

Smith makes VAT returns for calendar quarters, while Jones makes monthly returns. Each has a material inaccuracy in the return for the period to 30 April 1994. An officer discovering Smith's material inaccuracy in September 1994 can issue a PLN. However, an officer discovering Jones' material inaccuracy at the same time cannot issue a PLN since five prescribed accounting periods, commencing with that to 30 April 1994, have already expired.

DURATION OF PENALTY PERIOD

7.50   A penalty liability notice must specify a penalty period. This consists of eight consecutive prescribed accounting periods commencing with that in which the PLN is issued. The penalty period will therefore vary in duration between 8 and 24 months, depending on whether the trader makes monthly or quarterly returns (or eight years in the case of a trader on annual accounting).

7.51   The penalty period is determined when the PLN is issued, and this must be done on the basis of anticipated prescribed accounting periods based on current arrangements. It is not clear what happens if a trader making quarterly returns switches to monthly returns after a PLN has been issued. There is no apparent mechanism for adjusting the period covered by the PLN. The position on a change of stagger group (so that the penalty period expires part of the way through a prescribed accounting period) is also unclear.

MATERIAL INACCURACIES FOR PERIODS WITHIN PENALTY PERIOD

7.52   If there is a material inaccuracy for a period falling within the penalty period there is potentially a persistent misdeclaration penalty of 15% of the tax involved. However, no PMP is imposed for the first period within the currency of the PLN for which a material inaccuracy arises.

7.53   It should be noted that the imposition or otherwise of a PMP depends upon the order of the periods for which inaccuracies arise, not the order in which those inaccuracies are discovered. Also, the errors do not have to be discovered within the penalty period. Liability is determined solely by whether they relate to periods which fall within the penalty period.

EXAMPLE

A PLN is served on Bloggs covering periods 1 to 8.

A material inaccuracy of £10,000 is discovered for period 3.

Subsequently a further material inaccuracy of £7,000 is discovered for period 5. Bloggs is liable to a PMP of £1,050 (15% of £7,000).

If the second inaccuracy discovered had related to period 2 rather than period 5, it would have escaped penalty and the £10,000 inaccuracy for period 3, which had previously escaped penalty, would have attracted a PMP of £1,500 (15% of £10,000).

7.54   It should also be noted that the calculations have to be reviewed in the light of the discovery of further errors. For instance if, in the example above, over-declarations were subsequently discovered for period 3 such that there was no longer a material inaccuracy for that period, the period 5 inaccuracy would then be the first in the penalty period and the existing penalty would be repayable.

Transitional provisions

7.55   As indicated earlier, the new PMP regime will apply to periods commencing on or after a date to be fixed by statutory instrument. Any existing PLNs issued under the old system will expire as of the previous day, and earlier material inaccuracies will not count towards the new system.

5   MITIGATION OF PENALTIES

7.56   Perhaps the most significant change in the penalty system is the introduction of mitigation for:

(a)   serious misdeclaration penalty and persistent misdeclaration penalty;

(b)   penalties for belated notification and the unauthorised issue of tax invoices; and,

(c)   civil fraud penalty.

7.57   Mitigation is available, in the first instance, to the Commissioners, and it is open to them to mitigate the penalty by as much (or as little) as they think fit. There is a right of appeal to the VAT Tribunal on the amount of mitigation and, in such a case, it is open to the Tribunal to reduce the amount of mitigation as well as to increase it.

7.58   The power of mitigation has effect for penalties assessed on or after the date of Royal Assent (regardless of the period to which they relate). This means that mitigation is available for new assessments for penalties relating to periods not covered by the new rules on the basis for determining whether a serious or persistent misdeclaration penalty may be due. As an administrative matter, the Chancellor promised that misdeclaration penalties would not normally be assessed from Budget day until the new misdeclaration penalty rules are in force, which should make any new assessments eligible for mitigation.

LIMITATIONS ON MITIGATION

7.59   The provisions as enacted specifically prevent certain matters from being taken into account, by either the Commissioners or the Tribunals, in considering the question of mitigation. These are:

(a)   insufficiency of funds for paying either tax due or a penalty;

(b)   the fact that there has been no significant loss of tax (either looking at the specific case or at that case in conjunction with others); and,

(c)   the fact that those involved have acted in good faith.

7.60   It is clear from the whole thrust of the civil penalty system, and the Keith Report on which it is based, that it is intended to deter carelessness which might otherwise be excused because of the kinds of factors which are to be excluded from consideration. It seems at least likely that the Tribunals would spot this (and certain that the Commissioners would do so) and so adjust the weight given to these factors. It is difficult, therefore, to see the justification for excluding them from consideration altogether.

EXPRESSION OF MITIGATION

7.61   There are a number of ways in which mitigation might be expressed. Examples for, say, a serious misdeclaration penalty on a £100,000 under-declaration (with a basic penalty of, say, 15% or £15,000) are:

(a)   the penalty is reduced to £5,000; or,

(b)   the penalty is reduced by £10,000; or,

(c)   the penalty is reduced to one-third of the potential amount; or,

(d)   the penalty is reduced by two-thirds of the potential amount.

The Act does not specify any particular way of expressing the mitigation allowed, which may give rise to subsequent problems in calculating the position (see 7.62–7.67).

MULTIPLE ERRORS

7.62   The mitigation provisions are couched in terms of a single occasion on which a penalty may be charged. Clearly this is appropriate in terms of, say, belated notification of liability to register (although the lack of precision as to the expression of mitigation may still give problems here).

7.63   There are great difficulties inherent in the manner of expression when looking at misdeclaration penalties in which a number of different errors (as is commonly the case for larger organisations) make up a net misdeclaration for a period.

7.64   Assume, for instance, that a serious misdeclaration penalty arises for a period on an under-declaration of £100,000. The basic penalty is £15,000, and the Commissioners (or the Tribunal) mitigate this to £6,000.

7.65   Subsequently, a £50,000 over-declaration is discovered for the same period. The basic penalty for the period is therefore reduced to £7,500. Should the actual penalty, after mitigation, be reduced to £3,000 (40% of the new basic penalty of £7,500)? Or should the £6,000 penalty, being less than the basic penalty for the period, still stand?

7.66   Assume that a further under-declaration of £70,000 is then discovered, but that this is protected from penalty by reasonable excuse or disclosure, and a further £20,000 under-declaration is discovered which is not protected from penalty or eligible for any mitigation.

There is now a net under-declaration for the period of £140,000, made up as follows:

Under-declaration subject to mitigation	100,000
Under-declaration protected by reasonable excuse etc	70,000
Under-declaration not protected or mitigable	20,000
Gross under-declarations	190,000
Less: Over-declaration	50,000
Net under-declaration	£140,000

The basic penalty on this would be £16,000 (£140,000 @ 15%). However, the protected £70,000 may not give rise to a liability to a penalty (FA 1985 s 14(6)), which apparently reduces the basic penalty to £8,000. What should then be charged, bearing in mind the mitigation?

7.67   It may well be necessary to return to the Tribunal for reconsideration of the position for the period as a whole, in the absence of some statutory formula.

Having said all this, the introduction of mitigation must be welcome for traders, and their advisers, as giving some basis for making the penalty punishment fit the crime.

6 DEFAULT SURCHARGE

7.68   The maximum rate of default surcharge was reduced from 20% to 15% for defaults arising on or after 1 April 1993. The other changes described below take effect from 1 October 1993. However, the revised surcharge regime is a continuation of the old one, and any existing surcharge periods continue to run.

Being 'in default' and being liable to surcharge

7.69   A person is 'in default' if either the VAT return or some or all of the tax shown on it as due is not received by the Commissioners by the due date.

7.70   Under the new regime, a surcharge liability notice can be issued by the Commissioners (or the surcharge period can be extended) if a trader is in default. However, liability to the surcharge itself (or an increase in the rate of surcharge applicable to subsequent defaults) arises only if:

(a)   the trader is in default for a period which ends while a surcharge liability notice is in force; and,

(b)   some or all of the tax shown on the return is not received by the due date.

7.71   A repayment return submitted late cannot, therefore, give rise either to a surcharge or to an increase in the rate of surcharge for subsequent late returns, but it can trigger the issuing of a surcharge liability notice or the issuing of a notice extending an existing surcharge liability period.

Surcharge liability notice

7.72   The Commissioners may issue a surcharge liability notice (SLN) if a trader is in default for any prescribed accounting period. Previously the SLN could only be issued if the trader was in default twice within a year.

7.73   The surcharge liability notice specifies a surcharge period commencing on the day when the SLN is issued and ending on the first anniversary of the last day of the prescribed accounting period for which the trader is in default.

EXAMPLE

A trader's VAT return for the period ending on 31 December 1993 is due on 31 January 1994. It is not received by the Commissioners until 15 March 1994. The Commissioners issue a surcharge liability notice on 1 March 1994.

The surcharge period runs from 1 March 1994 to 31 December 1994.

If a further default occurs within a surcharge period, the Commissioners may issue a further notice extending the existing period.

Rate of surcharge

7.74   Liability to default surcharge arises if the trader is in default in respect of a period which ends within the surcharge period, and some or all of the tax due is not paid by the due date.

7.75   The surcharge is a flat percentage of the outstanding tax for the period (ie the amount, if any, of tax for which the trader is liable for the period which is not received by the due date), the rate of surcharge depending on the number of previous defaults within the surcharge period, as follows:

Default within period	Rate of surcharge
First default	2%
Second default	5%
Third default	10%
Fourth or subsequent default	15%

The minimum default surcharge liability is £30, and this amount is assessable if the percentage of the outstanding tax comes to less than £30.

7.76   The Chancellor has announced that, from 1 October 1993, the Commissioners will not in practice assess default surcharges amounting to less than £200 unless they are calculated at the 10% rate or higher (ie they relate to a third, or later, default within a surcharge period).

Practical points

7.77   A trader subject to a surcharge liability notice, and who is in difficulty in completing a further return, can avoid or minimise the surcharge for the further period by making an estimate of the tax due and paying this to the Commissioners on time. However, he will still be in default and subject to an extension of the surcharge period. A better plan, therefore, is for the trader to obtain permission to estimate the output tax (or input tax) for the period under the VAT (General) Regulations 1985 (SI 1985/886) reg 61 (or 62(2)), so that he can submit a 'correct' return on time.

7.78   The fact that a surcharge liability notice can be issued following a single default increases the risks for those traders tempted to submit one 'free' late return a year. Previously they have not been at immediate risk of surcharge liability for a further late return, only of having a surcharge period imposed. Now the surcharge period is a certainty following the first default, and a further default will give rise to a surcharge liability.

7   DEFAULT INTEREST

7.79   The maximum period for default interest is capped to a maximum of three years, being the last three years of the period for which interest would otherwise run. This applies for assessments made on or after a day to be fixed by statutory instrument.

It should be noted, however, that if the assessment of tax and interest is not then paid by the due date, interest will start to run once more.

8   DEEMED SUPPLIES

7.80   VATA 1983 Sch 2 para 5 provides that there is deemed to be a supply of goods if goods which are business assets are disposed of free of charge, or put to use for non-business purposes free of charge. However, some relief from this charge is given in the case of small gifts (costing less than £10) and industrial samples.

There are several changes to this provision, either contained in the Finance Act 1993 or implemented by Treasury Order.

Samples

7.81   The deemed supply on a gift of goods does not apply to a gift of an industrial sample to an actual or potential customer if the sample is in a form not ordinarily available for sale to the public (VATA 1983 Sch 2 para 5(2)(b)).

7.82   This is amended by section 47 of the Finance Act 1993, with effect from Royal Assent, so that the relief is available for 'a gift to any person of a sample of any goods'. In other words, the requirement that the sample be in a form not ordinarily available for sale has been removed, as has the requirement that the recipient be a customer or potential customer. This makes it possible to give samples free of VAT to, for instance, persons likely to provide publicity for the product.

7.83   The section goes on to withdraw the relief where a number of samples is given to one person (whether on one occasion or on different occasions) and the samples do not differ materially from each other. However, in this instance relief is still available for the first sample given.

7.84   The relevant EEC provision is Article 5(6) of the Sixth Directive (Directive 77/388/EEC), which provides for gifts of goods to be treated as supplies but goes on to say:

'However, applications for the giving of samples . . . for the purposes of the taxable person's business shall not be so treated.'

7.85   It will be seen that the Directive makes no stipulation as to the nature of the sample, the identity of the recipient, or the number of samples given. It seems, therefore, that the amendment brings the UK legislation partially into line with the Directive, but does not succeed in bringing it completely into line.

7.86   It is open to those giving several samples to one person (which may well happen where, for instance, the trader wishes to bring the product to the attention of a number of individuals working at a single organisation) to claim that the UK legislation fails to give effect to the Directive, and that the meaning of the Directive is clear and capable of having direct effect. A similar argument may be mounted by people who have been taxed on gifts of samples in the past, as not meeting the more stringent tests set by the UK legislation.

Gifts on which no input tax reclaimed

7.87   There is a further amendment to the UK legislation which provides that there is no deemed supply on a gift of goods unless the trader has been entitled to at least partial recovery of the input tax on the purchase, etc, of the goods.

This does no more than bring the UK legislation into line with the Directive (and with current practice).

Services – change of use

7.88   A further provision has been introduced by the VAT (Supply of Services) Order 1993 (SI 1993/1507), with effect from 1 August 1993, dealing with services.

This deems there to be a supply when the whole of the input tax is recovered on services, and those services are then put to some non-business use for no consideration.

The taxable amount is the cost of the non-business use, but is capped so that the output tax liability cannot exceed the amount of input tax recovered.

9   FUEL AND POWER

7.89   Section 42 of the Finance Act 1993 brings an end to the existing zero-rating for supplies of fuel and power for domestic use and for use by charities. It does this in two stages:

(a)   introducing a lower rate of 8% to have effect to supplies which are currently zero-rated and which take place from 1 April 1994 to 31 March 1995; and,

(b)   complete abolition of the zero-rating for supplies made from 1 April 1995 onwards.

The use of a lower rate, albeit temporarily, is interesting, and has led to some speculation whether it might be the precursor of a permanent lower rate to replace (or partially replace) zero-rating.

7.90   The increase in the tax base will no doubt lead to attempts to bring supplies forward, before each phase of the change, to avoid the increased charge. Attempts to do this merely by issuing invoices seem doomed to failure. It is generally accepted that an invoice for a zero-rated supply cannot be a tax invoice, because Reg 16 of the VAT (General) Regulations 1985 (SI 1985/886) specifically provides that Regs 12–15 (dealing with tax invoices) do not apply in the case of a zero-rated supply. Furthermore, Reg 12(1) only provides for tax invoices to be issued to persons who are taxable persons, so even an invoice for VAT at 8% is unlikely to rank as a tax invoice in a case where the customer is a private individual.

7.91   Payment for future supplies should be effective in bringing the tax point forward, and seems likely to be accepted as effective by the Commissioners. The treatment where, for instance, an individual makes an advance payment to the electricity board, then moves house before the advance payment has been used up, is problematical. It seems unlikely that the benefit of zero-rating can be passed on to a new customer purchasing under a new contract.

7.92   The use of an intermediate 'captive' electricity company might be attractive to some organisations affected. However, this approach may be rendered unworkable by statutory requirements placed on suppliers of electricity.

Index